Sir

Resources for the new Anglican lectionary and calendar from the Canterbury Press

Exciting Holiness – Collects and Readings for the Festivals and Lesser Festivals of the Church of England. *Compiled by Brother Tristam SSF*

Leading Intercessions – Prayers for Sundays, Holy Days and Festivals, Years A, B and C. *Raymond Chapman*

Word of Life – Commentary on the Lectionary Readings for the Principal Service on Sundays and Major Holy Days – Year C. *Martin Kitchen, Georgiana Heskins and Stepehn Motyer*

Sing His Glory

Hymns for the Three-Year Lectionary
Years A, B and C

Compiled by
Alan Luff, Alan Dunstan, Paul Ferguson,
Christopher Idle and Charles Stewart

CANTERBURY
PRESS
Norwich

© in this compilation Alan Luff, Alan Dunstan, Paul Ferguson,
Christopher Idle and Charles Stewart 1997

First published in 1997 by The Canterbury Press Norwich
(a publishing imprint of Hymns Ancient & Modern Limited,
a registered charity)
St Mary's Works, St Mary's Plain,
Norwich, Norfolk NR3 3BH

Reprinted 1998

British Library Cataloguing in Publication Data

A catalogue record for this book is available
from the British Library

ISBN 1-85311-175-9

Printed and bound in Great Britain by
Biddles Limited, Guildford and King's Lynn

Contents

PREFACE

Choosing hymns

This book is meant to help all those who have to choose hymns for worship. The compilers believe that this is a task of considerable importance – for at least two reasons. First, many people absorb their theology from, and are nurtured in the faith by, the words which they sing, and the tunes to which they sing those words. Secondly, although hymns can facilitate and adorn an act of worship, they can also be impediments and distractions within it.

Hymns need to be appropriate to the points at which they are sung – in any form of liturgy. This ought to be obvious, but it is still possible to find churches where the congregation is invited to sing 'O enter then his gates with praise' just as it is about to go home. And if hymn-singing is not to be monotonous, the choice for any service must reflect variety. There needs to be variety in such matters as the metre and subject-matter of the hymns and the style of the tunes. Further variety is achieved if the hymns range over the centuries – so that not all come from the eighteenth, nineteenth or twentieth centuries. And there has to be a balance in the delicate matter of what is well known and what may be new to the congregation.

The purpose of this book

It has seemed important to make these general points about hymn-choosing before stating the purpose of this book which is more specific. It is meant to be one companion to the Revised Common Lectionary in the form in which it has been accepted by the Church of England.

This lectionary follows a three-year cycle, and for each Sunday and Holy Day, three readings and a psalm are provided. Sometimes there are alternatives. The Easter season, for example, has no Old Testament readings, but an additional table of such readings is provided for those who require them. In the Sundays of 'Ordinary Time' there is a choice of two Old Testament readings, each paired with a psalm. We have taken into account these and many other options built into the lectionary, but have confined ourselves to the readings appointed for the principal Sunday service. We have tried to suggest hymns based upon, or in some way reflecting the message of, these readings. We do not suppose (or recommend) that a hymn is sung after every reading; we seek instead to offer suggestions about what is sung *when* it is needed.

Although the Revised Common Lectionary does not allocate themes for Sundays, there are sometimes connections between the readings, and hymns proposed for one might well be suitable for another. Sometimes a single reading is sufficiently varied in its content to evoke at least two hymns of different character, and the choice must therefore depend upon how the whole service for that day is planned. We have tried to be realistic about what is *likely* to be chosen – for example, rejecting Christmas hymns for some summer Sunday when one of the readings has a strongly incarnational thrust.

We have offered metrical versions for some of the psalms – recognising that there are congregations in which this is the only way in which psalms are likely to be *sung*. Where no suitable metrical version can be found, we have followed the principle applied to other parts of Scripture – that is, suggesting hymns which seem to reflect the message of the psalm in question.

The most obvious use of the hymns listed here will be before, between or after readings. Hymns so used can expound or interpret Scripture, and enable worshippers to make some response to what has been read. But the lists will be of particular use to preachers, and, again, hymns based upon the sermon will enable its hearers to make their response.

The selection of hymn books

For reasons of space, it has been necessary to restrict the number of hymn books from which material has been selected. In general, we have chosen the standard hymn books of the main Christian denominations. We have chosen the most recent versions of them so that the books mentioned here have been published in the last twenty years. An exception is the *Church Hymnary Third Edition* (1973) – in process of revision during the compilation of our book – which we thought right to include because the Revised Common Lectionary is printed in the current *Book of Common Order*. Because of its widespread use across the denominations, we have included *Mission Praise* (1990) and we have found a place for the new Anglican edition of *Hymns Old and New* (1996). We have not included the many collections of freer hymns and worship songs that are on the market, because the rapid turn-over of repertoire and editions would quickly cause these lists to be out of date. Nor have we included Roman Catholic hymnals – partly because of their number, and partly because the contents of the Roman Catholic lectionary differ somewhat from that on which we have based our work. Most of the hymns suggested here are found in more than one book, but we have made exceptions when a hymn found in only one collection seems particularly appropriate to a reading. It is surely desirable for congregations sometimes to sing hymns from a collection other than their own. If such hymns are presented on a sheet or on a screen, the rules of copyright must be observed.

The impetus for this work has been the authorisation of this lectionary for use in the Church of England from Advent 1997. But we hope that the value of this book will not be restricted to Anglicans or necessarily to those who use a lectionary on these lines. Hymns based upon this large selection of Biblical passages could be of wider service to Christian communities and encourage them to make additions from the hymn/song books which they use.

Using this book

It will be obvious that this book differs from what might be considered its predecessors in this field. In recent years, ecumenical hymn-guides and Sunday lists at the back of hymn books have concentrated on the themes originally proposed by the Joint Liturgical Group and amended slightly in the *Alternative Service Book 1980*. Earlier guides to individual hymn books not only provided what was suitable for particular Sundays, but sought to ensure a wide coverage of the hymns in the book.

We recognise that many people will consult these lists in order to find four or five hymns for a Sunday service. They may indeed be able to make such a selection from what is provided here, but we must emphasise again that the lists are based upon the readings in the lectionary. The points in worship at which hymns are sung is a matter of liturgy rather than lectionary. In the final editing an attempt has been made to include most of the hymns that are common to us all – in so far as that can be determined. But how and when they are used must be a matter for local parishes and congregations.

Choosing hymns for a particular service needs care and time; this book is intended to aid, not replace, that process. But we hope that the choice of hymns for worship will increasingly be regarded as a creative and refreshing exercise rather than as a chore to be endured. To facilitate this choice, we offer in conclusion two suggestions. First, we recommend that every church keeps a careful record of *what* is sung and *when*. This will avoid undue repetition and sometimes counter the complaint 'We don't know it'. Secondly, we believe that among all the considerations affecting the choice of hymns, there is an over-riding question: What is a hymn *meant* to do at *this* point in the worship of *this* church? If that question is faced, it will go some way towards securing a good selection and a positive use of hymnody.

How the list is set out

The hymn selections are set out according to the Sundays in the Lectionary, the three years being grouped together. In addition some Sundays or groups of Sundays have a list of hymns that might be considered for any of the years. We give the title of the Sunday in the new Church of England version of the lectionary, *The Christian Year: Calendar, Lectionary and Collects* (1997), but to aid users of other denominations we add the title as it appears in the original version of the Revised Common Lectionary. Where the title of a Sunday is different in the two lectionaries, the abbreviations CLC and RCL are used to distinguish them. This is particularly important in the weeks preceding Lent where the numbering of Sunday Propers does not correspond between the two lectionaries.

The hymns have been chosen with one, on a few occasions two, of the lections in mind and that is indicated by the letters:

o   Old Testament (or Apocrypha)
a   Acts (in Easter season)
p   Psalm
c   Canticle
e   Epistle or Revelation
r   Revelation (Dedication Festival Years A & B)
g   Gospel

Where there are alternative lections the letter may be followed by a numeral.

In addition there are added:

s   Hymns that may be used because of the season
l   Hymns which have a claim to be used for liturgical reasons or which need care in placing at a particular point in the liturgy.

Hymn texts have always been subject to editorial change and to the selection of verses by editors. We do not give the full variants but trust that the opening words given make the texts sufficiently recognisable for the user to wish to look up the number in the book in use and discover the variant offered there. In a number of cases what appear to be different hymns but which are translations of the same original texts are grouped together. A particular difficulty in selecting hymns to match lections is that in a number of cases (*All hail the power of Jesus' name* is a notable example) a hymn book may lack the verse that gave rise to the choice. All the appearances of a hymn are, however, noted and the user will need to decide whether to use the hymn as it is or to reproduce a more suitable version.

Certain fairly obvious differences between versions are not noted. Throughout the list 'Jesus' is used for both 'Jesus' and 'Jesu'. One version only of 'Alleluia' is used. Punctuation varies between books as does the use of capital letters; these have been kept to a minimum consistent with intelligibility.

The law of copyright has already been mentioned. Texts now remain copyright for 70 years after the death of the author. it should be noticed that some editors claim copyright for their revision of the texts of older hymns: this should be respected, but problems that this causes may be circumvented by using a different version of the text from another book.

The Hymn Books

The main selections are from the following hymn books

AMNS   Hymns Ancient and Modern New Standard Edition, 1983, The Canterbury Press Norwich. (This incorporates an abridged version of Hymns Ancient and Modern Revised 1950 and the whole of the two supplements Hundred Hymns for Today 1969 and More Hymns for Today 1980)

NEH   New English Hymnal, 1986, The English Hymnal Company/The Canterbury Press Norwich

HTC   Hymns for Today's Church (Second Edition), 1987, Jubilate Hymns/Hodder and Stoughton/Hodder Headline plc

HONA   Hymns Old and New (New Anglican Edition), 1996, Kevin Mayhew Ltd

MP   Mission Praise (Combined Words Edition), 1990, Marshall Pickering/HarperCollins Religious

H&P   Hymns and Psalms, 1983, Methodist Publishing House

R&S   Rejoice and Sing, 1991, United Reformed Church/Oxford University Press

BPW   Baptist Praise and Worship, 1991, Psalms and Hymns Trust/Oxford University Press

CH3   Church Hymnary (Third Edition), 1973, Oxford University Press

In addition individual hymns particularly suitable for a given reading have been selected from:

AHB   Anglican Hymn Book, 1965, Church Society/Oxford University Press

AMR   Hymns Ancient and Modern Revised, 1950, The Canterbury Press Norwich

BHB   Baptist Hymn Book, 1962, Psalms and Hymns Trust

BWF   Piece Together Praise (Brian Wren), 1996, Hope Publishing Company and Stainer and Bell Ltd

CFW   Church Family Worship, 1991, Jubilate Hymns/Hodder and Stoughton/Hodder Headline plc

CH   Christian Hymns, 1977, Evangelical Movement of Wales

EH   English Hymnal, 1933, A. R. Mowbray & Co Ltd/Oxford University Press

GH   Grace Hymns, 1977, Grace Publications Trust

HF   Hymns of Faith, 1964, CSSM and Scripture Union

HONR   Hymns Old and New, Roman Catholic New Century Edition, 1994, Kevin Mayhew Ltd

HSN   Heaven Shall Not Wait (Wild Goose Songs 1), Wild Goose Publications, The Iona Community

LFB   Love From Below, 1989 (Wild Goose Songs 3), Wild Goose Publications, The Iona Community

LPB   Let's Praise Book 2, 1994, Marshall Pickering/HarperCollins Religious

NSC   New Songs of Praise Book 3, 1987, Oxford University Press

PER   Singing to God (Michael Perry), 1995, Hope Publishing Company (Stainer and Bell Ltd)

PFT   Praise for Today, 1974, Jubilate Hymns/Hodder and Stoughton/Hodder Headline plc

SHF   Songs and Hymns of Fellowship, 1987, Thankyou Music and Kingsway Music/Kingsway's Thankyou Music

SS   Story Song, 1993, The Methodist Church Division of Education and Youth/Stainer and Bell Ltd

STG   Sing to God, 1971, Scripture Union

WAM   Worship Songs Ancient and Modern, 1992, The Canterbury Press Norwich

WOV   With One Voice (Australian Hymn Book), 1979, Collins/HarperCollins Religious

Collation of lists, preparation and layout of originals by Paul Ferguson.

The compilers express their gratitude for financial assistance from the Pratt Green Trust and Hymns Ancient and Modern in preparing this publication.

The convenor acknowledges his indebtedness in the final stages of checking the lists for comprehensiveness and accuracy to *HymnQuest, A Dictionary of Hymnody Volume One* (The Pratt Green Trust 1997) in both its printed and CD-Rom versions.

Year A
The First Sunday of Advent

Isaiah **2**: 1-5; Psalm **122**; Romans **13**: 11-14; Matthew **24**: 36-44

		AMNS	NEH	HTC	HON	MP	H&P	R&S	BPW	CH3
e	Awake, awake, fling off the night	342			49				404	
o	Behold, the mountain of the Lord						50	130	617	312
g	Christ is coming! Let creation									313
o	Christ is the world's true light	346	494	323	78		456	601	618	505
g	Come, thou/O long-expected Jesus	31	3	52	98	102	81	138	139	320
s	Creator of the earth and sky		152							
s	Creator of the starry height / stars of night	23	1		102					
o	Crown him with many crowns	147	352	174	103	109	255	262	37	298
g	Earth was waiting, spent and restless			54					141	
o	For the healing of the nations	361			139		402	620	621	
s	Hark, a herald/thrilling voice / Hark, a trumpet call	24	5	192	196					
g	Hark what a sound, and too divine for hearing						236	660		314
p	How pleased and blest was I						497	563	10	
p	I joyed when to the house of God / Pray that Jerusalem		441				510	727		489
g	Lo, he / Jesus comes with clouds descending	28	9	196	307	424	241	656	314	314
e	Lord, hear our prayer for this new year/day						357			
e	Lord, save thy world; in bitter need	397					425			
s	O come, O come, Emmanuel	26	11	66	358	493	85	126	144	165
g	O day of God, draw near/nigh In beauty	405						632	635	511
es	O heavenly word of God on high		2							
g	O quickly come, dread Judge of all		13							
e	Oft in danger, oft in woe / Christian soldiers, onward go	210	434	524	396	533	715			
g	Sing we the King who is coming to reign					602	244		318	
e	Stand up, stand up for Jesus	221	453	535	457	617	721			481
s	The advent of our King/God	25	14		470					
g	The day of the Lord shall come							637		
g	The Lord will come and not be slow	29	15		489		245	128		321
g	Thou Judge of quick and dead						247			
s	Wake, O wake / Sleepers, wake	32	16	199	529		249	132		315

Isaiah **64**: 1-9; Psalm **80**: 1-7, 17-19; 1 Corinthians **1**: 3-9; Mark **13**: 24-37

		AMNS	NEH	HTC	HON	MP	H&P	R&S	BPW	CH3
g	A safe stronghold/fortress/refuge	114		523		2	661	585	375	406/7
g	All for Jesus!		272	469	10		251		332	
e	All praise to our redeeming Lord					19	753		401	
e	As sons of the day and daughters of light			490						
g	Christ is coming! Let creation									313
g	Christian, seek not yet repose			355						
g	Come, thou/O long-expected Jesus	31	3	52	98	102	81	138	139	320
s	Creator of the starry height / stars of night	23	1		102					
g	Earth was waiting, spent and restless			54					141	
s	Hark, a herald/thrilling voice / Hark, a trumpet call	24	5	192	196					
g	Hark what a sound, and too divine for hearing						236	660		314
g	How firm a foundation			430	216	243		589	380	
o	Jesus, where'er thy people meet / Lord Jesus, when your people	162	390	371	282		549	476		
o	Lo, he / Jesus comes with clouds descending	28	9	196	307	424	241	656	314	314
e	March on, my soul, with strength						716	546		614
s	O come, O come, Emmanuel	26	11	66	358	493	85	126	144	165
g	O day of God, draw near/nigh In beauty	405						632	635	511
e	O Lord, I would delight in thee							593		
g	O quickly come, dread Judge of all		13							
g	Sing we the King who is coming to reign					602	244		318	
g	Sometimes a light surprises	108					571	595		
g	Songs of praise the angels sang	196	451	350			512	667		38
s	The advent of our King/God	25	14		470					
g	The day of the Lord shall come							637		
g	The Lord will come and not be slow	29	15		489		245	128		321
g	Thou Judge of quick and dead						247			
s	Wake, O wake / Sleepers, wake	32	16	199	529		249	132		315
g	Will your anchor hold				561	770	689	598	549	412

Year C
The First Sunday of Advent

Jeremiah **33**: 14-16; Psalm **25**: 1-10; 1 Thessalonians **3**: 9-13; Luke **21**: 25-36

		AMNS	NEH	HTC	HON	MP	H&P	R&S	BPW	CH3
g	Christ is coming! Let creation									313
g	Come and see the shining hope			188		86			271	
g	Come, thou/O long-expected Jesus	31	3	52	98	102	81	138	139	320
s	Creator of the starry height / stars of night	23	1		102					
g	Earth was waiting, spent and restless			54				141		
g	Great God, what do I see and hear			189						
gs	Hark, a herald/thrilling voice / Hark, a trumpet call	24	5	192	196					
g	Hark what a sound, and too divine for hearing						236	660		314
g	Jesus, priceless treasure			461	262		259			
g	Lo, he / Jesus comes with clouds descending	28	9	196	307	424	241	656	314	314
e	My hope is built on nothing less			462		473				411
s	O come, O come, Emmanuel	26	11	66	358	493	85	126	144	165
o	Come, O thou / O come, our all-victorious Lord			441			418			
g	O day of God, draw near/nigh In beauty	405						632	635	511
g	O quickly come, dread Judge of all		13							
p	Show me thy ways, O Lord									74
g	Sing we the King who is coming to reign					602	244		318	
s	The advent of our King/God	25	14		470					
g	The day of the Lord shall come							637		
g	The Lord will come and not be slow	29	15		489		245	128		321
g	Thou Judge of quick and dead						247			
s	Wake, O wake / Sleepers, wake	32	16	199	529		249	132		315

Year A
The Second Sunday of Advent

Isaiah **11**: 1-10; Psalm **72**: 1-7, 18-19; Romans **15**: 4-13; Matthew **3**: 1-12

		AMNS	NEH	HTC	HON	MP	H&P	R&S	BPW	CH3
g	Christ, when for us you were baptized	442					129		405	
e	God, who has caused to be written thy word	467					472			
e	God who spoke in the beginning	468						60		
p	Hail to the Lord's anointed	142	55	190	193	204	125	127	142	317
g	Hark, a herald/thrilling voice / Hark, a trumpet call	24	5	192	196					
p	His large and great dominion shall									167
e	How beauteous/gracious are their feet	301					449	133		
p	Jesus shall reign where'er the sun	143	388	516	277	379	239	269	313	413
g	Lo, from the desert homes	316								
g	Lo, in the wilderness a voice	384	170							
e	Lord, I have made thy word my choice	490					475	316		
e	Lord, thy word abideth / Lord, your word shall guide us	166	407	251	318	446	476	317	102	130
o	My heart and voice I raise						268			
o	O come, O come, Emmanuel	26	11	66	358	493	85	126	144	165
o	O day of God, draw near/nigh In beauty	405						632	635	511
gs	On Jordan's bank the Baptist's cry	27	12	601	401	538	84	134	147	208
e	Rise and hear! the Lord is speaking	509								
g	Sing we the praises of the great forerunner / On this high feast day	315	168							
o	Spirit divine, attend/inspire our prayers			240		614	327	303		107
o	Spirit of wisdom, turn our eyes						385			
e	Thanks/Praise to God whose word	423	438	255			483	319	106	
gs	The advent of our King/God	25	14		470					
o	The day of the Lord shall come							637		
g	The Kingdom of God is justice and joy		333			651	139	200	321	
p	The Lord will come and not be slow	29	15		489		245	128		321
e	The prophets spoke in days of old	513								
e	When Christ was lifted from the earth	525	335					655		
g	When he was baptized in Jordan								234	
g	When Jesus came to Jordan	526					132			

See also Bible Sunday, pages 166-168

Year B
The Second Sunday of Advent

Isaiah **40**: 1-11; Psalm **85**: 1-2, 8-13; 2 Peter **3**: 8-15a; Mark 1: 1-8

		AMNS	NEH	HTC	HON	MP	H&P	R&S	BPW	CH3
s	Before all time the Word existed									162
g	Christ, when for us you were baptized	442					129		405	
s	Earth was waiting, spent and restless			54					141	
s	Hail to the Lord's anointed	142	55	190	193	204	125	127	142	317
g	Hark, a herald/thrilling voice / Hark, a trumpet call	24	5	192	196					
s	Hills of the north, rejoice	470	7		209		237		311	
e	How firm a foundation			430	216	243		589	380	
o	Judge eternal, throned in splendour		490	329	285	395	409	626	627	519
g	Lo, from the desert homes	316								
g	Lo, in the wilderness a voice	384	170							
s	Long ago, prophets knew	484	10				83			
p	Lord, thine heart in love hath yearned							704		75
e	Love divine, all loves excelling	131	408	217	321	449	267	663	559	437
o	March on, my soul, with strength						716	546		614
e	O/Our God, our help in ages past	99	417	37	366	498	358	705	389	611
e	On all the earth thy Spirit shower						321			
gs	On Jordan's bank the Baptist's cry	27	12	601	401	538	84	134	147	208
g	Sing we the praises of the great forerunner / On this high feast day	315	168							
gs	The advent of our King/God	25	14		470					
s	The great Creator of the worlds	511								
g	The Kingdom of God is justice and joy			333		651	139	200	321	
p	The Lord will come and not be slow	29	15		489		245	128		321
s	The voice of God goes out to all the world						140	131		
o	Thou Shepherd of Israel and mine						750			
g	When he was baptized in Jordan								234	
g	When Jesus came to Jordan	526					132			
s	Ye/You servants of the Lord	150	18	598	566		248			319

See also Bible Sunday, pages 166-168

Year C
The Second Sunday of Advent

Baruch 5: 1-9 or Malachi 3: 1-4; (Canticle) Benedictus; Philippians 1: 3-11; Luke 3: 1-6

		AMNS	NEH	HTC	HON	MP	H&P	R&S	BPW	CH3
e	All praise to our redeeming Lord					19	753		401	
s	Before all time the Word existed									162
g	Christ, when for us you were baptized	442					129		405	
s	Earth was waiting, spent and restless			54					141	
e	Father, we thank thee, who hast planted / you now for planting	357	284					444	434	586
o	God is in his temple					186	494	32	7	
s	Hail to the Lord's anointed	142	55	190	193	204	125	127	142	317
g	Hark, a herald/thrilling voice / Hark, a trumpet call	24	5	192	196					
s	Hills of the north, rejoice	470	7		209		237		311	
g	Lo, from the desert homes	316								
g	Lo, in the wilderness a voice	384	170							
s	Long ago, prophets knew	484	10				83			
o	Love divine, all loves excelling	131	408	217	321	449	267	663	559	437
c	O bless the God of Israel			599						
g	O Spirit of the living God			513			322	577	579	496
g	On Jordan's bank the Baptist's cry	27	12	601	401	538	84	134	147	208
g	Sing we the praises of the great forerunner / On this high feast day	315	168							
g	The advent of our King/God	25	14		470					
s	The great Creator of the worlds	511								
g	The Kingdom of God is justice and joy			333		651	139	200	321	
s	The voice of God goes out to all the world						140	131		
g	When he was baptized in Jordan								234	
g	When Jesus came to Jordan	526					132			
s	Ye/You servants of the Lord	150	18	598	566		248			319

See also Bible Sunday, pages 166-168

Year A
The Third Sunday of Advent

Isaiah **35**: 1-10; Psalm **146**: 5-10 or (Canticle) Magnificat; James **5**: 7-10; Matthew **11**: 2-11

		AMNS	NEH	HTC	HON	MP	H&P	R&S	BPW	CH3
o	A great and mighty wonder	43	21	49	2		90		140	192
s	Blest are the saints/is the man / How blest are they						670	541		324
e	Great God, what do I see and hear			189						
g	Hark, a herald/thrilling voice / Hark, a trumpet call	24	5	192	196					
s	How beauteous/gracious are their feet	301					449	133		
p	I'll praise my Maker while I've breath			20		320	439	734	127	
e	Judge eternal, throned in splendour		490	329	285	395	409	626	627	519
o	Let the desert sing			198						
g	Lo, from the desert homes	316								
g	Lo, in the wilderness a voice	384	170							
s	O day of God, draw near/nigh In beauty	405						632	635	511
g	O for a thousand tongues to sing	125	415	219	362	496	744	285	59	371
e	Rejoice! the Lord is King	139	443	180	432	575	243	657	317	296
g	Sing we the praises of the great forerunner / On this high feast day	315	168							
e	Teach me, my God and King	240	456		466		803	538		692
e	Tell out, my soul, the greatness of the Lord	422	186	42	467	631	86	740	391	164
o	The day of the Lord shall come							637		
g	The Kingdom of God is justice and joy			333		651	139	200	321	
s	The race that long / The people that in darkness	52	57	71	491		89	129		168
s	Thy/Your kingdom come, O God	177	499	334	519		783	638	644	322
e	Wait for the Lord (Taizé)				528				148	
o	When the King shall come again			200						

Year B
The Third Sunday of Advent

Isaiah **61**: 1-4, 8-11; Psalm **126** or (Canticle) Magnificat; 1 Thessalonians **5**: 16-24; John **1**: 6-8, 19-28

		AMNS	NEH	HTC	HON	MP	H&P	R&S	BPW	CH3
e	As sons of the day and daughters of light			490						
e	Be thou my vision / Lord be my vision	343	339	545	56	51	378	489	521	87
s	Blest are the saints/is the man / How blest are they						670	541		324
e	Father, who on man dost shower						341			515
o	God is working his purpose out		495	191	172	189	769	573		303
o	Hail to the Lord's anointed	142	55	190	193	204	125	127	142	317
g	Hark, a herald/thrilling voice / Hark, a trumpet call	24	5	192	196					
e	Holy Spirit, ever dwelling/living		141				303	324	290	334
s	How beauteous/gracious are their feet	301					449	133		
p	I will sing, I will sing a song			S15		313		279		
o	I'll praise my Maker while I've breath			20		320	439	734	127	
o	Jesus shall reign where'er the sun	143	388	516	277	379	239	269	313	413
g	Lo, from the desert homes	316								
g	Lo, in the wilderness a voice	384	170							
e	Lord of the Church, we pray for our renewing			499		442			486	
s	O day of God, draw near/nigh In beauty	405						632	635	511
g	On Jordan's bank the Baptist's cry	27	12	601	401	538	84	134	147	208
o	Rejoice, O people, in the mounting years						657			
e	Shepherd divine, our wants relieve	228					558			
g	Sing we the praises of the great forerunner / On this high feast day	315	168							
e	Soldiers of Christ, arise	219	449	533	449	604	719	370	580	441
e	Spirit divine, attend/inspire our prayers			240		614	327	303		107
c	Tell out, my soul, the greatness of the Lord	422	186	42	467	631	86	740	391	164
s	The race that long / The people that in darkness	52	57	71	491		89	129		168
o	The voice of God goes out to all the world						140	131		
o	Thou/God whose almighty / Father your mighty word	180	466	506	514	699	29	38	591	494
s	Thy/Your kingdom come, O God	177	499	334	519		783	638	644	322
p	When Sion's bondage God turned back									393

Year C
The Third Sunday of Advent

Zephaniah 3: 14-20; (Canticle) Isaiah 12: 2-6; Philippians 4: 4-7; Luke 3: 7-18

		AMNS	NEH	HTC	HON	MP	H&P	R&S	BPW	CH3
s	Blest are the saints/is the man / How blest are they						670	541		324
o	Christ is the King! O friends rejoice	345	345	492				571	475	474
g	Christ, when for us you were baptized	442					129		405	
c	Christ's Church shall glory in his power			522						
o	Glorious things of thee/you are spoken	172	362	494	158	173	817	560	480	421
g	Hark, a herald/thrilling voice / Hark, a trumpet call	24	5	192	196					
s	How beauteous/gracious are their feet	301					449	133		
o	Jesus is Lord of all the earth			53	24	30	250	234	31	
e	Like a mighty river flowing			32		419			632	
g	Lo, from the desert homes	316								
g	Lo, in the wilderness a voice	384	170							
e	May the mind of Christ my Saviour			550	334	463	739		537	432
s	O day of God, draw near/nigh In beauty	405						632	635	511
g	O Spirit of the living God			513			322	577	579	496
g	On Jordan's bank the Baptist's cry	27	12	601	401	538	84	134	147	208
e	Rejoice in the Lord always (1v chorus)				430	577		286		
o	Rejoice! the Lord is King	139	443	180	432	575	243	657	317	296
g	Sing we the praises of the great forerunner / On this high feast day	315	168							
g	The advent of our King/God	25	14		470					
g	The Kingdom of God is justice and joy			333		651	139	200	321	
s	The race that long / The people that in darkness	52	57	71	491		89	129		168
s	Thy/Your kingdom come, O God	177	499	334	519		783	638	644	322
c	To God be the glory			584	522	708	463	289	566	374
e	We praise you, Lord, for all that's true and pure							516		
e	What a friend we have in Jesus			373	541	746	559	413	603	
g	When he was baptized in Jordan								234	
g	When Jesus came to Jordan	526					132			

Year A
The Fourth Sunday of Advent

Isaiah **7**: 10-16; Psalm **80**: 1-7, 17-19; Romans **1**: 1-7; Matthew **1**: 18-25

		AMNS	NEH	HTC	HON	MP	H&P	R&S	BPW	CH3
o	A Virgin most pure, as the prophets do tell						93			
g	All hail the power of Jesus' name	140	332	587/203	13	13	252		29	382
o	And art thou come with us to dwell						415	136		
s	Behold, the mountain of the Lord						50	130	617	312
g	Come and join the celebration					83	97	166	160	
g	Earth was waiting, spent and restless			54					141	
g	Glory be to God on high						101			
p	Great Shepherd of thy/your people, hear	164		363			490	387		
g	Had he not loved us			57						
s	Hark the glad sound! The Saviour comes	30	6	193	198	210	82	137	143	160
g	Jesus, hope of every nation			58						
s	Joy to the world, the Lord is come			197	283	393	77	135	315	
g	Let earth and heaven combine						109	190		
s	Lift up your heads, ye/you mighty gates	483	8				240			12
e	Long ago, prophets knew	484	10				83			
e	May the grace of Christ our Saviour	181		370	333		762		110	634
s	O come, O come, Emmanuel	26	11	66	358	493	85	126	144	165
g	The darkness turns to dawn			68						
s	The Lord will come and not be slow	29	15		489		245	128		321
g	The race that long / The people that in darkness	52	57	71	491		89	129		168
s	There's a light upon the mountains					679	246		149	
s	Thy kingdom come! on bended knee	178	500		520					323
g	To the Name of our / that brings salvation	121	470	222	523		80	291		373
eg	What Adam's disobedience cost	524					430			
g	Where do Christmas songs begin								180	
g	Where is this stupendous stranger	527	41					174		
g	Within a crib my Saviour lay			70						

Year B
The Fourth Sunday of Advent

2 Samuel **7**: 1-11, 16; (Canticle) Magnificat or Psalm **89**: 1-4, 19-26; Romans **16**: 25-27; Luke **1**: 26-38

		AMNS	NEH	HTC	HON	MP	H&P	R&S	BPW	CH3
o	Amazing grace			28	27	31	215	92	550	
g	At the name of Jesus	148	338	172	46	41	74	261	370	300
s	Behold, the mountain of the Lord						50	130	617	312
o	Behold the servant of the Lord						788			
g	Come all you good people			80						
g	Gabriel's message does away		4							
e	God of God the uncreated			56						
s	Hark the glad sound! The Saviour comes	30	6	193	198	210	82	137	143	160
g	Jesus, the name high over all			213		385	264			
s	Joy to the world, the Lord is come			197	283	393	77	135	315	
s	Lift up your heads, ye/you mighty gates	483	8				240			12
g	Long ago, prophets knew	484	10				83			
o	Lord, you need no house			546					349	
e	May the mind of Christ my Saviour			550	334	463	739		537	432
g	Now tell us, gentle Mary							142		
s	O come, O come, Emmanuel	26	11	66	358	493	85	126	144	165
p	O greatly blest the people are									390
e	Of the Father's love/heart begotten / God of God	33	33	56	395		79	181	145	198
c	Tell out, my soul, the greatness of the Lord	422	186	42	467	631	86	740	391	164
g	The angel Gabriel from heaven came				471		87	139	177	
s	The Lord will come and not be slow	29	15		489		245	128		321
s	There's a light upon the mountains					679	246		149	
s	Thy kingdom come! on bended knee	178	500		520					323
p	Timeless love! we sing the story			47		707	60			
g	To the Name of our / that brings salvation	121	470	222	523		80	291		373

Year C
The Fourth Sunday of Advent

Micah **5**: 2-5a; (Canticle) Magnificat or Psalm **80**: 1-7; Hebrews **10**: 5-10; Luke **1**: 39-45 [46-55]

		AMNS	NEH	HTC	HON	MP	H&P	R&S	BPW	CH3
g	A great and mighty wonder	43	21	49	2		90		140	192
g	All hail the power of Jesus' name	140	332	587/203	13	13	252		29	382
s	Behold, the mountain of the Lord						50	130	617	312
o	Bethelem, of noblest / Earth has many	48	48		113		122			199
g	Come and join the celebration					83	97	166	160	
g	Earth was waiting, spent and restless			54					141	
o	From east to west, from shore to shore		20				99	172		189
g	From heaven above to earth I come						100	154		
g	Glory be to God on high						101			
g	Had he not loved us			57						
s	Hark the glad sound! The Saviour comes	30	6	193	198	210	82	137	143	160
g	Jesus, hope of every nation			58						
s	Joy to the world, the Lord is come			197	283	393	77	135	315	
eg	Let earth and heaven combine						109	190		
s	Lift up your heads, ye/you mighty gates	483	8				240			12
s	O come, O come, Emmanuel	26	11	66	358	493	85	126	144	165
o	O little town of Bethlehem	40	32	88	377	503	113	145	170	172
c	Tell out, my soul, the greatness of the Lord	422	186	42	467	631	86	740	391	164
g	The darkness turns to dawn			68						
s	The Lord will come and not be slow	29	15		489		245	128		321
g	The race that long / The people that in darkness	52	57	71	491		89	129		168
s	There's a light upon the mountains					679	246		149	
s	Thy kingdom come! on bended knee	178	500		520					323
g	To the Name of our / that brings salvation	121	470	222	523		80	291		373
g	What Adam's disobedience cost	524					430			
g	When came in flesh the incarnate word		17							
g	Where do Christmas songs begin								180	
g	Where is this stupendous stranger	527	41					174		
g	Within a crib my Saviour lay			70						

Years A, B, C
Christmas Midnight

For readings see Christmas Day

		AMNS	NEH	HTC	HON	MP	H&P	R&S	BPW	CH3
s	A great and mighty wonder	43	21	49	2		90		140	192
I	All my heart this night rejoices			76			91	143		171
s	Angels from the realms of glory	39		77	34	35	92	163	155	182
s	Away in a manger		22	72	51	47	94	146	157	195
I	Before the world began							180		
sg	Christians, awake	36	24	78	84	80	96	158	159	190
I	Come and sing the Christmas story			81					161	
s	Come, thou Redeemer of the earth		19							
I	Come, thou/O long-expected Jesus	31	3	52	98	102	81	138	139	320
s	Hark! the herald angels sing	35	26	59	199	211	106	159	165	169
s	In the bleak midwinter	42	28	600	248	337	107	162	166	178
I	It came upon the midnight clear	41	29	87	253	345	108	144	168	170
s	O come all ye/you faithful	34	30	597	357	491	110	160	169	191
s	O little town of Bethlehem	40	32	88	377	503	113	145	170	172
s	Of the Father's love/heart begotten / God of God	33	33	56	395		79	181	145	198
I	On Christmas night all Christians sing				400	537	115	153		181
s	Once in royal David's city	46	34	67	403	539	114	167	172	193
lg	Silent night / Still the night		35	95	444	597	112	147	176	176
sg	While shepherds watched their flocks / While humble shepherds	37	42	94	554	764	120	155	182	174

Years A, B, C: Christmas Day

Set I: Isaiah 9: 2-7; Psalm 96; Titus 2: 11-14; Luke 2: 1-14 [15-20]

Set II: Isaiah 62: 6-12; Psalm 97; Titus 3: 4-7; Luke 2: [1-7] 8-20

Set III: Isaiah 52: 7-10; Psalm 98; Hebrews 1: 1-4 [5-12]; John 1: 1-14 (to be used at some service)

		AMNS	NEH	HTC	HON	MP	H&P	R&S	BPW	CH3
o1	A great and mighty wonder	43	21	49	2		90		140	192
s	Away in a manger		22	72	51	47	94	146	157	195
l	Born in the night, Mary's child				65	62	95	188	156	
s	Child in the manger			51	75	71		150	158	180
lg	Christians, awake	36	24	78	84	80	96	158	159	190
s	Cloth for the cradle				86					
l	Come and join the celebration					83	97	166	160	
l	Good Christian men / Good Christians all, rejoice		107	154	181	196	104	238	250	183
s	Hark! the herald angels sing	35	26	59	199	211	106	159	165	169
o3	How beauteous/gracious are their feet	301					449	133		
o3	How lovely on the mountains are the feet of him				219	249			310	
g1	Infant holy, infant lowly			86	251	342		149	167	186
s	It came upon the midnight clear	41	29	87	253	345	108	144	168	170
o2	Make way, make way, for Christ the King				329	457		141		
s	O come all ye/you faithful	34	30	597	357	491	110	160	169	191
s	O little one sweet, O little one mild		31		376		111			
s	O little town of Bethlehem	40	32	88	377	503	113	145	170	172
s	Of the Father's love/heart begotten / God of God	33	33	56	395		79	181	145	198
s	Once in royal David's city	46	34	67	403	539	114	167	172	193
sg	See him lying on a bed of straw			91	440	589	118	151	174	
o1	The darkness turns to dawn			68						
s	The first Nowell		36	93	477	644	119		178	173
e1	The grace of God has dawned upon the world							741		
o1	The race that long / The people that in darkness	52	57	71	491		89	129		168
s	Thou who wast rich / Lord, you were rich			63		700				
o1	To us a child of royal birth	45		64						
o1	Unto us a Child / boy/ Jesus Christ the Lord is born		39	83	526	714	127	169	181	187
s	What child is this?		40		542	749		170		
s	While shepherds watched their flocks / While humble shepherds	37	42	94	554	764	120	155	182	174

Year A
The First Sunday of Christmas

Isaiah **63**: 7-9; Psalm **148**; Hebrews **2**: 10-18; Matthew **2**: 13-23

		AMNS	NEH	HTC	HON	MP	H&P	R&S	BPW	CH3
s	A great and mighty wonder	43	21	49	2		90		140	192
s	Angels from the realms of glory	39		77	34	35	92	163	155	182
s	Before the world began							180		
s	Behold the great Creator makes	44	23	50	58			171		197
s	Child in the manger			51	75	71		150	158	180
s	Child of the stable's secret birth		43	53			124			
e	Christ is the world's true light	346	494	323	78		456	601	618	505
s	Go tell it on the mountain				165	179	135	164	571	
s	God from on high hath/has heard	38					102	176		
s	God rest you merry, gentlemen		25	84	176		103		163	184
s	Had he not loved us			57						
s	Holy child, how still you lie			60		236				
s	In the bleak midwinter	42	28	600	248	337	107	162	166	178
s	Jesus, hope of every nation			58						
s	Lord, who left the highest heaven			97						
s	Love came down at Christmas			62	320	451	105	614	171	194
s	O little one sweet, O little one mild		31		376		111			
s	O sing a song of Bethlehem	413						201		220
s	Of the Father's love/heart begotten / God of God	33	33	56	395		79	181	145	198
s	Once in royal David's city	46	34	67	403	539	114	167	172	193
p	Praise the Lord, his glories show			345			14	102		359
s	See him lying on a bed of straw			91	440	589	118	151	174	
s	See, amid the winter's snow / in yonder manger low			90	439		117	157	173	179
s	The first Nowell		36	93	477	644	119		178	173
s	The growing limbs of God the Son / The heavenly child	50	45							
s	Thou didst leave thy throne	250	465		513	697	154	192	179	
s	To us a child of royal birth	45		64						
g	Unto us a Child / boy/ Jesus Christ the Lord is born		39	83	526	714	127	169	181	187
s	What child is this?		40		542	749		170		
s	Who would think that what was needed				558			178		

Isaiah 61:10 — 62:3; Psalm 148; Galatians 4: 4-7; Luke 2: 15-21

		AMNS	NEH	HTC	HON	MP	H&P	R&S	BPW	CH3
s	A song was heard at Christmas			75						
s	Angels from the realms of glory	39		77	34	35	92	163	155	182
s	Before the world began							180		
s	Child in the manger			51	75	71		150	158	180
s	Child of the stable's secret birth		43	53			124			
e	Father God, I wonder how I managed to exist				119	128				
s	Go tell it on the mountain				165	179	135	164	571	
s	God from on high hath/has heard	38					102	176		
s	God rest you merry, gentlemen		25	84	176		103		163	184
s	Had he not loved us			57						
s	Holy child, how still you lie			60		236				
s	How brightly shines/beams the morning star		27					182		202
s	In the bleak midwinter	42	28	600	248	337	107	162	166	178
s	Infant holy, infant lowly			86	251	342		149	167	186
s	Jesus, hope of every nation			58						
s	Lord, who left the highest heaven			97						
s	Love came down at Christmas			62	320	451	105	614	171	194
g	O come all ye/you faithful	34	30	597	357	491	110	160	169	191
s	Once in royal David's city	46	34	67	403	539	114	167	172	193
p	Praise the Lord, his glories show			345			14	102		359
s	See him lying on a bed of straw			91	440	589	118	151	174	
s	See, amid the winter's snow / in yonder manger low			90	439		117	157	173	179
s	The first Nowell		36	93	477	644	119		178	173
s	The growing limbs of God the Son / The heavenly child	50	45							
s	The Maker of the sun and moon		38					173		
s	Thou didst leave thy throne	250	465		513	697	154	192	179	
s	To us a child of royal birth	45		64						
s	Unto us a Child / boy/ Jesus Christ the Lord is born		39	83	526	714	127	169	181	187
s	What child is this?		40		542	749		170		
g	While shepherds watched their flocks / While humble shepherds	37	42	94	554	764	120	155	182	174
s	Who would think that what was needed				558			178		

Year C
The First Sunday of Christmas

1 Samuel **2**: 18-20, 26; Psalm **148**; Colossians **3**: 12-17; Luke **2**: 41-52

		AMNS	NEH	HTC	HON	MP	H&P	R&S	BPW	CH3
s	Before the world began							180		
s	Angels from the realms of glory	39		77	34	35	92	163	155	182
s	Behold the great Creator makes	44	23	50	58			171		197
s	Child in the manger			51	75	71		150	158	180
s	Child of the stable's secret birth		43	53			124			
s	Go tell it on the mountain				165	179	135	164	571	
s	God from on high hath/has heard	38					102	176		
s	God rest you merry, gentlemen		25	84	176		103		163	184
s	Had he not loved us			57						
s	Holy child, how still you lie			60		236				
s	I cannot tell why/how he whom angels worship		194	226	266	238	265	381		
s	In the bleak midwinter	42	28	600	248	337	107	162	166	178
s	Jesus, hope of every nation			58						
s	Lord, who left the highest heaven			97						
s	Love came down at Christmas			62	320	451	105	614	171	194
s	Of the Father's love/heart begotten / God of God	33	33	56	395		79	181	145	198
s	Once in royal David's city	46	34	67	403	539	114	167	172	193
p	Praise the Lord, his glories show		345				14	102		359
s	See him lying on a bed of straw			91	440	589	118	151	174	
s	See, amid the winter's snow / in yonder manger low			90	439		117	157	173	179
s	The first Nowell		36	93	477	644	119		178	173
s	The great God of heaven		37							
s	The growing limbs of God the Son / The heavenly child	50	45							
s	The Maker of the sun and moon		38					173		
s	Thou didst leave thy throne	250	465		513	697	154	192	179	
s	To us a child of royal birth	45		64						
s	Unto us a Child / boy/ Jesus Christ the Lord is born		39	83	526	714	127	169	181	187
s	What child is this?		40		542	749		170		
s	Who would think that what was needed				558			178		

New Year

		AMNS	NEH	HTC	HON	MP	H&P	R&S	BPW	CH3
s	Be thou / O Lord, my/our guardian	217	64	374	55					
s	Be thou my vision / Lord be my vision	343	339	545	56	51	378	489	521	87
s	Breathe on me, Breath of God	157	342	226	69	67	280	295	282	103
s	Christ be the Lord of all our days			256						
s	Father, let us dedicate			257						
s	For thy/your mercy and thy/your grace			258	140					612
s	God is working his purpose out		495	191	172	189	769	573		303
s	Great God, we sing that mighty / your guiding hand						356	63	552	613
s	Great is thy/your faithfulness			260	186	200	66	96	553	
s	How good is the God we adore / This, this is the God			450	217	244	277	542	338	
s	Lead us, heavenly Father, lead us	224	393	595	293	400	68	543	597	90
s	Lord, for the years			328	310	428		603	535	
s	Lord of our growing years			259					514	
s	Lord of the changing year			261						
s	Make me a channel of your peace			S19	328	456	776	629	634	
s	New every morning is the love	2	238	270	349	480	636	536		47
s	O Christ the same, through all our story's pages		258	263						
s	O God of Bethel / O God of Jacob	216	416	35	364		442	71	599	72
s	O/Our God, our help in ages past	99	417	37	366	498	358	705	389	611
s	Through all the changing scenes of life	209	467	46	516	702	73	685	544	
s	When morning gilds the skies	146	473	223	551	756	276	292	73	370

See also The Naming and Circumcision of Jesus, page 188

Years A, B, C
The Second Sunday of Christmas

Jeremiah **31**: 7-14; Psalm **147**: 12-20; Ephesians **1**: 3-14; John **1**: [1-9] 10-18

or Ecclesiasticus **24**: 1-12; (Canticle) Wisdom **10**: 15-21; Ephesians **1**: 3-14; John **1**: [1-9] 10-18

		AMNS	NEH	HTC	HON	MP	H&P	R&S	BPW	CH3
s	A great and mighty wonder	43	21	49	2		90		140	192
s	A song was heard at Christmas			75						
s	Angel-voices ever singing	163	336	307	33	34	484	405	1	455
s	Before the world began							180		
s	Child in the manger			51	75	71		150	158	180
s	Go tell it on the mountain				165	179	135	164	571	
o	God is working his purpose out		495	191	172	189	769	573		303
s	Had he not loved us			57						
g	Hark! the herald angels sing	35	26	59	199	211	106	159	165	169
s	Holy child, how still you lie			60		236				
s	How brightly shines/beams the morning star		27					182		202
s	Infant holy, infant lowly			86	251	342		149	167	186
s	Jesus, hope of every nation			58						
s	Lord, who left the highest heaven			97						
s	Love came down at Christmas			62	320	451	105	614	171	194
s	O little one sweet, O little one mild		31		376		111			
s	Once in royal David's city	46	34	67	403	539	114	167	172	193
ge	Praise be to Christ in whom we see			220						
s	See, amid the winter's snow / in yonder manger low			90	439		117	157	173	179
s	See him lying on a bed of straw			91	440	589	118	151	174	
s	Son of the Lord most high	420					152	202	210	219
s	The first Nowell		36	93	477	644	119		178	173
s	The great God of heaven		37							
s	The growing limbs of God the Son / The heavenly child	50	45							
s	Thou didst leave thy throne	250	465		513	697	154	192	179	
s	To us a child of royal birth	45		64						
s	What child is this?		40		542	749		170		
s	Who can measure heaven and earth			27						
s	Who would think that what was needed				558			178		
g	You laid aside your majesty					795				

StF

Isaiah **60**: 1-6; Psalm **72**: [1-9] 10-15; Ephesians **3**: 1-12; Matthew **2**: 1-12

		AMNS	NEH	HTC	HON	MP	H&P	R&S	BPW	CH3
s	Angel-voices ever singing	163	336	307	33	34	484	405	1	455
s	As with gladness	51	47	99	41	39	121	184	189	200
o	Be thou my vision / Lord be my vision	343	339	545	56	51	378	489	521	87
s	Behold the great Creator makes	44	23	50	58			171		197
s	Bethelem, of noblest / Earth has many	48	48		113		122			199
s	Brightest and best of the sons of the morning	47	49	338	71	65	123	183	190	201
s	Child of the stable's secret birth		43	53			124			
o	City of God, Jerusalem			187						
g	Faithful vigil ended	453	44	55	118	125				
g	From the eastern mountains	327	50							
g	Hail, thou source of every blessing		51							
p	Hail to the Lord's anointed	142	55	190	193	204	125	127	142	317
g	Holy child, how still you lie			60		236				
s	In the bleak midwinter	42	28	600	248	337	107	162	166	178
s	Jesus, good above all other	378	387	96	269		732	528		111
l	Let all mortal flesh keep silence	256	295	61	295		266	454	441	577
s	Let earth and heaven combine						109	190		
s	Lord, when the wise men came from far							186		
s	Lord, who left the highest heaven			97						
l	O worship / Worship the Lord in the beauty of holiness	49	52	344	394	529	505	187	22	40
s	Shepherds came, their praises / Angel voices, richly	180		74				156	192	175
s	Songs of thankfulness and praise	53	56	98	451			191		
s	The first Nowell		36	93	477	644	119		178	173
o	The race that long / The people that in darkness	52	57	71	491		89	129		168
s	What child is this?		40		542	749		170		
s	Why, Herod, so unpitying / impious Herod / How vain		46					189		209
s	Wise men, seeking Jesus						128	185		222
s	Wise men, they came to look for wisdom			100						

Year A
The Baptism of Christ (The First Sunday of Epiphany)

Isaiah **42**: 1-9; Psalm **29**; Acts **10**: 34-43; Matthew **3**: 13-17

		AMNS	NEH	HTC	HON	MP	H&P	R&S	BPW	CH3
e	A man there lived in Galilee	334			3					
a	All hail the power of Jesus' name	140	332	587/203	13	13	252		29	382
e	Awake, awake, fling off the night	342			49				404	
o	Be thou my vision / Lord be my vision	343	339	545	56	51	378	489	521	87
g	Christ, when for us you were baptized	442					129		405	
g	Crown him with many crowns	147	352	174	103	109	255	262	37	298
g	Name of all majesty			218		481				
l	Now is eternal life	402	114		351		203	432		
g	O love, how deep, how broad, how high	119	425		383		229	283	207	223
s	O worship / Worship the Lord in the beauty of holiness	49	52	344	394	529	505	187	22	40
g	On Jordan's bank the Baptist's cry	27	12	601	401	538	84	134	147	208
g	Songs of thankfulness and praise	53	56	98	451			191		
g	Spirit of God, unseen as the wind								295	
e	The Church's one foundation	170	484	501	473	640	515	566	393	420
o	The Kingdom of God is justice and joy			333		651	139	200	321	
o	The race that long / The people that in darkness	52	57	71	491		89	129		168
g	The sinless one to Jordan came		58							
g	To the Name of our / that brings salvation	121	470	222	523		80	291		373
e	We have a gospel to proclaim	431	486	519	532	728	465		585	
g	When Jesus came to Jordan	526					132			
g	Why, Herod, so unpitying / impious Herod / How vain		46					189		209
o	With joy we meditate the grace	530				774	235	206	275	

Year B
The Baptism of Christ (The First Sunday of Epiphany)

Genesis **1**: 1-5; Psalm **29**; Acts **19**: 1-7; Mark **1**: 4-11

		AMNS	NEH	HTC	HON	MP	H&P	R&S	BPW	CH3
e	Awake, awake, fling off the night	342			49				404	
o	Be thou my vision / Lord be my vision	343	339	545	56	51	378	489	521	87
e	Breathe on me, Breath of God	157	342	226	69	67	280	295	282	103
e	Christ on whom the Spirit rested			228						
g	Christ, when for us you were baptized	442					129		405	
g	Christians, lift up your hearts … Praise for the Spirit	444		229						
e	Come, gracious Spirit, heavenly dove	153	347							116
g	Crown him with many crowns	147	352	174	103	109	255	262	37	298
og	Give to our God immortal praise	460		31	155	171	22	94	47	
l	God, that madest earth and heaven	12	245		178		641			
s	Hail to the Lord's anointed	142	55	190	193	204	125	127	142	317
g	How sweet the name of Jesus sounds	122	374	211	220	251	257	277	339	376
o	Morning has broken		237	265	337	467	635	45	132	
g	Name of all majesty			218		481				
l	Now is eternal life	402	114		351		203	432		
e	O Breath of life, come sweeping / O Breath of love, come breathe			237	356	488	777	302	293	339
g	O love, how deep, how broad, how high	119	425		383		229	283	207	223
s	O worship / Worship the Lord in the beauty of holiness	49	52	344	394	529	505	187	22	40
g	On Jordan's bank the Baptist's cry	27	12	601	401	538	84	134	147	208
g	Songs of thankfulness and praise	53	56	98	451			191		
og	Spirit divine, attend/inspire our prayers			240		614	327	303		107
g	Spirit of the living God, fall afresh on me			S23	454	612	295	308	298	
og	Thanks/Praise to God whose word	423	438	255			483	319	106	
o	The race that long / The people that in darkness	52	57	71	491		89	129		168
g	The sinless one to Jordan came		58							
o	Thou/God whose almighty / Father your mighty word	180	466	506	514	699	29	38	591	494
g	To the Name of our / that brings salvation	121	470	222	523		80	291		373
g	Why, Herod, so unpitying / impious Herod / How vain		46					189		209

Year C
The Baptism of Christ (The First Sunday of Epiphany)

Isaiah **43**: 1-7; Psalm **29**; Acts **8**: 14-17; Luke **3**: 15-17, 21-22

		AMNS	NEH	HTC	HON	MP	H&P	R&S	BPW	CH3
o	Amazing grace			28	27	31	215	92	550	
e	Awake, awake, fling off the night	342			49				404	
e	Be thou my vision / Lord be my vision	343	339	545	56	51	378	489	521	87
l	Christ, when for us you were baptized	442					129		405	
g	Christians, lift up your hearts ... Praise for the Spirit	444		229						
g	Come, gracious Spirit, heavenly dove	153	347							116
s	Crown him with many crowns	147	352	174	103	109	255	262	37	298
s	Hail to the Lord's anointed	142	55	190	193	204	125	127	142	317
o	How firm a foundation			430	216	243		589	380	
g	My song is love unknown	63	86	136	346	478	173	207	204	224
g	Name of all majesty			218		481				
l	Now is eternal life	402	114		351		203	432		
e	O Breath of life, come sweeping / O Breath of love, come breathe			237	356	488	777	302	293	339
g	O love, how deep, how broad, how high	119	425		383		229	283	207	223
s	O worship / Worship the Lord in the beauty of holiness	49	52	344	394	529	505	187	22	40
g	On Jordan's bank the Baptist's cry	27	12	601	401	538	84	134	147	208
g	Spirit divine, attend/inspire our prayers			240		614	327	303		107
e	Spirit of the living God, fall afresh on me			S23	454	612	295	308	298	
o	The race that long / The people that in darkness	52	57	71	491		89	129		168
g	The sinless one to Jordan came		58							
g	To the Name of our / that brings salvation	121	470	222	523		80	291		373
g	When Jesus came to Jordan	526					132			

Year A
The Second Sunday of Epiphany

Isaiah **49**: 1-7; Psalm **40**: 1-11; 1 Corinthians **1**: 1-9; John **1**: 29-42

		AMNS	NEH	HTC	HON	MP	H&P	R&S	BPW	CH3
g	Christ on whom the Spirit rested			228						
g	Christ, when for us you were baptized	442					129		405	
g	Come, let us join our cheerful songs	144	349	206	94	93	810	382	6	
g	Crown him with many crowns	147	352	174	103	109	255	262	37	298
g	Glory, glory in the highest					174				
o	God is our strength and refuge		527			188			308	
o	God is working his purpose out		495	191	172	189	769	573		303
e	God of gods, we sound his praises			340				46		
e	God of grace and God of glory	367		324	174	192	712	344	572	88
e	Great is thy/your faithfulness			260	186	200	66	96	553	
s	Hail to the Lord's anointed	142	55	190	193	204	125	127	142	317
g	Jesus calls us: o'er/in the tumult	312	200	104	266	359	141	355		211
s	Jesus, hope of every nation			58						
s	Jesus, the name high over all			213		385	264			
g	Just as I am, without one plea	246	294	440	287	396	697	364	346	79
o	Like a river glorious			463		421				
o	Safe in the shadow of the Lord			445		583				
s	Songs of thankfulness and praise	53	56	98	451			191		
s	The race that long / The people that in darkness	52	57	71	491		89	129		168
g	The sinless one to Jordan came		58							
g	There is a Redeemer				500	673				
g	When Jesus came to Jordan	526					132			
o	Ye/You servants of God, your Master proclaim	149	476	520	565	784	278	293	76	372

Year B
The Second Sunday of Epiphany

1 Samuel **3**: 1-10 [11-20]; Psalm **139**: 1-6, 13-18; Revelation **5**: 1-10; John **1**: 43-51

		AMNS	NEH	HTC	HON	MP	H&P	R&S	BPW	CH3
e	All heaven declares				14	14				
e	Alleluia! sing to Jesus	262	271	170	26	207	592		270	
o	Be still and know that I am God				52	48			280	
o	Be still and know that I am God, and there							347		
e	Bright the vision that delighted / Round the Lord	96	343	578	70		445	665	71	353
e	Come, let us join our cheerful songs	144	349	206	94	93	810	382	6	
l	Forth in thy/your name, O Lord	239	235	306	143	159	381	521	526	463
e	Hail thou/our once-despisèd/rejected Jesus			175	192	203	222		273	
s	Hail to the Lord's anointed	142	55	190	193	204	125	127	142	317
o	Hushed was the evening hymn					253	523	526		123
g	I cannot tell why/how he whom angels worship			194	226	266	238	265	381	
o	I, the Lord of sea and sky				235					
g	Jesus calls us: o'er/in the tumult	312	200	104	266	359	141	355		211
g	Just as I am, without one plea	246	294	440	287	396	697	364	346	79
e	Lion of Judah: SHF 330									
e	Lord, enthroned in heavenly splendour	263	296	416	309	431	616			583
o	Lord, speak to me, that I may speak			510		444	553	613	611	485
p	Lord, you have searched and known my ways						71	70	564	
e	O worship the King all glorious above	101	433	24	393	528	28	47	63	35
s	Songs of thankfulness and praise	53	56	98	451			191		
o	Speak, Lord, in the stillness			253		608			105	
s	The race that long / The people that in darkness	52	57	71	491		89	129		168
e	There is a Redeemer				500	673				
o	When heaven's voice was still: SS71									
g	Will you come and follow me?				560			558	363	
g	You are the King of glory				570	790		271	74	

Year C
The Second Sunday of Epiphany

Isaiah **62**: 1-5; Psalm **36**: 5-10; 1 Corinthians **12**: 1-11; John **2**: 1-11

		AMNS	NEH	HTC	HON	MP	H&P	R&S	BPW	CH3
e	Christ from whom all blessings flow			491			764	561		
e	Come down, O Love Divine	156	137	231	90	89	281	294	283	115
e	Filled with the Spirit's power	359		233	131		314			
e	Gracious Spirit, Holy Ghost / Holy Spirit, gracious Guest	154	367	474	184	198	301	310	288	438
s	Hail to the Lord's anointed	142	55	190	193	204	125	127	142	317
e	Holy Spirit, come, confirm us	471	140		214		288	298	289	
p	Immortal, invisible, God only wise	199	377	21	242	327	9	67	383	32
g	Jesus, come! for we invite you			109						
e	Jesus is Lord! creation's voice proclaims it			S17	270	367	260	268	384	
g	Jesus, Lord, we pray	475		302			365			
g	Lord Jesus Christ, invited guest and Saviour			297						
e	O thou/Lord who came[st]	233	431	552/596	392	525	745	433	355	110
e	Of all the Spirit's gifts to me	503					320			
g	Songs of thankfulness and praise	53	56	98	451			191		
e	Spirit of holiness, wisdom and faithfulness			246		611				
e	Take my life, and let it be	249		554	464	624	705	371	358	462
o	The Church's one foundation	170	484	501	473	640	515	566	393	420
s	The race that long / The people that in darkness	52	57	71	491		89	129		168
e	The Spirit came, as promised			244					297	
g	Why, Herod, so unpitying / impious Herod / How vain		46					189		209

Year A
The Third Sunday of Epiphany

Isaiah **9**: 1-4; Psalm **27**: 1, 4-9; 1 Corinthians **1**: 10-18; Matthew **4**: 12-23

		AMNS	NEH	HTC	HON	MP	H&P	R&S	BPW	CH3
s	As the bridegroom/bride is	340					30	517		
e	Christ from whom all blessings flow			491			764	561		
es	Christ is the King! O friends rejoice	345	345	492				571	475	474
p	Christ is the world's true light	346	494	323	78		456	601	618	505
o	Christ, whose glory fills the skies	4	234	266	82	79	457	380		114
g	Dear Lord and Father of mankind	115	353	356	106	111	673	492	84	76
es	Father, Lord of all creation	356			122				620	
e	Father make us one					137				
l	Forth in the peace of Christ we go	458	361	542	142			602	607	589
es	God is love, and where true love is / Here in Christ we gather	465	513				757	473		
s	Hail to the Lord's anointed	142	55	190	193	204	125	127	142	317
es	I come with joy to meet my Lord	473		408	227		610	447	437	
g	I want to walk with Jesus Christ			S16		302		367		
g	Jesus calls us: o'er/in the tumult	312	200	104	266	359	141	355		211
g	Jesus who walked beside the lake: SS81									
g	Jesus, hope of every nation			58						
es	Jesus, Lord, we look to thee	380	481				759	564		
o	O God beyond all praising			36	363					
e	O thou who at thy eucharist / O Christ at your first eucharist	265	302	420	391		779			492
s	Songs of thankfulness and praise	53	56	98	451			191		
g	'The Kingdom is upon you!'	512								
g	The Kingdom of God is justice and joy			333		651	139	200	321	
o	The light of Christ					652				
o	The race that long / The people that in darkness	52	57	71	491		89	129		168
g	Thy kingdom come! on bended knee	178	500		520					323
e	When I survey the wondrous cross	67	95	147	549	755	180	217	233	254
es	Where love and loving-kindness dwell	528								
g	Will you come and follow me?				560			558	363	

Year B
The Third Sunday of Epiphany

Genesis **14**: 17-20; Psalm **128**; Revelation **19**: 6-10; John **2**: 1-11

		AMNS	NEH	HTC	HON	MP	H&P	R&S	BPW	CH3
e	Alleluia, for the Lord our God					205				
o	Behold the eternal King and Priest			397						
es	Christ is the King! O friends rejoice	345	345	492				571	475	474
e	Deck thyself/yourself, my soul, with gladness	257	280	400	108		606	446		567
es	Father, Lord of all creation	356			122				620	
I	Forth in the peace of Christ we go	458	361	542	142			602	607	589
e	Glory, love, and praise, and honour	461	287		160		35			
es	God is love, and where true love is / Here in Christ we gather	465	513				757	473		
s	Hail to the Lord's anointed	142	55	190	193	204	125	127	142	317
e	Here, Lord, we take the broken bread			404			604	448	440	
e	Here, O my Lord, I see thee/you	274		406		230	608		436	573
es	I come with joy to meet my Lord	473		408	227		610	447	437	
o	I will call upon the Lord					306				
g	Jesus, come! for we invite you			109						
es	Jesus, Lord, we look to thee	380	481				759	564		
g	Jesus, Lord, we pray	475		302			365			
e	Lift high the cross	72		508	303	417	170	422	575	550
g	Lord Jesus Christ, invited guest and Saviour			297						
I	O thou who at thy eucharist / O Christ at your first eucharist	265	302	420	391		779			492
g	One shall tell another				406	541				
e	Rejoice! the Lord is King	139	443	180	432	575	243	657	317	296
g	Songs of thankfulness and praise	53	56	98	451			191		
e	The Lord is King! lift up thy/your voice	107		183	485	656	58	76	322	36
I	The race that long / The people that in darkness	52	57	71	491		89	129		168
g	We come as guests invited			602		723				
es	Where love and loving-kindness dwell	528								

Year C
The Third Sunday of Epiphany

Nehemiah **8**: 1-3, 5-6, 8-10; Psalm **19**; 1 Corinthians **12**: 12-31a; Luke **4**: 14-21

		AMNS	NEH	HTC	HON	MP	H&P	R&S	BPW	CH3
e	Christ from whom all blessings flow			491			764	561		
es	Christ is the King! O friends rejoice	345	345	492				571	475	474
o	Father of mercies, in thy/your word	167		247					99	
es	Father, Lord of all creation	356			122			620		
l	Forth in the peace of Christ we go	458	361	542	142			602	607	589
o	God has spoken — by his prophets			248			64		100	
es	God is love, and where true love is / Here in Christ we gather	465	513				757	473		
g	God of glory, we exalt				191					
g	God's Spirit is deep in my heart			180			315	576	574	
o	God, who has caused to be written thy word	467					472			
g	Hark the glad sound! The Saviour comes	30	6	193	198	210	82	137	143	160
o	How sure the Scriptures are			249						
es	I come with joy to meet my Lord	473		408	227		610	447	437	
es	Jesus, Lord, we look to thee	380	481				759	564		
g	Jesus, the name high over all			213		385	264			
o	Lord, be thy word my rule / Lord, make your word	232		250						
o	Lord, I have made thy word my choice	490					475	316		
e	Lord of the Church, we pray for our renewing			499		442			486	
o	Lord, thy word abideth / Lord, your word shall guide us	166	407	251	318	446	476	317	102	130
g	Make way, make way, for Christ the King				329	457		141		
g	O for a thousand tongues to sing	125	415	219	362	496	744	285	59	371
g	O thou who at thy eucharist / O Christ at your first eucharist	265	302	420	391		779			492
s	Songs of thankfulness and praise	53	56	98	451			191		
og	Thanks/Praise to God whose word	423	438	255			483	319	106	
p	The heavens declare thy/your glory, Lord	168		254			481	320		
g	The Kingdom of God is justice and joy			333		651	139	200	321	
s	The race that long / The people that in darkness	52	57	71	491		89	129		168
es	Where love and loving-kindness dwell	528								

Year A
The Fourth Sunday of Epiphany

1 Kings 17: 8-16; Psalm 36: 5-10; 1 Corinthians 1: 18-31; John 2: 1-11

		AMNS	NEH	HTC	HON	MP	H&P	R&S	BPW	CH3
e	Be thou my vision / Lord be my vision	343	339	545	56	51	378	489	521	87
s	Christ is our corner-stone	161	206	564	77					
e	Disposer supreme and judge of the earth	298	216		110					
e	Firmly I believe and truly	118	360	429	133					400
e	Glorious things of thee/you are spoken	172	362	494	158	173	817	560	480	421
s	Hail to the Lord's anointed	142	55	190	193	204	125	127	142	317
p	Immortal, invisible, God only wise	199	377	21	242	327	9	67	383	32
e	In the Cross of Christ I glory		379		249	338	167	224	344	259
g	Jesus, come! for we invite you			109						
g	Jesus, Lord, we pray	475		302			365			
e	Lift high the cross	72		508	303	417	170	422	575	550
g	Lord Jesus Christ, invited guest and Saviour			297						
e	Nature with open volume stands	497	87				174	219		
o	O Lord my God, when I in awesome wonder [How great thou art]				380	506		117	62	
g	Songs of thankfulness and praise	53	56	98	451			191		
s	The race that long / The people that in darkness	52	57	71	491		89	129		168
g	We come as guests invited			602		723				
e	We rest on thee / We trust in you			446		735				
e	We sing the praise of him who died	138	94	146	536	738	182	229	231	258
e	When I survey the wondrous cross	67	95	147	549	755	180	217	233	254
g	Why, Herod, so unpitying / impious Herod / How vain		46					189		209

Year B
The Fourth Sunday of Epiphany

Deuteronomy 18: 15-20; Psalm 111; Revelation 12: 1-5a; Mark 1: 21-28

		AMNS	NEH	HTC	HON	MP	H&P	R&S	BPW	CH3
s	Christ is our corner-stone	161	206	564	77					
o	Father of heaven, whose love profound	97	358	359	124		519			77
g	Firmly I believe and truly	118	360	429	133					400
s	Hail to the Lord's anointed	142	55	190	193	204	125	127	142	317
o	How sweet the name of Jesus sounds	122	374	211	220	251	257	277	339	376
g	Jesus Christ is waiting				268				534	
g	Jesus, the name high over all			213		385	264			
g	Join all the glorious names			214		392	78	280	557	304
o	Judge eternal, throned in splendour		490	329	285	395	409	626	627	519
g	King of glory, King of peace	194	391	603	288	397	499	97	53	364
g	O for a thousand tongues to sing	125	415	219	362	496	744	285	59	371
g	Son of God, eternal Saviour	132	498	102				605	639	454
s	Songs of thankfulness and praise	53	56	98	451			191		
g	'The Kingdom is upon you!'	512								
s	The race that long / The people that in darkness	52	57	71	491		89	129		168
g	There is a Redeemer				500	673				
g	Thine arm, O Lord, in days of old	285	324		502		397			214
e	Thy/Your kingdom come, O God	177	499	334	519		783	638	644	322

Year C
The Fourth Sunday of Epiphany

Ezekiel 43:27 — 44:4; Psalm 48; 1 Corinthians 13: 1-13; Luke 2: 22-40

		AMNS	NEH	HTC	HON	MP	H&P	R&S	BPW	CH3
e	A/The new commandment I give			S26	4	1		745	470	
s	Christ is our corner-stone	161	206	564	77					
e	Christ is the King! O friends rejoice	345	345	492				571	475	474
p	City of God, Jerusalem			187						
e	Come, praise the name of Jesus			538					331	
g	Fairest Lord Jesus			209				273	334	375
g	Faithful vigil ended	453	44	55	118	125				
s	Glorious things of thee/you are spoken	172	362	494	158	173	817	560	480	421
e	Gracious Spirit, Holy Ghost / Holy Spirit, gracious Guest	154	367	474	184	198	301	310	288	438
g	Hail to the Lord who comes	314	157				126			
g	Hail to the Lord's anointed	142	55	190	193	204	125	127	142	317
e	Help us to help each other / Jesus, united by thy grace	374		540	208		773	500		
o	Jerusalem the golden	184	381	573	259			662	312	537
g	Jesus, hope of every nation			58						
g	Lord, now let your servant			611						
e	Love divine, all loves excelling	131	408	217	321	449	267	663	559	437
e	O perfect love	280	320		387	517	370		509	
s	Songs of thankfulness and praise	53	56	98	451			191		
s	The race that long / The people that in darkness	52	57	71	491		89	129		168
e	Though gifts of knowledge and of tongues							307		
o	We see the Lord					736				

See Third Sunday of Epiphany for hymns on Christian Unity

Presentation of Christ in the Temple (Candlemas)

Malachi 3: 1-5; Psalm 24: [1-6] 7-10; Hebrews 2: 14-18; Luke 2: 22-40

		AMNS	NEH	HTC	HON	MP	H&P	R&S	BPW	CH3
I	Angels from the realms of glory	39		77	34	35	92	163	155	182
s	Christ, whose glory fills the skies	4	234	266	82	79	457	380		114
g	Come, thou/O long-expected Jesus	31	3	52	98	102	81	138	139	320
s	Earth was waiting, spent and restless			54					141	
s	Fairest Lord Jesus			209				273	334	375
g	Faithful vigil ended	453	44	55	118	125				
e	Hail thou/our once-despisèd/rejected Jesus			175	192	203	222		273	
g	Hail to the Lord who comes	314	157				126			
g	Jesus, hope of every nation			58						
e	Join all the glorious names			214		392	78	280	557	304
e	Lead us, heavenly Father, lead us	224	393	595	293	400	68	543	597	90
p	Lift up your heads, ye/you mighty gates	483	8				240			12
g	Lord, now let your servant			611						
s	Love divine, all loves excelling	131	408	217	321	449	267	663	559	437
o	Make way, make way, for Christ the King				329	457		141		
e	Praise to the Holiest in the height	117	439	140	426	563	231	103	562	238
o	Purify my heart / Refiner's fire				428					
o	Restore, O Lord, the honour of your name				434	579			324	
s	Virgin-born, we bow before thee	311	187		527					
e	What a friend we have in Jesus			373	541	746	559	413	603	
e	Where high the heavenly temple stands	130		184				259		295
e	With joy we meditate the grace	530				774	235	206	275	

Year A
CLC: Ordinary Time: Proper 1
RCL: Fifth Sunday after the Epiphany

Isaiah **58**: 1-9a[b-12]; Psalm **112**: 1-9 [10]; 1 Corinthians **2**: 1-12 [13-16]; Matthew **5**: 13-20

		AMNS	NEH	HTC	HON	MP	H&P	R&S	BPW	CH3
o	Almighty Father, who for us thy Son didst give	338					401	621		
g	Blest are the pure in heart	238	341	110	63		724		588	113
e	Can we/man by searching find out God	438					76	80		
g	Dearest Jesus, we are here / Look upon us, blessed Lord	269			107					129
o	Eternal Ruler of the ceaseless round	353	355		115			623	477	514
g	Father of mercies, in thy/your word	167		247				99		
e	Glory be to Jesus	66	83	126	159					
o	God of freedom, God of justice							625	623	
o	Judge eternal, throned in splendour		490	329	285	395	409	626	627	519
g	Lord Jesus, once you spoke	392		112					598	
g	Lord, I have made thy word my choice	490					475	316		
g	Lord, speak to me, that I may speak			510		444	553	613	611	485
e	Nature with open volume stands	497	87				174	219		
g	O changeless Christ, for ever new			108				206		
o	O Christ the Lord, O Christ the King		496				406	630		
o	O day of God, draw near/nigh In beauty	405						632	635	511
g	O Lord, you are the life of the world							510		
o	The Church of Christ in every age						804	636	613	
g	The Kingdom of God is justice and joy			333		651	139	200	321	
o	This we can do for justice and for peace							639		
o	Thy/Your kingdom come, O God	177	499	334	519		783	638	644	322
o	We pray for peace						413	641		
e	We sing the praise of him who died	138	94	146	536	738	182	229	231	258
o	We utter our cry: that peace may prevail							642		
g	When Jesus walked upon this earth			317						

Year B
CLC: Ordinary Time: Proper 1
RCL: Fifth Sunday after the Epiphany

Isaiah **40**: 21-31; Psalm **147**: 1-11, 20c; 1 Corinthians **9**: 16-23; Mark **1**: 29-39

		AMNS	NEH	HTC	HON	MP	H&P	R&S	BPW	CH3
g	A stranger once did bless the earth	335						198		
g	At even[ing], ere/when the sun was/had set	9	243	315	43	43	142	644	616	52
o	Awake our souls, away our fears	436					663	488		
p	Fill your hearts with joy and gladness			30	130	147			40	
g	From the town's dusty clamour: SS84									
e	Go forth and tell			505	164	178	770	574	570	
og	God is love: let heaven adore him	365	364		170	187	36	95	374	
o	Hast thou not known						446	61		
g	Heal me, hands of Jesus			319						
g	Jesus' hands were kind hands						393	197		228
g	Lord Christ, who on thy heart didst bear	388			308		394			
e	Lord, if at thy command						771			
e	Lord, speak to me, that I may speak			510		444	553	613	611	485
g	O Christ the healer, we have come						395			
g	O God, by whose almighty plan	406					396	651		
g	O God, whose will is life and good	408								
e	O Spirit of the living God			513			322	577	579	496
p	Praise ye the Lord; for it is good									136
p	Praise ye the Lord! 'Tis good to raise						338	50		
e	Send out/forth the gospel			517		593			584	
e	Shout it in the street						782			
e	Speak forth thy/your word, O Father								581	468
e	Tell all the world of Jesus			521					582	
g	Thine arm, O Lord, in days of old	285	324		502		397			214
g	Thou to whom the sick and dying		325							
e	Thou/Lord, you have given thyself/yourself for our healing					698			576	
e	We have a gospel to proclaim	431	486	519	532	728	465		585	
e	We've a story to tell to the nations					744			586	
g	When Jesus walked upon this earth			317						
g	Your will for us and others, Lord						398			

Year C
CLC: Ordinary Time: Proper 1
RCL: Fifth Sunday after the Epiphany

Isaiah 6: 1-8 [9-13]; Psalm 138; 1 Corinthians 15: 1-11; Luke 5: 1-11

		AMNS	NEH	HTC	HON	MP	H&P	R&S	BPW	CH3
e	And can it be			452/588	30	33	216	366	328	409
e	As man and woman we were made						364	466	506	
o	Bright the vision that delighted / Round the Lord	96	343	578	70		445	665	71	353
e	Christ is the world's Redeemer						219	272		301
e	Come, let us with our Lord arise	449	254	375			575	383		
e	Come, thou everlasting Spirit						298	315		
o	Eternal Light! Eternal Light!			454			458	83	85	357
g	Fisherman, come and fish for men							196		
ol	Forth in the peace of Christ we go	458	361	542	142			602	607	589
gl	Forth in thy/your name, O Lord	239	235	306	143	159	381	521	526	463
o	God of gods, we sound his praises			340					46	
o	God of love and truth and beauty	368					403			
o	God, we praise you! God, we bless you!			341				49		
o	God, your glory we have seen in your Son						459	746		469
g	Hear us, O Lord, from heaven						346			
o	Holy, holy, holy, Lord God almighty	95	146	7/594	212	237	7	34	51	352
o	How shall they hear the word of God			507						
o	How shall they hear who have not heard					250				
o	Immortal, invisible, God only wise	199	377	21	242	327	9	67	383	32
o	Let all mortal flesh keep silence	256	295	61	295		266	454	441	577
o	My God, how wonderful thou art / you are	102	410	369	343	468	51	408		356
o	Saviour from sin, I wait to prove						747			
o	Spirit of truth, essential God						480	313		
o	Stand up, and bless the Lord	201	452	351	456	615	513	391		39
e	The Saviour died, but rose again						233	597		293
e	The strife is o'er/past	78	119	163	495	670	214	250	261	266
o	We praise, we worship thee/you, O God						443	755	490	
e	We sing the praise of him who died	138	94	146	536	738	182	229	231	258
g	Wise men, seeking Jesus						128	185		222

Year A
CLC: Proper 2
RCL: Sixth Sunday after the Epiphany, Proper 1

Deuteronomy **30**: 15-20 or Ecclesiasticus **15**: 15-20; Psalm **119**: 1-8; 1 Corinthians **3**: 1-9; Matthew **5**: 21-37

		AMNS	NEH	HTC	HON	MP	H&P	R&S	BPW	CH3
e	Bless and keep us, Lord, in your love united							471		
e	Christ from whom all blessings flow			491			764	561		
e	Christ is the world's light	440		321			455	600	34	
e	Christ's Church shall glory in his power			522						
o	Come, let us to the Lord our God						33	81		69
ol	Fill thou/now my/our life	200		541	129	146	792	406	569	457
g	Forgive our sins as we forgive	362	66	111	141		134	84	83	
o	Freedom and life are ours			544					528	
e	God our Father, bless your people			496						
e	God, you meet us in our weakness							475		
g	I come with joy to meet my Lord	473		408	227		610	447	437	
o	In full and glad surrender			557	245	330				
e	Jesus, where'er thy people meet / Lord Jesus, when your people	162	390	371	282		549	476		
e	Jesus, with thy Church abide									490
ol	Lord, as I wake I turn to you	485	236	267			634	534		
e	Lord Christ, the Father's mighty Son	386						568		
o	Lord Jesus, let these eyes of mine			549						
e	Lord of our life, and God of our salvation		404	529	315	441				491
e	Lord of the Church, we pray for our renewing			499		442			486	
g	Lord, speak to me, that I may speak			510		444	553	613	611	485
o	My God, accept my heart this day	279	318	551	341		701			429
o	O happy day that fixed my choice			442	369	499	702	359	539	
e	O Jesus Christ, grow thou in me / within me grow						742	508	540	
el	O thou who at thy eucharist / O Christ at your first eucharist	265	302	420	391		779			492
e	Risen Lord, whose name we cherish			500						
o	Take my life, and let it be	249		554	464	624	705	371	358	462
p	Teach me, O Lord, the perfect way									127
g	The Kingdom of God is justice and joy			333		651	139	200	321	
o	Thy/Your way, not mine			555	521					
e	We are your people	519						483		

Year B
CLC: Proper 2
RCL: Sixth Sunday after the Epiphany, Proper 1

2 Kings **5**: 1-14; Psalm **30**; 1 Corinthians **9**: 24-27; Mark **1**: 40-45

		AMNS	NEH	HTC	HON	MP	H&P	R&S	BPW	CH3
g	A man there lived in Galilee	334			3					
e	Awake, my soul, stretch every nerve							487		
e	Christ's Church shall glory in his power			522						
g	Father of mercy, God of consolation		323					645		
e	Fight the good fight	220	359	526	128	143	710	496	524	442
g	From thee/you all skill and science flow	286		310			389			525
g	He/they want/lack not friends	183	371				495	481		
g	Heal me, hands of Jesus			319						
o	I greet thee, who my sure Redeemer art						391	501		86
g	Inspired by love and anger				252					
g	Jesus, lover of my soul	123	383	438	261	372	528	332	345	78
g	Lord Christ, who on thy heart didst bear	388			308		394			
g	Love inspired the anger: SS90									
o	O Christ the healer, we have come						395			
g	O God, by whose almighty plan	406					396	651		
e	O Lord my / Thee will I love, my strength, my tower			485						678
g	The crippled hands reached out: SS95									
e	Thee will I love, my God and King						40			403
g	Thine arm, O Lord, in days of old	285	324		502		397			214
g	We give God thanks for those who knew			318						
g	With loving hands at work among the suffering			106						
g	Your will for us and others, Lord						398			

Year C
CLC: Proper 2
RCL: Sixth Sunday after the Epiphany, Proper 1

Jeremiah **17**: 5-10; Psalm **1**; 1 Corinthians **15**: 12-20; Luke **6**: 17-26

		AMNS	NEH	HTC	HON	MP	H&P	R&S	BPW	CH3
o	All my hope on God is founded	336	333	451	15	16	63	586	327	405
g	Christ is the world's light	440		321			455	600	34	
o	Christ is the world's Redeemer						219	272		301
e	Hail the day that sees him rise	87	130	176	191	202	197	252	272	
p	Happy are they who walk in God's wise way							669		
g	Heal us, Immanuel! Hear our prayer						390	335		
g	How blest the poor who love the Lord								197	
o	I hunger and I thirst			409			730	449		
g	Jesus, thy far-extended fame						148			
g	Lord Jesus, once you spoke to men	392		112					598	
o	Lord of the Church, we pray for our renewing			499		442			486	
e	Now lives the Lamb of God			159					255	
g	O changeless Christ, for ever new			108					206	
g	O Christ the healer, we have come						395			
o	Open, Lord, my inward ear						540			
e	This joyful Eastertide		121	165	509		213	248	258	271
g	When Jesus walked upon this earth			317						
e	Ye/You choirs of new Jerusalem	73	124	168	563		823			
g	You gave us, Lord, by word and deed								89	

Year A
CLC: Proper 3
RCL: Seventh Sunday after the Epiphany, Proper 2

Leviticus **19**: 1-2, 9-18; Psalm **119**: 33-40; 1 Corinthians **3**: 10-11, 16-23; Matthew **5**: 38-48

		AMNS	NEH	HTC	HON	MP	H&P	R&S	BPW	CH3
g	A stranger once did bless the earth	335						198		
g	At even[ing], ere/when the sun was/had set	9	243	315	43	43	142	644	616	52
g	Beloved, let us love			468				610		
e	Christ is made the sure foundation / Blessed city, heavenly Salem	283/332	204/205	559	76		485	559	474	10
e	Christ is our corner-stone	161	206	564	77					
e	Come down, O Love Divine	156	137	231	90	89	281	294	283	115
e	Come, thou/O fount of every blessing			337			517	360		
o	Creator of the earth and skies	351		320			419	82		
o	Father of all, whose laws have stood			539					335	
o	For the fruits of his/all creation	457		286	138	153	342	42	123	
g	From the town's dusty clamour: SS84									
g	God is here! As we his people	464		560			653			
o	God's glory fills the universe							275		
g	Heal me, hands of Jesus			319						
o	Here, Lord, we come to you			327						
o	Holy, holy, holy, Lord God almighty	95	146	7/594	212	237	7	34	51	352
e	How firm a foundation			430	216	243		589	380	
g	I am trusting thee/you, Lord Jesus			433	233	258			340	685
g	Jesus' hands were kind hands						393	197		228
o	Judge eternal, throned in splendour		490	329	285	395	409	626	627	519
g	Lord Christ, who on thy heart didst bear	388			308		394			
g	Love of the Father	159	409		323					335
e	My God, accept my heart this day	279	318	551	341		701			429
g	O Christ the healer, we have come						395			
o	O Christ the Lord, O Christ the King		496				406	630		
o	O day of God, draw near/nigh In beauty	405						632	635	511
g	O God, by whose almighty plan	406					396	651		
g	O God, whose will is life and good	408								
o	One holy apostolic Church			514						
o	Remember, Lord, the world you made			332						
l	Strengthen for service, Lord, the hands	421	306	423	460		626	461	453	588
p	Teach me, O Lord, the perfect way									127

continued on next page

		AMNS	NEH	HTC	HON	MP	H&P	R&S	BPW	CH3
o	The Church of Christ in every age						804	636	613	
e	The Church's one foundation	170	484	501	473	640	515	566	393	420
o	The Kingdom of God is justice and joy			333		651	139	200	321	
e	The Lord is King! lift up thy/your voice	107		183	485	656	58	76	322	36
g	Thine arm, O Lord, in days of old	285	324		502		397			214
o	This we can do for justice and for peace						639			
g	Thou to whom the sick and dying		325							
o	Thy/Your kingdom come, O God	177	499	334	519		783	638	644	322
g	We are your people	519					483			
o	When Christ was lifted from the earth	525		335			655			
g	When Jesus walked upon this earth			317						
g	Where love and loving-kindness dwell	528								
g	Your will for us and others, Lord						398			

Year B
CLC: Proper 3
RCL: Seventh Sunday after the Epiphany, Proper 2

Isaiah 43: 18-25; Psalm 41; 2 Corinthians 1: 18-22; Mark 2: 1-12

		AMNS	NEH	HTC	HON	MP	H&P	R&S	BPW	CH3
e	A debtor to mercy alone			449						
e	A mighty mystery we set forth						579		403	
g	Come, O thou all-victorious Lord / O come, our all-victorious			441			418			
g	Four friends brought to Capernaum: SS94									
o	How good is the God we adore / This, this is the God			450	217	244	277	542	338	
g	Open, Lord, my inward ear						540			
g	The love of God comes close							107		
o	Through the night of doubt and sorrow	211	468	466	517		441		546	423
o	To Abraham and Sarah							553		
o	Will you come and follow me?				560			558	363	

See also hymns for CLC Year B Proper 1, page 35

Year C
CLC: Proper 3
RCL: Seventh Sunday after the Epiphany, Proper 2

Genesis 45: 3-11, 15; Psalm 37: 1-11, 39-40; 1 Corinthians 15: 35-38, 42-50; Luke 6: 27-38

		AMNS	NEH	HTC	HON	MP	H&P	R&S	BPW	CH3
g	Brother, sister, let me serve you				73			474	473	
g	Forgive our sins as we forgive	362	66	111	141		134	84	83	
o	Glory, love, and praise, and honour	461	287		160		35			
g	God! when human bonds are broken							652		
g	God, you have / who hast given us power	469					345			452
o	Great God, we sing that mighty / your guiding hand						356	63	552	613
g	Help us to help each other / Jesus, united by thy grace	374		540	208		773	500		
e	In Adam we have all been one	474					420			
g	Lord/Great God, your love has called us here	489		480			500	339	442	
g	Lord, save thy world; in bitter need	397					425			
e	Low in the grave he lay			158	326	453	202		256	
e	Now lives the Lamb of God			159					255	
g	O matchless beauty of our God							101		
g	Peace with the Father, peace with Christ his Son							616		
o	Praise and thanksgiving be to our creator	506								
e	Praise to the Holiest in the height	117	439	140	426	563	231	103	562	238
o	Put thou thy trust / Commit thou all thy griefs	223			429		672	550		669
e	Seed, secret sown in the earth: SS26									
e	Spirit of God within me			243			294	304	296	
g	Take this moment, sign and space								360	
g	The great Creator of the worlds	511								
e	The Lord made man, the Scriptures tell			143						
g	The love of God is broad							108		
e	What Adam's disobedience cost	524					430			

Year A: Genesis 1:1 — 2:3; Psalm **136**: all or 1-9, 23-26; Romans **8**: 18-25; Matthew **6**: 25-34

Year B: Proverbs **8**: 1, 22-31; Psalm **104**: 24-35; Colossians **1**: 15-20; John **1**: 1-14

Year C: Genesis **2**: 4b-9, 15-25; Psalm **65**; Revelation 4; Luke **8**: 22-25

		AMNS	NEH	HTC	HON	MP	H&P	R&S	BPW	CH3
s	All creatures of our God and King	105	263	13	9	7	329	39	28	30
s	Bless the Lord, creation sings			604						
s	Carpenter, carpenter, make me a tree								118	
s	Come, let us praise the Lord					92			119	
s	Creating God, your fingers trace							56		
s	Creation sings a new song						332			
p	Give to our God immortal praise	460		31	155	171	22	94	47	
s	God in his love for us lent us this planet						343	85		
s	God is a name my soul adores						24	31		
s	God who spoke in the beginning	468						60		
s	How wonderful this world of thine						336			152
s	I sing the almighty power of God					293	334	43		
s	Let us, with a gladsome mind / Let us gladly with one mind	204	397	23	302	415	27		56	33
s	Lord, bring the day to pass						347	87		
s	Lord of beauty, thine the splendour	106	265		314					120
s	Lord of the boundless curves of space	493	405				335	44		
s	Lord of the changing year			261						
s	Now praise the protector of heaven			19						
s	O God, the joy of heaven above									149
s	O Lord of every shining constellation	411		314					130	141
s	O praise him! O praise him! O praise him!						503	46		
p	Praise, O praise our God and King	288			423		359			
s	Praise ye the Lord! 'Tis good to raise						338	50		
s	The Lord of heaven confess									135
s	The spacious firmament	103	267		493		339			143
s	The works of the Lord are created in wisdom			26						
o	Thou/God whose almighty / Father your mighty word	180	466	506	514	699	29	38	591	494
s	With wonder, Lord we see your works	531					353			

Year A
RCL only: Eighth Sunday after Epiphany, Proper 3

Isaiah **49**: 8-16a; Psalm **131**; 1 Corinthians **4**: 1-5; Matthew **6**: 24-34

		AMNS	NEH	HTC	HON	MP	H&P	R&S	BPW	CH3
g	All my hope on God is founded	336	333	451	15	16	63	586	327	405
e	Almighty Father, who for us thy Son didst give	338					401	621		
o	Be thou my vision / Lord be my vision	343	339	545	56	51	378	489	521	87
e	Come, thou/O long-expected Jesus	31	3	52	98	102	81	138	139	320
o	Faithful Shepherd, feed me		282	29	117					
o	Hark, my soul, it is the Lord / Christian, do you hear the Lord	244		472	197	209	521	348		676
e	Hark what a sound, and too divine for hearing						236	660		314
o	Here from all nations, all tongues, and all peoples			571					309	
o	Hills of the north, rejoice	470	7		209		237		311	
o	Immortal, invisible, God only wise	199	377	21	242	327	9	67	383	32
g	In heavenly love abiding			458	246	331	678	590	555	681
e	Lo, he / Jesus comes with clouds descending	28	9	196	307	424	241	656	314	314
g	Mine eyes have seen the glory				336		242			318
o	O Lord, I would delight in thee							593		
o	O Lord of heaven and earth and sea	287	422	287			337		387	145
e	O thou, my Judge and King									666
o	O what shall I do my Saviour to praise						569			
g	Put thou thy trust / Commit thou all thy griefs	223			429		672	550		669
g	Seek ye first the Kingdom of God				442	590	138	512	357	
o	Sometimes a light surprises	108					571	595		
e	The Lord will come and not be slow	29	15		489		245	128		321
e	Thou Judge of quick and dead						247			
g	We plough the fields and scatter	290	262	292	534	732	352	124	135	620
e	Ye/You servants of the Lord	150	18	598	566		248			319

Year B
RCL only: Eighth Sunday after Epiphany, Proper 3

Hosea **2**: 14-20; Psalm **103**: 1-13, 22; 2 Corinthians **3**: 1-6; Mark **2**: 13-22

		AMNS	NEH	HTC	HON	MP	H&P	R&S	BPW	CH3
g	And can it be			452/588	30	33	216	366	328	409
g	At the name of Jesus	148	338	172	46	41	74	261	370	300
o	Church of God, elect and glorious			504					406	
g	He gave his life in selfless love			405		214			435	
e	Help us, O Lord, to learn	373	370	493			474			
g	Here, Lord, we take the broken bread			404			604	448	440	
gl	Here, O my Lord, I see thee/you	274		406		230	608		436	573
g	Jesus calls us: o'er/in the tumult	312	200	104	266	359	141	355		211
g	Jesus came — the heavens adoring			195						
g	Jesus who walked beside the lake: SS81									
g	Jesus, whose all-redeeming love	383								215
p	O bless the Lord, my soul, his saving								129	
p	O bless the Lord, my soul, let all			34						
o	O Christ the great foundation			502						
p	O Lord of every shining constellation	411		314					130	141
g	O Lord of the kingdom where losing is winning								316	
e	O Spirit of the living God			513			322	577	579	496
p	O thou my soul, bless God the Lord							715		351
p	Praise, my soul, the King of heaven	192	436	38	422	560	13	104	65	360
p	Praise to the Lord, the Almighty	207	440	40	427	564	16	74	68	9
g	Shout for joy, loud and long			348						
o	The Church's one foundation	170	484	501	473	640	515	566	393	420
g	The great love of God						45	105		415
g	The Kingdom of God is justice and joy			333		651	139	200	321	
p	When all thy/your mercies	109	472	39	544	751	573	109		150

RCL only: Eighth Sunday after Epiphany, Proper 3

Sirach **27**: 4-7 or Isaiah **55**: 10-13; Psalm **92**: 1-4, 12-15; 1 Corinthians **15**: 51-58; Luke **6**: 39-49

		AMNS	NEH	HTC	HON	MP	H&P	R&S	BPW	CH3
e	Abide with me	13	331	425	6	4	665	336	515	695
e	Christ above all glory seated						189			
e	Christ the Lord is risen today / Love's redeeming work is done / All creation	83	113	150	324	76	193	232	246	275
e	Come, let us worship Christ			S10		96				
e	For this purpose					155			372	
e	God, that madest earth and heaven	12	245		178		641			
e	Great God, what do I see and hear		189							
e	In Christ shall all be made alive		459							
e	Jesus lives! Thy/Your terrors now	82	112	156	272	373	198	239	253	605
e	Let saints on earth / Come let us join our friends above	182	396	574	297	409	812	472		543
o2	Lord, thy word abideth / Lord, your word shall guide us	166	407	251	318	446	476	317	102	130
g	My hope is built on nothing less			462		473				411
e	Name of all majesty			218		481				
e	Now is eternal life	402	114		351		203	432		
g	O changeless Christ, for ever new			108				206		
e	Rejoice! the Lord is King	139	443	180	432	575	243	657	317	296
e	Ride on Jesus, all-victorious						272			
g	Risen Lord, whose name we cherish			500						
g	Rock of ages	135	445	593	437	582	273	365	545	83
e	Sing we the King who is coming to reign					602	244		318	
e	Sing we the song of those who stand						821	666		
e	The strife is o'er/past	78	119	163	495	670	214	250	261	266
e	Thine/Yours be/is the glory	428	120	167	503	689	212	247	260	279
p	To render thanks unto the Lord									29
e	When the Lord in glory comes			201		758				
o2	You shall go out with joy				571	796		415		

Year A

RCL only: Ninth Sunday after the Epiphany, Proper 4

Deuteronomy 11: 18-21, 26-28; Psalm 31: 1-5, 19-24; Romans 1: 16-17, 3: 22b-28 (29-31); Matthew 7: 21-29

		AMNS	NEH	HTC	HON	MP	H&P	R&S	BPW	CH3
g	All my hope on God is founded	336	333	451	15	16	63	586	327	405
e	Amazing grace			28	27	31	215	92	550	
e	And can it be			452/588	30	33	216	366	328	409
e	Approach, my soul, the mercy-seat									667
g	Christ, our King before creation			428			75			
e	Father, whose everlasting love						520			
g	Firmly I believe and truly	118	360	429	133					400
g	Glorious things of thee/you are spoken	172	362	494	158	173	817	560	480	421
o	God of the morning, at whose voice								9	
e	Have faith in God, my heart	372		431	201		675	499	336	
g	How firm a foundation			430	216	243		589	380	
e	I'm not ashamed to own/name my Lord			448	240	323	677	428	343	591
g	Jesus, lover of my soul	123	383	438	261	372	528	332	345	78
e	Jesus, our Lord and King							429		
e	Just as I am, without one plea	246	294	440	287	396	697	364	346	79
g	Lord, dismiss us with thy blessing						652			638
g	My hope is built on nothing less			462		473				411
g	Come, O thou / O come, our all-victorious Lord			441			418			
o	O happy day that fixed my choice			442	369	499	702	359	539	
e	Out of the depths I cry to thee						429	331		
pg	Rock of ages	135	445	593	437	582	273	365	545	83
e	Souls of men / Restless souls / There's a wideness	251	461	443	501	607,683	230	353	573	218
o	Take my life, and let it be	249		554	464	624	705	371	358	462
e	Thy ceaseless, unexhausted love						48	106		
g	We come unto our fathers'/faithful God					724	453	484	488	14
o	Who is on the Lord's side?					769	722		615	479

Year B

RCL only: Ninth Sunday after the Epiphany, Proper 4

Deuteronomy **5**: 12-15; Psalm **81**: 1-10; 2 Corinthians **4**: 5-12; Mark **2**:23 — **3**:6

		AMNS	NEH	HTC	HON	MP	H&P	R&S	BPW	CH3
e	All praise to thee/Christ, for thou / our Lord and King divine	337	335	204	18		253	750		297
el	Author of life divine	258	274	395	48		596	440		587
e	Before the heaven and earth			612						
e	Christ, whose glory fills the skies	4	234	266	82	79	457	380		114
e	Come, Holy Ghost, our hearts inspire (Wesley)	448	348		91		469	312	97	122
g	Come, let us with our Lord arise	449	254	375			575	383		
e	Eternal light, shine in my heart			339						
og	Father of all, whose laws have stood			539					335	
g	First of the week and finest day			376						
g	Jesus, stand among us in thy/your risen power			364	280	380	530	388	88	11
g	Let the Lord's people, heart and voice uniting	479								
e	Lord of all being, throned afar		403			439	11	69		34
g	Most glorious Lord of life, that on this day		255							44
e	O Jesus, King most wonderful	120	386	484			269	356	353	378
g	On this day, the first of days		256		402					
e	Out of darkness let light shine			447						
g	Sweet is the work, my God, my King			377		620	514			
g	The first day of the week	424					576			
e	The Son of God proclaim	427		415			627	458	455	
g	Thine arm, O Lord, in days of old	285	324		502		397			214
g	This is the day of light	21		380						46
g	This is the day the Lord hath/has made	22	257	379			577	376		
g	This is the day, this is the day			S28	508	691	578	377	21	

Year C
RCL only: Ninth Sunday after the Epiphany, Proper 4

1 Kings **8**: 22-23, 41-43; Psalm **96**: 1-9; Galatians **1**: 1-12; Luke **7**: 1-10

		AMNS	NEH	HTC	HON	MP	H&P	R&S	BPW	CH3
o	Christ is made the sure foundation / Blessed city, heavenly Salem	283/332	204/205	559	76		485	559	474	10
e	Go forth and tell			505	164	178	770	574	570	
o	God of light and life's creation			561						
g	I am not worthy, holy Lord			407						570
p	Let all the world in every corner sing	202	394	342	296	404	10	114	54	361
g	Lord Christ, who on thy heart didst bear	388			308		394			
g	Lord of all power, I give you my will / Lord of creation, to you be all praise	395		547		440	699	532		428
e	Lord, thy Church on earth is seeking						774	579		
g	Lord/Great God, your love has called us here	489		480			500	339	442	
e	May the grace of Christ our Saviour	181		370	333		762		110	634
p	New songs of celebration render	498		343	350		491	709		
g	O for a heart to praise my God	230	74	483	361	495	536	514	538	85
o	O God, in whom we live and move							409		
p	O sing a new song to the Lord									22
e	Revive thy work / Revive your church			515		578	780			
o	Saviour, and can it be						541			
o	Send out/forth the gospel			517		593			584	
o	That mighty, resurrected Word						658			
e	The Church of Christ in every age						804	636	613	
o	The heaven of heavens / Where the appointed		312					78		
g	We cannot measure how you heal							653		
e	We have a gospel to proclaim	431	486	519	532	728	465		585	

Years A, B, C
CLC: The Sunday next before Lent
RCL: Last Sunday after the Epiphany (Transfiguration Sunday)

Year A: Exodus **24**: 12-18; Psalm **2** or **99**; 2 Peter **1**: 16-21; Matthew **17**: 1-9

Year B: 2 Kings **2**: 1-12; Psalm **50**: 1-6; 2 Corinthians **4**: 3-6; Mark **9**: 2-9

Year C: Exodus **34**: 29-35; Psalm **99**; 2 Corinthians 3:12 — 4:2; Luke **9**: 28-36 [37-43]

		AMNS	NEH	HTC	HON	MP	H&P	R&S	BPW	CH3
s	Christ is the world's true light	346	494	323	78		456	601	618	505
s	Christ upon the mountain peak	441	177	115			155		195	
s	Christ, whose glory fills the skies	4	234	266	82	79	457	380		114
s	Come, praise the name of Jesus			538					331	
s	Eternal Light! Eternal Light!			454			458	83	85	357
s	How/It's/'Tis good, Lord, to be here	318	178				156	203	201	
s	Jesus, these eyes have never seen	245	389					592		674
s	Lord Jesus, once you spoke to men	392		112					598	
s	O raise your eyes	502								
s	O splendour of God's glory						461	537		
s	O vision blest / O wondrous type		176					204		217
s	Once on a mountain top						157			
s	Our Saviour Christ once knelt in prayer			116						
s	Stay, Master, stay upon this heavenly hill						158			
s	The brightness of God's glory			221						
sl	Thee we adore	254	308		497			459		584
s	When Jesus led his chosen three			117						

Years A, B, C
Ash Wednesday

Joel **2**: 1-2, 12-17 or Isaiah **58**: 1-12; Psalm **51**: 1-17; 2 Corinthians 5:20b — **6**:10;
Matthew **6**: 1-6, 16-21 or John **8**: 1-11

		AMNS	NEH	HTC	HON	MP	H&P	R&S	BPW	CH3
s	Approach, my soul, the mercy-seat									667
l	Awake, my soul, and with the sun	1	232	264	50		632	378		42
e	Be thou my vision / Lord be my vision	343	339	545	56	51	378	489	521	87
s	Begone, unbelief						667			
s	Christian, dost thou see them	55	65							
e	Christian, seek not yet repose			355						
s	Come, let us to the Lord our God						33	81		69
s	Dear Lord and Father of mankind	115	353	356	106	111	673	492	84	76
s	Father of heaven, whose love profound	97	358	359	124		519			77
e	Fight the good fight	220	359	526	128	143	710	496	524	442
s	Forgive our sins as we forgive	362	66	111	141		134	84	83	
s	Forty days and forty nights	56	67	103	145	160	130		218	210
l	Great Shepherd of thy/your people, hear	164		363			490	387		
s	How can we sing with joy to God			362					86	
s	Into a desert place: SS23									
s	Into our world from God: SS78									
p	Jesus, lover of my soul	123	383	438	261	372	528	332	345	78
o	Judge eternal, throned in splendour		490	329	285	395	409	626	627	519
s	Lord Jesus, think on/of me	129	70	316	312		533	363		80
p	Lord of our life, and God of our salvation		404	529	315	441				491
l	Lord, as I wake I turn to you	485	236	267			634	534		
l	Now is the healing time decreed		59							
s	O for a heart to praise my God	230	74	483	361	495	536	514	538	85
s	O Jesus, I have promised	235	420	531	372	501	704	509	352	434
o	O Lord, the clouds are gathering					509				
s	O love, how deep, how broad, how high	119	425		383		229	283	207	223
g	Prayer is the soul's sincere/supreme desire		442	372		567	557			
p	Rock of ages	135	445	593	437	582	273	365	545	83
e	Soldiers of Christ, arise	219	449	533	449	604	719	370	580	441
e	Stand up, stand up for Jesus	221	453	535	457	617	721			481
s	Who would true valour / He who would valiant / Who honours courage	212	372	537/590	205	224	688	557	362	443

Year A
The First Sunday of Lent

Genesis **2**: 15-17, **3**: 1-7; Psalm **32**; Romans **5**: 12-19; Matthew **4**: 1-11

		AMNS	NEH	HTC	HON	MP	H&P	R&S	BPW	CH3
g	A safe stronghold/fortress/refuge	114		523		2	661	585	375	406/7
o	All hail the power of Jesus' name	140	332	587/203	13	13	252		29	382
l	At even[ing], ere/when the sun was/had set	9	243	315	43	43	142	644	616	52
s	Awake our souls, away our fears	436					663	488		
s	Be thou / O Lord, my/our guardian	217	64	374	55					
. s	Christian, dost thou see them	55	65							
s	Father, hear the prayer we offer	113	357	360	120	132	436	495	523	
g	Father of all, whose laws have stood			539					335	
s	Father of heaven, whose love profound	97	358	359	124		519			77
g	Forty days and forty nights	56	67	103	145	160	130		218	210
o	From the sinews of the earth: SS4									
s	He lives in us, the Christ of God			457					554	
g	Into a desert place: SS23									
s	Jesus, grant me this I pray	136	382		260					
g	Lead us, heavenly Father, lead us	224	393	595	293	400	68	543	597	90
s	'Lift up your hearts!' We lift them	241	398	366	304		405			440
g	Lord, who throughout these forty days						131			
g	O happy band of pilgrims	208	418	530	368					
s	O Jesus, I have promised	235	420	531	372	501	704	509	352	434
o	O lift us up, strong Son of God						427	337		
s	O love, how deep, how broad, how high	119	425		383		229	283	207	223
o	Praise to the Holiest in the height	117	439	140	426	563	231	103	562	238
p	Restore, O Lord, the honour of your name				434	579			324	
g	Seek ye first the Kingdom of God				442	590	138	512	357	
g	Shepherd divine, our wants relieve	228					558			
o	The Lord made man, the Scriptures tell			143						
o	Walking in a garden	518	123					334		
s	What a friend we have in Jesus			373	541	746	559	413	603	
o	What Adam's disobedience cost	524					430			
s	Where high the heavenly temple stands	130		184				259		295
s	With joy we meditate the grace	530				774	235	206	275	

Year B
The First Sunday of Lent

Genesis 9: 8-17; Psalm 25: 1-10; 1 Peter 3: 18-22; Mark 1: 9-15

		AMNS	NEH	HTC	HON	MP	H&P	R&S	BPW	CH3
s	As pants the hart	226	337		38		416	689		
s	Be thou / O Lord, my/our guardian	217	64	374	55					
p	Blest are the pure in heart	238	341	110	63		724		588	113
e	Christ is the world's Redeemer						219	272		301
s	Christian, dost thou see them	55	65							
p	Christian, seek not yet repose			355						
o	Creatures, once in safety held: SS5									
s	Forty days and forty nights	56	67	103	145	160	130		218	210
s	How firm a foundation			430	216	243		589	380	
g	I bind unto myself / myself to God today / Christ be with me		159	5	225		695	36		402
g	Into a desert place: SS23									
e	Jesus, lover of my soul	123	383	438	261	372	528	332	345	78
s	Lord Jesus, think on/of me	129	70	316	312		533	363		80
p	Lord of our life, and God of our salvation		404	529	315	441				491
g	My dear Redeemer and my Lord							205	205	
s	O for a closer walk with God	231	414	368	360	494		551		663
s	O love, how deep, how broad, how high	119	425		383		229	283	207	223
o	O love that will/wilt not let me go			486	384	515	685	511	541	677
g	On Jordan's bank the Baptist's cry	27	12	601	401	538	84	134	147	208
s	Shepherd divine, our wants relieve	228					558			
g	Songs of thankfulness and praise	53	56	98	451			191		
g	Spirit divine, attend/inspire our prayers			240		614	327	303		107
o	The Kingdom of God is justice and joy			333		651	139	200	321	
g	The sinless one to Jordan came		58							
p	Thy/Your way, not mine			555	521					
g	When he was baptized in Jordan								234	
g	When Jesus came to Jordan	526					132			

Year C
The First Sunday of Lent

Deuteronomy **26**: 1-11; Psalm **91**: 1-2, 9-16; Romans **10**: 8b-13; Luke **4**: 1-13

		AMNS	NEH	HTC	HON	MP	H&P	R&S	BPW	CH3
s	Awake our souls, away our fears	436					663	488		
s	Christian, dost thou see them	55	65							
s	Father of heaven, whose love profound	97	358	359	124		519			77
g	Forty days and forty nights	56	67	103	145	160	130		218	210
e	He is Lord, he is Lord			S7	204	220	256	264	378	
s	He lives in us, the Christ of God			457					554	
p	I bind unto myself / myself to God today / Christ be with me		159	5	225		695	36		402
e	I'm not ashamed to own/name my Lord			448	240	323	677	428	343	591
g	Into a desert place: SS23									
e	Jesus is Lord! creation's voice proclaims it			S17	270	367	260	268	384	
p	Jesus, lover of my soul	123	383	438	261	372	528	332	345	78
e	Jesus, the very thought of thee/you is sweet	120	291/385	478	264	386	265	509	352	377
e	Jesus, thou/the joy of loving hearts	255	292	413	265	383	258	389	439	571
g	Lead us, heavenly Father, lead us	224	393	595	293	400	68	543	597	90
e	Lord of the Church, we pray for our renewing			499		442			486	
s	Lord, in this thy mercy's day		69							
o	My father was a wandering Aramean: SS54									
e	Name of all majesty			218		481				
g	O happy band of pilgrims	208	418	530	368					
s	O Jesus, I have promised	235	420	531	372	501	704	509	352	434
e	O Jesus, King most wonderful	120	386	484			269	356	353	378
e	O Spirit of the living God			513			322	577	579	496
p	Safe in the shadow of the Lord			445		583				
e	Saviour, again to thy/your dear name	15	250	281	438	584	643	640		649
g	Seek ye first the Kingdom of God				442	590	138	512	357	
e	Spirit of faith, come down						325			
s	Still near me, O my Saviour			464						
s	What a friend we have in Jesus			373	541	746	559	413	603	
e	What shall our greeting be						806			

Year A
The Second Sunday of Lent

Genesis **12**: 1-4a; Psalm **121**; Romans **4**: 1-5, 13-17; John **3**: 1-17

		AMNS	NEH	HTC	HON	MP	H&P	R&S	BPW	CH3
g	Blessed assurance				62	59	668		329	
g	Born by the Holy Spirit's breath			225		61	279		281	
g	Born of the water			382						
g	Christ for the world we sing	344					789	599		500
o	Deep in the shadows of the past						447			
e	Father of Jesus Christ, my Lord						693	351		
o	Fill thou/now my/our life	200		541	129	146	792	406	569	457
g	Give to our God immortal praise	460		31	155	171	22	94	47	
p	I lift my eyes to the quiet hills					281		64	595	
p	I to the hills will lift mine eyes						496	726	126	139
g	Immortal Love, for ever full	133	378	105	243	328	392	267	198	306
g	Name of all majesty			218		481				
g	O lift us up, strong Son of God						427	337		
g	O praise ye the Lord / Sing praise to the Lord	203	427	354	388	518		49	70	
s	Oft in danger, oft in woe / Christian soldiers, onward go	210	434	524	396	533	715			
g	Spirit divine, attend/inspire our prayers			240		614	327	303		107
g	Spirit of God within me			243			294	304	296	
o	The God of Abraham praise	331	148	9	478	645	452	121	131	358
s	Thy/Your hand, O God, has guided	171	485	536	518	705	784	567	398	424
o	Thy/Your way, not mine			555	521					
o	To Abraham and Sarah							553		
g	To God be the glory			584	522	708	463	289	566	374
g	Under the cloak of evening: SS67									
p	Unto the hills around			48						
g	We give immortal praise	520		11			18	37	72	
g	We know that Christ is raised and dies no more			389				426		
g	When Christ was lifted from the earth	525		335				655		
g	With loving hands at work among the suffering			106						

Year B
The Second Sunday of Lent

Genesis **17**: 1-7, 15-16; Psalm **22**: 23-31; Romans **4**: 13-25; Mark **8**: 31-38

		AMNS	NEH	HTC	HON	MP	H&P	R&S	BPW	CH3
s	Art thou weary: AHB 467									
g	At the name of Jesus	148	338	172	46	41	74	261	370	300
s	Christ's Church shall glory in his power			522						
e	Father of Jesus Christ, my Lord						693	351		
p	I, the Lord of sea and sky				235					
g	I'm not ashamed to own/name my Lord			448	240	323	677	428	343	591
g	It was easy up to Caesarea Philippi: SS27									
s	Jesus, grant me this I pray	136	382		260					
e	Jesus, if still the same thou art						529			
s	Jesus, Lord of life and glory		68							
g	Light of the minds that know him		400	477				529		
g	Lord Christ, we praise your sacrifice	487		132			532	611		
s	Lord Christ, when first thou cam'st to men	387						270		255
s	My God, how wonderful thou art / you are	102	410	369	343	468	51	408		356
s	My spirit longs for thee	57	299					333		
g	New every morning is the love	2	238	270	349	480	636	536		47
g	Take up thy/your cross	237	76	114	465					430
o	The God of Abraham praise	331	148	9	478	645	452	121	131	358
p	The Lord is King! lift up thy/your voice	107		183	485	656	58	76	322	36
s	This day God gives me	516						79		
o	To Abraham and Sarah							553		
g	When things began to happen			69						
g	Will you come and follow me?				560			558	363	
p	Ye/You servants of God, your Master proclaim	149	476	520	565	784	278	293	76	372

Year C
The Second Sunday of Lent

Genesis **15**: 1-12, 17-18; Psalm **27**; Philippians 3:17 — **4**:1; Luke **13**: 31-35 or [RCL] **9**: 28-36

		AMNS	NEH	HTC	HON	MP	H&P	R&S	BPW	CH3
o	A safe stronghold/fortress/refuge	114		523		2	661	585	375	406/7
s	All my hope on God is founded	336	333	451	15	16	63	586	327	405
g	All who love and serve your city WOV562									
s	All ye who seek a comfort / for sure relief	64	63		22					
o	Christ is the world's true light	346	494	323	78		456	601	618	505
e	Church of God, elect and glorious			504					406	
s	Come, O thou traveller unknown	243	350				434			
o	Creatures, once in safety held: SS5									
e	Fight the good fight	220	359	526	128	143	710	496	524	442
s	In the Cross of Christ I glory		379		249	338	167	224	344	259
e	Light's abode, celestial Salem	185	401		305					
o	Lord, be thy word my rule / Lord, make your word	232		250						
e	Lord of the Cross of shame			548		443				
s	Maker of Earth, to thee alone		71							
s	My faith looks up to thee		72		339	469	683			81
s	My Lord, you wore no royal crown			118						
s	Now is the healing time decreed		59							
l	O Christ who art the light and day		61							652
p	O God beyond all praising			36	363					
l	O kind creator, bow thine ear		60							
s	Souls of men / Restless souls / There's a wideness	251	461	443	501	607,683	230	353	573	218
o	The God of Abraham praise	331	148	9	478	645	452	121	131	358
e	Thou Judge of quick and dead						247			
o	Timeless love! we sing the story			47		707	60			
o	To Abraham and Sarah							553		

Year A
The Third Sunday of Lent

Exodus 17: 1-7; Psalm 95; Romans 5: 1-11; John 4: 5-42

		AMNS	NEH	HTC	HON	MP	H&P	R&S	BPW	CH3
l	A Virgin most pure, as the prophets do tell						93			
g	Broken promises: SS11									
e	Come down, O Love Divine	156	137	231	90	89	281	294	283	115
g	Come, thou/O fount of every blessing			337			517	360		
p	Come with all joy to sing to God			16						
p	Come worship God who is worthy			18					36	
o	Father, hear the prayer we offer	113	357	360	120	132	436	495	523	
g	Glorious things of thee/you are spoken	172	362	494	158	173	817	560	480	421
g	God is here! As we his people	464		560			653			
o	Guide me, O thou/my great Redeemer/Jehovah	214	368	528	188	201	437	345	593	89
g	Holy Spirit, Truth divine			235			289	301	292	106
p	How sure the Scriptures are			249						
g	How sweet the name of Jesus sounds	122	374	211	220	251	257	277	339	376
g	I cannot tell why/how he whom angels worship			194	226	266	238	265	381	
og	I have no bucket							340		
g	I heard the voice of Jesus say	247	376		231	275	136	349		212
o	I hunger and I thirst			409			730	449		
e	Jesus my Lord, my God, my all		384	476						
g	Jesus our hope, our heart's desire	86		178						302
g	Jesus, lover of my soul	123	383	438	261	372	528	332	345	78
g	Jesus, the very thought of thee/you is sweet	120	291,385	478	264	386	265	509	352	377
g	Jesus, thou/the joy of loving hearts	255	292	413	265	383	258	389	439	571
l	Jesus, where'er thy people meet / Lord Jesus, when your people	162	390	371	282		549	476		
p	Let all the world in every corner sing	202	394	342	296	404	10	114	54	361
p	Let us sing to the God of salvation								15	
g	Lord of the Church, we pray for our renewing			499		442			486	
e	My God, I love thee/you; not because	65	73	479	344		171	357		379
e	Not what these hands / I bless the Christ of God			435		487				410

continued on next page

p	O worship / Worship the Lord in the beauty of holiness	49	52	344	394	529	505	187	22	40
g	Rock of ages	135	445	593	437	582	273	365	545	83
e	The Kingdom of God is justice and joy			333		651	139	200	321	
g	There was a woman: SS83									
e	To God be the glory			584	522	708	463	289	566	374
g	Woman in the night: SS76									

Year B
The Third Sunday of Lent

Exodus **20**: 1-17; Psalm **19**; 1 Corinthians **1**: 18-25; John **2**: 13-22

		AMNS	NEH	HTC	HON	MP	H&P	R&S	BPW	CH3
e	All my hope on God is founded	336	333	451	15	16	63	586	327	405
e	Be thou my vision / Lord be my vision	343	339	545	56	51	378	489	521	87
g	Come to us, creative Spirit			308			377			
p	Creator of the earth and skies	351		320			419	82		
o	Father of all, whose laws have stood			539					335	
p	Father of mercies, in thy/your word	167		247				99		
p	From all that/who dwell/live beneath	98		580	146		489	723		362
p	God be in my head	236	328	543	166		694	498	592	433
g	God our Father and Creator			562						
e	Here hangs a man discarded							225		
g	I greet thee, who my sure Redeemer art						391	501		86
p	I know that my Redeemer lives, what joy			169	232	278	196	278	251	
p	Jesus, Lord of life and glory		68							
o	Lord, I have made thy word my choice	490					475	316		
p	Lord, thy word abideth / Lord, your word	166	407	251	318	446	476	317	102	130
g	Love inspired the anger: SS90									
e	Nature with open volume stands	497	87				174	219		
p	O for a heart to praise my God	230	74	483	361	495	536	514	538	85
p	O for a thousand tongues to sing	125	415	219	362	496	744	285	59	371
g	O thou/Lord who came[st]	233	431	552/596	392	525	745	433	355	110
p	Powerful in making us wise to salvation			252			479			
e	Rejoice, O people, in the mounting years						657			
o	Sweet is the work, my God, my King			377		620	514			
p	Tell all the world of Jesus			521					582	
p	The heavens declare thy/your glory, Lord	168		254			481	320		
p	The spacious firmament	103	267		493		339			143
e	We sing the praise of him who died	138	94	146	536	738	182	229	231	258

Year C
The Third Sunday of Lent

Isaiah **55**: 1-9; Psalm **63**: 1-8; 1 Corinthians **10**: 1-13; Luke **13**: 1-9

		AMNS	NEH	HTC	HON	MP	H&P	R&S	BPW	CH3
p	As water to the thirsty			470						
e	Blessed Jesu, Mary's Son		275							
e	Bread of heaven, on thee we feed	271	276	398	67			442		
l	Bread of the world in mercy broken	270	277	396	68		599	443	428	574
e	Christ is the heavenly food	439								
g	Come, O thou all-victorious Lord / O come, our all-victorious			441			418			
g	Come, we that love the Lord						487	384	525	
l	Draw nigh and take / Draw near and take		281	401						
l	Faithful Shepherd, feed me		282	29	117					
o	Father of mercies, in thy/your word	167		247					99	
e	For all the saints	305	197	567	134	148	814	658	478	534
e	Glorious things of thee/you are spoken	172	362	494	158	173	817	560	480	421
o	Great God of wonders! All thy ways					197	38			
e	Guide me, O thou/my great Redeemer/Jehovah	214	368	528	188	201	437	345	593	89
e	How sweet the name of Jesus sounds	122	374	211	220	251	257	277	339	376
l	I am not worthy, holy Lord			407						570
e	I come with joy to meet my Lord	473		408	227		610	447	437	
e	I hunger and I thirst			409			730	449		
p	Jesus, priceless treasure			461	262		259			
p	Jesus, thou/the joy of loving hearts	255	292	413	265	383	258	389	439	571
e	Jesus, the very thought of thee/you is sweet	120	291,385	478	264	386	265	509	352	377
o	Leader of faithful souls and guide						819			
e	Lord, enthroned in heavenly splendour	263	296	416	309	431	616			583
e	O bless the Lord, my soul, let all			34						
l	O bread to pilgrims given / O food of men wayfaring		300				620	456		
l	O for a closer walk with God	231	414	368	360	494		551		663
l	O God, unseen yet ever near	272		421	367					
e	Rock of ages	135	445	593	437	582	273	365	545	83
e	Through the night of doubt and sorrow	211	468	466	517		441		546	423

Year A
The Fourth Sunday of Lent

1 Samuel **16**: 1-13; Psalm **23**; Ephesians **5**: 8-14; John **9**: 1-41

		AMNS	NEH	HTC	HON	MP	H&P	R&S	BPW	CH3
s	Ah, holy Jesus, how hast thou offended		62	123	8		164	215	215	251
g	Amazing grace			28	27	31	215	92	550	
e	Awake, awake, fling off the night	342			49				404	
e	Awake, my soul, and with the sun	1	232	264	50		632	378		42
g	Christ is the world's light	440		321			455	600	34	
g	Christ is the world's true light	346	494	323	78		456	601	618	505
g	Christ, whose glory fills the skies	4	234	266	82	79	457	380		114
g	Come, Holy Ghost, our souls inspire	93	138	589	92	90	283	751		342
p	Faithful Shepherd, feed me		282	29	117					
g	Father of mercies, in thy/your word	167		247					99	
g	He gave his life in selfless love			405		214			435	
g	His eyes will guide my footsteps			301						
g	I heard the voice of Jesus say	247	376		231	275	136	349		212
g	I saw the grass: SS91									
p	I will sing the wondrous story			212	237	315	223		382	381
g	I'll praise my Maker while I've breath			20		320	439	734	127	
g	In heavenly love abiding			458	246	331	678	590	555	681
g	Just as I am, without one plea	246	294	440	287	396	697	364	346	79
g	Lord, I was blind			437		433	423	358	558	
o	Lord, you have searched and known my ways						71	70	564	
p	My Father, for another night	3		269	340					
p	My God, and/now is thy table spread	259		418	342					
g	O Jesus, King most wonderful	120	386	484			269	356	353	378
p	The God of love my shepherd is	110	77		479		43	677		
p	The King of love my shepherd is	126	457	44	484	649	69	552	394	388
p	The Lord my pasture shall prepare	111	458							
p	The Lord's my shepherd, I'll not want	426	459	591/45	490	660	70	679	395	387
g	Thou/God whose almighty / Father your mighty word	180	466	506	514	699	29	38	591	494
g	To God be the glory			584	522	708	463	289	566	374
e	Wake, O wake / Sleepers, wake	32	16	199	529		249	132		315

See also Mothering Sunday, page 64

Year B
The Fourth Sunday of Lent

Numbers **21**: 4-9; Psalm **107**: 1-3, 17-22; Ephesians **2**: 1-10; John **3**: 14-21

		AMNS	NEH	HTC	HON	MP	H&P	R&S	BPW	CH3
e	All hail the power of Jesus' name	140	332	587/203	13	13	252		29	382
e	Amazing grace			28	27	31	215	92	550	
g	And can it be			452/588	30	33	216	366	328	409
o	Bread of heaven, on thee we feed	271	276	398	67			442		
e	Come, thou/O fount of every blessing			337			517	360		
g	Downtrodden Christ			125						
g	Eternal Light! Eternal Light!			454			458	83	85	357
p	Give to our God immortal praise	460		31	155	171	22	94	47	
g	It is a thing most wonderful	70	84	131	255	346	224	503	219	385
e	Jesus my Lord, my God, my all		384	476						
e	Jesus! the name high over all			213		385	264			
g	Lift high the cross	72		508	303	417	170	422	575	550
e	Lord, I was blind			437		433	423	358	558	
e	Lord/Great God, your love has called us here	489		480			500	339	442	
g	Man of sorrows			130	330	458	228		350	380
g	Name of all majesty			218		481				
e	Not what these hands / I bless the Christ of God			435		487				410
g	O God of truth, whose living word	222								
g	O lift us up, strong Son of God						427	337		
e	Rock of ages	135	445	593	437	582	273	365	545	83
g	Sing, my tongue, the glorious battle / Here proclaim the glorious	59	78	142	446		177	228	226	256
e	Souls of men / Restless souls / There's a wideness	251	461	443	501	607,683	230	353	573	218
e	Tell all the world of Jesus			521					582	
g	To God be the glory			584	522	708	463	289	566	374
g	We give immortal praise	520		11			18	37	72	
g	When all the world to life is waking		240							
g	When Christ was lifted from the earth	525		335				655		
g	With loving hands at work among the suffering			106						

See also Mothering Sunday, page 64

Year C
The Fourth Sunday of Lent

Joshua **5**: 9-12; Psalm **32**; 2 Corinthians **5**: 16-21; Luke **15**: 1-3, 11b-32

		AMNS	NEH	HTC	HON	MP	H&P	R&S	BPW	CH3
s	All for Jesus!		272	469	10		251		332	
g	Amazing grace			28	27	31	215	92	550	
s	Forgive our sins as we forgive	362	66	111	141		134	84	83	
g	Give me joy in my heart / oil in my lamp	459		S11	153	167	492	523	530	
g	God makes his rain to fall: SS96									
g	Hail thou/our once-despisèd/rejected Jesus			175	192	203	222		273	
e	He gave his life in selfless love			405		214			435	
e	Holy Spirit, come, confirm us	471	140		214		288	298	289	
p	How firm a foundation			430	216	243		589	380	
g	I cannot tell why/how he whom angels worship			194	226	266	238	265	381	
g	I will sing the wondrous story			212	237	315	223		382	381
e	In Christ there is no east or west	376	480	322	244	329	758	647	482	425
g	Jesus came — the heavens adoring			195						
g	Just as I am, without one plea	246	294	440	287	396	697	364	346	79
e	Lord/Great God, your love has called us here	489		480			500	339	442	
g	Lord, I was blind			437		433	423	358	558	
g	Lord of all power, I give you my will / Lord of creation, to you be all praise	395		547		440	699	532		428
e	Love divine, all loves excelling	131	408	217	321	449	267	663	559	437
e	No weight of gold or silver			138						
p	None other Lamb						271			
o	O bread to pilgrims given / O food of men wayfaring		300				620	456		
e	O Spirit of the living God			513			322	577	579	496
e	O what shall I do my Saviour to praise						569			
g	O where, O where's my silver piece: SS97									
l	On this day, the first of days		256			402				
e	One there is above all others					542	149		560	
e	Stupendous height of heavenly love						462			
e	The Church's one foundation	170	484	501	473	640	515	566	393	420
g	The Kingdom of God is justice and joy			333		651	139	200	321	
o	We come unto our fathers'/faithful God					724	453	484	488	14

See also Mothering Sunday, page 64

Years A, B, C
Mothering Sunday

Exodus **2**: 1-10 or 1 Samuel **1**: 20-28; Psalm **34**: 11-20 or Psalm **127**: 1-4;

2 Corinthians **1**: 3-7 or Colossians **3**: 12-17; Luke **2**: 33-35 or John **19**: 25-27

		AMNS	NEH	HTC	HON	MP	H&P	R&S	BPW	CH3
s	All things bright and beautiful	116	264	283	21	23	330		116	154
s	Children of the heavenly King	213	344	566	63					
s	Come and praise the Lord our King			S8						
s	Come down, O Love Divine	156	137	231	90	89	281	294	283	115
s	Father on high, to whom we pray			296					499	
s	For the beauty of the earth	104	285	298	137	152	333	41	121	367
s	From east to west, from shore to shore		20				99	172		189
s	Glorious things of thee/you are spoken	172	362	494	158	173	817	560	480	421
s	God is our strength and refuge			527		188			308	
l	God, we praise you! God, we bless you!			341					49	
s	Great God, we praise the mighty love			299						
s	Happy are they, they that/who love God	176	369	473	195		711			408
s	Happy the home that welcomes you			300			366			
s	He's got the whole world in his hands				206	225				
l	I come with joy to meet my Lord	473		408	227		610	447	437	
s	Jerusalem the golden	184	381	573	259			662	312	537
x	Jesus' hands were kind hands						393	197		228
s	Jesus, good above all other	378	387	96	269		732	528		111
p	Lift up your heads, ye/you mighty gates	483	8				240			12
s	Lord of all hopefulness	394	239	101	313		552	531	517	92
s	Lord of our growing years			259					514	
s	Lord of the home, your only Son	494					367		500	
g	Lord, who left the highest heaven			97						
s	Now thank we all our God	205	413	33	354	486	566	72	128	368
p	O God in heaven, whose loving plan	407					369			
s	O Lord of heaven and earth and sea	287	422	287			337		387	145
s	Once in royal David's city	46	34	67	403	539	114	167	172	193
p	Our Father, by whose name	505					371			522
s	Son of God, eternal Saviour	132	498	102				605	639	454
o	Tell out, my soul, the greatness of the Lord	422	186	42	467	631	86	740	391	164
e	When, in our music, God is glorified				550		388	414		

See also the Fourth Sunday of Lent, pages 61-63

Year A
The Fifth Sunday of Lent (Passiontide begins)

Ezekiel **37**: 1-14; Psalm **130**; Romans **8**: 6-11; John **11**: 1-45

		AMNS	NEH	HTC	HON	MP	H&P	R&S	BPW	CH3
o	Breathe on me, Breath of God	157	342	226	69	67	280	295	282	103
e	Come down, O Love Divine	156	137	231	90	89	281	294	283	115
o	Come, let us with our Lord arise	449	254	375			575	383		
g	Eternal light, shine in my heart			339						
e	Father of heaven, whose love profound	97	358	359	124		519			77
o	Father of Jesus Christ, my Lord						690	351		
e	First of the week and finest day			376						
g	God our Father and Creator			562						
g	Hark, my soul, it is the Lord / Christian, do you hear the Lord	244		472	197	209	521	348		676
o	Here within this house of prayer			563						
e	Holy Spirit, come, confirm us	471	140		214		288	298	289	
g	In Christ shall all be made alive			459						
g	It is a thing most wonderful	70	84	131	255	346	224	503	219	385
g	Jesus the Lord said/says, I am the Bread					384	137	199	202	
g	Jesus, the name high over all			213		385	264			
g	Jesus, thy/your blood and righteousness			460			225			
g	Light of the minds that know him		400	477				529		
g	Lord, I was blind			437		433	423	358	558	
o	O Breath of life, come sweeping / O Breath of love, come breathe			237	356	488	777	302	293	339
e	O for a thousand tongues to sing	125	415	219	362	496	744	285	59	371
o	O Spirit of the living God			513			322	577	579	496
o	O Trinity, O Trinity			6						
p	Out of our failure to create							88		
g	Poor Lazarus is sick: SS29									
o	Revive thy work / Revive your church			515		578	780			
p	Souls of men / Restless souls / There's a wideness	251	461	443	501	607,683	230	353	573	218
o	Spirit of God most high			242						
e	Spirit of God within me			243			294	304	296	
o	This is the day of light	21		380						46
g	Thou art / You are the way	128	464	113	512	695	234	554		121
g	We give immortal praise	520		11			18	37	72	

Year B
The Fifth Sunday of Lent (Passiontide begins)

Jeremiah **31**: 31-34; Psalm **51**: 1-12 or Psalm **119**: 9-16; Hebrews **5**: 5-10; John **12**: 20-33

		AMNS	NEH	HTC	HON	MP	H&P	R&S	BPW	CH3
e	A debtor to mercy alone			449						
g	As we break the bread			393				439		
p	Christian, seek not yet repose			355						
o	Creatures, once in safety held: SS5									
g	God's glory fills the universe							275		
g	Great God, we praise the mighty love			299						
o	Help us, O Lord, to learn	373	370	493			474			
e	It is a thing most wonderful	70	84	131	255	346	224	503	219	385
o	Jesus, lover of my soul	123	383	438	261	372	528	332	345	78
e	Join all the glorious names			214		392	78	280	557	304
e	Lead us, heavenly Father, lead us	224	393	595	293	400	68	543	597	90
g	Lift high the cross	72		508	303	417	170	422	575	550
g	Man of sorrows			130	330	458	228		350	380
s	Meekness and majesty				335	465			58	
o	My hope is built on nothing less			462		473				411
p	My Lord, what love is this				345	476				
g	Now the green blade rises/riseth	501	115		355		204	243	257	278
p	O for a heart to praise my God	230	74	483	361	495	536	514	538	85
p	O God, be gracious to me in thy/your love							695		64
g	O Jesus, I have promised	235	420	531	372	501	704	509	352	434
g	O lift us up, strong Son of God						427	337		
g	O my Saviour, lifted	248			386	516				
g	Seed, secret sown in the earth: SS26									
g	Sing, my tongue, the glorious battle / Here proclaim the glorious	59	78	142	446		177	228	226	256
e	The Lord ascendeth up on high		135				210			287
s	The royal banners forward go / As royal banners are unfurled	58	79		492		179	216	228	257
g	When Christ was lifted from the earth	525		335				655		
e	Where high the heavenly temple stands	130		184				259		295
g	With joy we meditate the grace	530				774	235	206	275	
e	With loving hands at work among the suffering			106						

Year C
The Fifth Sunday of Lent (Passiontide begins)

Isaiah **43**: 16-21; Psalm **126**; Philippians **3**: 4b-14; John **12**: 1-8

		AMNS	NEH	HTC	HON	MP	H&P	R&S	BPW	CH3
e	And can it be			452/588	30	33	216	366	328	409
e	Awake, my soul, stretch every nerve							487		
e	Beneath the cross of Jesus				59	55	165			684
e	Can we/man by searching find out God	438					76	80		
e	Fight the good fight	220	359	526	128	143	710	496	524	442
p	Forth in thy/your name, O Lord	239	235	306	143	159	381	521	526	463
p	Go forth and tell			505	164	178	770	574	570	
e	Here, O my Lord, I see thee/you	274		406		230	608		436	573
g	How good a thing it is			497						
p	I will sing, I will sing a song			S15		313		279		
e	In Christ shall all be made alive			459						
e	Jesus, the name high over all			213		385	264			
e	Jesus, the very thought of thee/you is sweet	120	291,385	478	264	386	265	509	352	377
e	Jesus, thou/the joy of loving hearts	255	292	413	265	383	258	389	439	571
e	Jesus, thy/your blood and righteousness			460			225			
o	Lord, for the years			328	310	428		603	535	
e	My hope is built on nothing less			462		473				411
s	Never further than thy cross							507		
e	No more, my God, I boast							369		
e	O happy band of pilgrims	208	418	530	368					
e	One thing I know: STG 128									
g	Said Judas to Mary: SS32									
e	Thou hidden source of calm repose						275			
p	To God be the glory			584	522	708	463	289	566	374
e	To him we come			518		709			547	
e	We sing the praise of him who died	138	94	146	536	738	182	229	231	258
e	When I survey the wondrous cross	67	95	147	549	755	180	217	233	254
o	When the King shall come again			200						

Palm Sunday: Liturgy of the Palms

Year A: Matthew **21**: 1-11; Psalm **118**: 1-2, 19-29
Year B: Mark **11**: 1-11 or John **12**: 12-16; Psalm **118**: 1-2, 19-24
Year C: Luke **19**: 28-40; Psalm **118**: 1-2, 19-29

		AMNS	NEH	HTC	HON	MP	H&P	R&S	BPW	CH3
g	A stable lamp is lighted: PFT 1									
g	All glory, laud, and honour / All glory, praise	60/328	509	120	11	9	160	208	216	233
p	All people that on earth do dwell	100	334	14	17	20	1	712	2	1
g	Children of Jerusalem					70	163			236
p	Christ is made the sure foundation / Blessed city, heavenly Salem	283/332	204/205	559	76		485	559	474	10
p	Christ is our corner-stone	161	206	564	77					
p	Come, let us with our Lord arise	449	254	375			575	383		
g	Give me joy in my heart / oil in my lamp	459		S11	153	167	492	523	530	
g	Hail to the Lord's anointed	142	55	190	193	204	125	127	142	317
g	Hark the glad sound! The Saviour comes	30	6	193	198	210	82	137	143	160
g	Here comes Jesus: SS79									
g	Hosanna, hosanna, hosanna in the highest				215	242				
p	I will enter his gates				236	307		386	11	
g	Lift up your heads, ye/you mighty gates	483	8				240			12
g	Listen to the shouts of praises								222	
p	Lord, enthroned in heavenly splendour	263	296	416	309	431	616			583
g	Make way, make way, for Christ the King				329	457		141		
g	My song is love unknown	63	86	136	346	478	173	207	204	224
s	O thou who through this holy week		96							
g	Ride on, ride on in majesty	61	511	119	435	580	159	209	225	234
g	The glory of our King was seen						161	230		
p	This earth belongs to God: CFW 584									
p	This is the day the Lord hath/has made	22	257	379			577	376		
p	This is the day, this is the day			S28	508	691	578	377	21	
g	Trotting, trotting through Jerusalem						162			
p	We are marching in the light of God							555	487	
g	You are the King of glory				570	790		271	74	

Year A
Palm Sunday: Liturgy of the Passion

Isaiah **50**: 4-9a; Psalm **31**: 9-16; Philippians **2**: 5-11; Matthew **26**:14 — **27**:66 or Matthew **27**: 11-54

Lists for the three years overlap only slightly; but many hymns are interchangeable as the Gospel is the only variable reading. Distinctive features of the Gospels are taken into account.

		AMNS	NEH	HTC	HON	MP	H&P	R&S	BPW	CH3
e	And can it be			452/588	30	33	216	366	328	409
e	At the name of Jesus	148	338	172	46	41	74	261	370	300
e	Empty he came			127						
g	Great God, what do I see and hear			189						
e	He gave his life in selfless love			405		214			435	
o	He lives in us, the Christ of God			457					554	
s	Jesus, meek and lowly		85							
s	Light of the lonely pilgrim's heart		399							
g	Lord, teach us how to pray aright	227	406	367	316		551			
e	Morning glory, starlit sky	496						99		
g	My Lord of light, who made the worlds			4						
e	Name of all majesty			218		481				
s	Nature with open volume stands	497	87				174	219		
s	O love, how deep, how broad, how high	119	425		383		229	283	207	223
o	O sacred head	68	90	139	389	520	176	220	223	253
s	O sing a song of Bethlehem	413						201		220
s	O thou who through this holy week		96							
g	Praise to the Holiest in the height	117	439	140	426	563	231	103	562	238
o	See, Christ was wounded for our sake			137					229	
s	Son of God, eternal Saviour	132	498	102				605	639	454
g	That night at table: SS36									
g	The hands of Christ			141						
e	The head that was once crowned with thorns	141	134	182	480	647	209	257	274	286
g	This is the night, dear friends: SS37									
g	Thy/Your way, not mine			555	521					
s	To Christ, the Prince of peace	127								
g	To mock your reign	517						221		
s	We sing the praise of him who died	138	94	146	536	738	182	229	231	258
s	With glorious clouds encompassed round						184			

Isaiah 50: 4-9a; Psalm 31: 9-16; Philippians 2: 5-11; Mark 14:1 — 15:47 or Mark 15: 1-39 [40-47]

Lists for the three years overlap only slightly; but many hymns are interchangeable as the Gospel is the only variable reading. Distinctive features of the Gospels are taken into account.

		AMNS	NEH	HTC	HON	MP	H&P	R&S	BPW	CH3
s	A man there lived in Galilee	334			3					
e	All praise to thee/Christ, for thou / our Lord and King divine	337	335	204	18		253	750		297
s	All ye who seek a comfort / for sure relief	64	63		22					
e	Before the heaven and earth			612						
g	Christ is the world's light	440		321			455	600	34	
o	Christ triumphant, ever reigning			173	81	77			306	
g	Christian, seek not yet repose			355						
l	Forth in thy/your name, O Lord	239	235	306	143	159	381	521	526	463
g	From heaven you came (The servant King)				148	162		522	529	
l	Glory in the highest		363	582						
g	God of unexampled grace						166			
g	Hail thou/our once-despised/rejected Jesus			175	192	203	222		273	
s	I am not skilled to understand			432		257	221			687
s	In the Cross of Christ I glory		379		249	338	167	224	344	259
s	Lord Christ, we praise your sacrifice	487		132			532	611		
g	My heart and voice I raise						268			
g	My Lord, you wore no royal crown			118						
g	My song is love unknown	65	86	136	346	478	173	207	204	224
g	Now, my soul, thy voice uprising		88							
g	O crucified Redeemer	404					424	604		
g	Stand up, stand up for Jesus	221	453	535	457	617	721			481
g	The head that was once crowned with thorns	141	134	182	480	647	209	257	274	286
s	The royal banners forward go / As royal banners are unfurled	58	79		492		179	216	228	257
l	The sun is sinking fast	14								50
g	Thy/Your way, not mine			555	521					
g	Won, the victor's crown			185						

Year C
Palm Sunday: Liturgy of the Passion

Isaiah **50**: 4-9a; Psalm **31**: 9-16; Philippians **2**: 5-11; Luke **22**:14 — **23**:56 or Luke **23**: 1-49

Lists for the three years overlap only slightly; but many hymns are interchangeable as the Gospel is the only variable reading. Distinctive features of the Gospels are taken into account.

		AMNS	NEH	HTC	HON	MP	H&P	R&S	BPW	CH3
g	Alas! and did my Saviour bleed			124						
g	All hail the power of Jesus' name	140	332	587/203	13	13	252		29	382
s	Come, ye faithful / Alleluia, raise the anthem	145	351	205	99	103	813		269	
g	Forgive our sins as we forgive	362	66	111	141		134	84	83	
g	Hail Redeemer, King divine			210						
g	I cannot tell why/how he whom angels worship			194	226	266	238	265	381	
g	I will sing the wondrous story			212	237	315	223		382	381
g	Look, ye/you saints, the sight is glorious			179		426	201			289
g	Lord Jesus Christ, you have come to us	391	297	417	311	435	617	373	444	
g	Lord Jesus, are we one with thee: AHB 269									
g	Lord Jesus, for my sake you come			133					224	
g	Lord Jesus, think on/of me	129	70	316	312		533	363		80
g	Lord, who left the highest heaven				97					
s	My Lord, what love is this				345	476				
s	No weight of gold or silver			138						
l	O Sacrifice of Calvary			424						
s	O the bitter shame and sorrow			487		524	538			
g	So dies this man, this carpenter: SS41									
g	The hands of Christ			141						
s	There is a fountain			144		671				
g	They borrowed a bed: SS77									
g	Thou didst leave thy throne	250	465		513	697	154	192	179	
s	Thou who wast rich / Lord, you were rich			63		700				
s	To the Name of our / that brings salvation	121	470	222	523		80	291		373
g	We have a gospel to proclaim	431	486	519	532	728	465		585	
g	We were not there to see you come			121						
g	When my love to God/Christ grows weak						183	218		
g	When you prayed beneath the trees: WAM 98									

Years A, B, C
Maundy Thursday

Exodus **12**: 1-4 [5-10] 11-14; Psalm **116**: 1-2, 12-19; 1 Corinthians **11**: 23-26; John **13**: 1-17, 31b-35

		AMNS	NEH	HTC	HON	MP	H&P	R&S	BPW	CH3
e	According to thy gracious word		270							585
g	An upper room did our Lord prepare	434			29		594	438	429	
g	At the supper, Christ the Lord			394						
l	Blest by the sun, the olive tree		512							
s	By gracious powers so wonderfully sheltered							486	117	
e	Draw nigh and take / Draw near and take		281	401						
e	Father, it is right and fitting								433	
e	For the bread which you have broken	456		403						
e	He gave his life in selfless love			405		214			435	
e	I come with joy to meet my Lord	473		408	227		610	447	437	
g	Jesus, in dark Gethsemane							213		
s	Jesus in the olive grove						169			
e	Jesus, we thus / Now Jesus we obey	477					614	450	446	
g	Kneels at the feet of his friends / Jesus, Jesus						145	648	606	
e	Let us break bread together	480			299	414	615	452	443	
g	Lord/Great God, your love has called us here	489		480			500	339	442	
e	Lord Jesus Christ, you have come to us	391	297	417	311	435	617	373	444	
g	Love is his word			481	322				445	
g	Meekness and majesty				335	465			58	
e	My God, and/now is thy table spread	259		418	342					
e	Now/Sing my tongue / Of the glorious body	252	268		353		624	457	449	578
g	O thou who at thy eucharist / O Christ at your first eucharist	265	302	420	391		779			492
e	The church is like a table							480		
e	The heavenly Word proceeding forth	253	269							
e	The Son of God proclaim	427		415			627	458	455	
g	There's a spirit in the air	515		245			326	329	300	
g	This is the night, dear friends: SS37									
e	We come as guests invited			602		723				
s	When you prayed beneath the trees: WAM 98									

Years A, B, C
Good Friday

Isaiah **52**:13 — **53**:12; Psalm **22**; Hebrews **10**: 16-25 or Hebrews **4**: 14-16, **5**: 7-9; John **18**:1 — **19**:42

(See also Palm Sunday — Liturgy of the Passion Years A, B, C)

		AMNS	NEH	HTC	HON	MP	H&P	R&S	BPW	CH3
g	A purple robe			122						
g	Ah, holy Jesus, how hast thou offended		62	123	8		164	215	215	251
g	Alas! and did my Saviour bleed			124						
g	Alone thou goest / you once went / now going forth, O Lord							212	217	242
g	At the cross, her station keeping	69	97		44					246
g	Before the cock crew twice							214		
g	Beneath the cross of Jesus				59	55	165			684
g	Downtrodden Christ			125						
g	Glory be to Jesus	66	83	126	159					
g	He stood before the court			129						
g	It is a thing most wonderful	70	84	131	255	346	224	503	219	385
g	It is finished! Blessed Jesus		99							
o	Lord Christ, we praise your sacrifice	487		132			532	611		
g	Man of sorrows			130	330	458	228		350	380
s	My God, I love thee/you; not because	65	73	479	344		171	357		379
g	My song is love unknown	63	86	136	346	478	173	207	204	224
g	O Christ, the master carpenter			135						
g	O come and mourn with me awhile	114								243
g	O come and stand beneath the cross		98							
g	O dearest Lord, thy/your sacred head	71	89	134	359		172	222	351	252
g	O love divine, what hast thou done						175			
g	O perfect life of love [Also AHB 175]									249
g	O sacred head	68	90	139	389	520	176	220	223	253
s	Praise to the Holiest in the height	117	439	140	426	563	231	103	562	238
g	Rock of ages	135	445	593	437	582	273	365	545	83
o	See, Christ was wounded for our sake			137					229	
g	Sing, my tongue, the glorious battle / Here proclaim the glorious	59	78	142	446		177	228	226	256
s	There is a green hill far away	137	92	148	499	674	178	223	230	241
g	Throned upon the awesome/aweful tree [Also AHB 177]									247
s	When I survey the wondrous cross	67	95	147	549	755	180	217	233	254

Year A
Easter Day

Acts **10**: 34-43 or Jeremiah **31**: 1-6; Psalm **118**: 1-2, 14-24; Colossians **3**: 1-4 or Acts **10**: 34-43; John **20**: 1-18 or Matthew **28**: 1-10

		AMNS	NEH	HTC	HON	MP	H&P	R&S	BPW	CH3
g1	At break of day three women came: SS45									
e	Away with gloom	437					187			292
a	Christ the Lord is risen again	79	105	153	80		192	233		
o	Come ye faithful, raise the strain / Spring has come	76	106	160	100		194	236	248	269
g	Comes Mary to the grave			152						
g1	Early morning. 'Come, prepare him'	451								
g1	Good Joseph had a garden						195			280
s	Hail thee festival day [Easter]		109							
s	Jesus Christ is risen today	77	110	155	267	357			252	264
e	Lift up your hearts to things above						820			
s	Light's glittering morn	329		157						
p	O set ye open unto me									263
g	See how a light shines: SS46									
g	The day of resurrection	75	117	161	474		208	246		267
g	Thine/Yours be/is the glory	428	120	167	503	689	212	247	260	279
o	This hallowed chosen morn		122							
p	This is the day the Lord hath/has made	22	257	379			577	376		
p	This is the day, this is the day			S28	508	691	578	377	21	
g1	Too early for the blackbird							249		
s	Welcome, happy morning			166						272
e	Ye faithful souls who Jesus know						751			
s	Ye/You choirs of new Jerusalem	73	124	168	563		823			

Year B
Easter Day

Acts **10**: 34-43 or Isaiah **25**: 6-9; Psalm **118**: 1-2, 14-24; 1 Corinthians **15**: 1-11 or Acts **10**: 34-43;
John **20**: 1-18 or Mark **16**: 1-8

		AMNS	NEH	HTC	HON	MP	H&P	R&S	BPW	CH3
a	Christ the Lord is risen again	79	105	153	80		192	233		
s	Come ye faithful, raise the strain / Spring has come	76	106	160	100		194	236	248	269
g	Comes Mary to the grave			152						
g1	Early morning. 'Come, prepare him'	451								
g1	Good Joseph had a garden						195			280
s	Hail thee festival day [Easter]		109							
g	It fell upon a summer day				254					213
g2	Jesus Christ is risen today	77	110	155	267	357			252	264
s	Light's glittering morn	329		157						
p	O set ye open unto me									263
g	See how a light shines: SS46									
s	The day of resurrection	75	117	161	474		208	246		267
oa	The strife is o'er/past	78	119	163	495	670	214	250	261	266
s	Thine/Yours be/is the glory	428	120	167	503	689	212	247	260	279
p	This is the day the Lord hath/has made	22	257	379			577	376		
p	This is the day, this is the day			S28	508	691	578	377	21	
g1	Too early for the blackbird							249		
s	Welcome, happy morning			166						272
e	When Easter to the dark world came						200	251		
s	Ye/You choirs of new Jerusalem	73	124	168	563		823			

Year C
Easter Day

Acts **10**: 34-43 or Isaiah **65**: 17-25; Psalm **118**: 1-2, 14-24; 1 Corinthians **15**: 19-26 or Acts **10**: 34-43; John **20**: 1-18 or Luke **24**: 1-12

		AMNS	NEH	HTC	HON	MP	H&P	R&S	BPW	CH3
g2	All ye that seek the Lord who died						188			
g	At break of day three women came: SS45									
g2	Christ is alive! Let Christians sing						190	260	244	
a	Christ the Lord is risen again	79	105	153	80		192	233		
s	Come ye faithful, raise the strain / Spring has come	76	106	160	100		194	236	248	269
g	Comes Mary to the grave			152						
g1	Early morning. 'Come, prepare him'	451								
g1	Good Joseph had a garden						195			280
s	Hail thee festival day [Easter]		109							
s	Jesus Christ is risen today	77	110	155	267	357			252	264
e	Jesus lives! Thy/Your terrors now	82	112	156	272	373	198	239	253	605
s	Light's glittering morn	329		157						
e	Now is eternal life	402	114		351		203	432		
p	O set ye open unto me									263
g	See how a light shines: SS46									
s	The day of resurrection	75	117	161	474		208	246		267
a	The strife is o'er/past	78	119	163	495	670	214	250	261	266
s	Thine/Yours be/is the glory	428	120	167	503	689	212	247	260	279
p	This is the day the Lord hath/has made	22	257	379			577	376		
p	This is the day, this is the day			S28	508	691	578	377	21	
g1	Too early for the blackbird							249		
s	Welcome, happy morning			166						272
o	Ye/You choirs of new Jerusalem	73	124	168	563		823			

Year A
The Second Sunday of Easter

Acts **2**: 14a, 22-32; Psalm **16**; 1 Peter **1**: 3-9; John **20**: 19-31

		AMNS	NEH	HTC	HON	MP	H&P	R&S	BPW	CH3
s	At the Lamb's high feast we sing	81	104		45					
g	Blessed Thomas, doubt no longer		173							
e	Blest be the everlasting God						669	588		530
s	Christ the Lord is risen today / Love's redeeming work is done / All creation	83	113	150	324	76	193	232	246	275
s	Come ye faithful, raise the strain / Spring has come	76	106	160	100		194	236	248	269
s	Easter glory fills the sky									276
s	Good Christian men / Good Christians all, rejoice		107	154	181	196	104 (191	238	250	183
s	He is Lord, he is Lord			S7	204	220	256	264	378	
g	Jesus, Lord, Redeemer						199	240		283
g	Jesus, stand among us in thy/your risen power			364	280	380	530	388	88	11
e	Jesus, these eyes have never seen	245	389					592		674
g	My daughters and my sons: SS48									
p	Now is eternal life	402	114		351		203	432		
g	O Lord, we long to see your face	412								
g	O sons and daughters, let us sing	74	125				205	244		277
g	Rushing wind that fills: SS51									
g	That Easter-tide with joy was bright	329iii								
s	The Lamb's high banquet we await		101							
a	The strife is o'er/past	78	119	163	495	670	214	250	261	266
g	These things did Thomas: SS49									
s	This joyful Eastertide		121	165	509		213	248	258	271
g	When Easter to the dark world came						200	251		
s	When fear and grief had barred the door								259	

For those who require an Old Testament reading on the Sundays in Eastertide, provision is made in the table on page 60 of *Calendar, Lectionary and Collects*

Year B
The Second Sunday of Easter

Acts **4**: 32-35; Psalm **133**; 1 John 1:1 — **2**:2; John **20**: 19-31

		AMNS	NEH	HTC	HON	MP	H&P	R&S	BPW	CH3
s	At the Lamb's high feast we sing	81	104		45					
g	Blessed Thomas, doubt no longer		173							
e	Christ is the world's true light	346	494	323	78		456	601	618	505
s	Christ the Lord is risen today / Love's redeeming work is done / All creation	83	113	150	324	76	193	232	246	275
s	Come ye faithful, raise the strain / Spring has come	76	106	160	100		194	236	248	269
e	Eternal Light! Eternal Light!			454			458	83	85	357
s	Good Christian men / Good Christians all, rejoice		107	154	181	196	~~194~~ 191	238	250	183
a	Help us to help each other / Jesus, united by thy grace	374		540	208		773	500		
g	Jesus, Lord, Redeemer						199	240		283
a	Jesus, Lord, we look to thee	380	481				759	564		
g	Jesus, stand among us in thy/your risen power			364	280	380	530	388	88	11
p	O Holy Spirit, Lord of grace	152	419		371		310			
g	O Lord, we long to see your face	412								
e	O sons and daughters, let us sing	74	125				205	244		277
g	That Easter-tide with joy was bright	329iii								
s	The Lamb's high banquet we await		101							
g	These things did Thomas: SS49									
s	This joyful Eastertide		121	165	509		213	248	258	271
g	When Easter to the dark world came						200	251		
g	When fear and grief had barred the door								259	

For those who require an Old Testament reading on the Sundays in Eastertide, provision is made in the table on page 60 of *Calendar, Lectionary and Collects*

Year C
The Second Sunday of Easter

Acts **5**: 27-32; Psalm **118**: 14-29 or Psalm **150**; Revelation **1**: 4-8; John **20**: 19-31

		AMNS	NEH	HTC	HON	MP	H&P	R&S	BPW	CH3
s	At the Lamb's high feast we sing	81	104		45					
s	At the name of Jesus	148	338	172	46	41	74	261	370	300
g	Blessed Thomas, doubt no longer		173							
s	Come ye faithful, raise the strain / Spring has come	76	106	160	100		194	236	248	269
g	Good Christian men / Good Christians all, rejoice		107	154	181	196	184 191	238	250	183
g	Jesus, Lord, Redeemer						199	240		283
g	Jesus, stand among us in thy/your risen power			364	280	380	530	388	88	11
s	Lord, enthroned in heavenly splendour	263	296	416	309	431	616			583
g	O Lord, we long to see your face	412								
p2	O praise ye the Lord / Sing praise to the Lord	203	427	354	388	518		49	70	
p	O set ye open unto me									263
g	O sons and daughters, let us sing	74	125				205	244		277
p2	Praise the Lord, his glories show			345			14	102		359
p2	Praise to the Lord, the Almighty	207	440	40	427	564	16	74	68	9
g	That Easter-tide with joy was bright	329iii								
s	The Lamb's high banquet we await		101							
g	These things did Thomas: SS49									
s	This is the day the Lord hath/has made	22	257	379			577	376		
g	This joyful Eastertide		121	165	509		213	248	258	271
s	Thou Shepherd of Israel and mine						750			
s	We have a gospel to proclaim	431	486	519	532	728	465		585	
g	When Easter to the dark world came						200	251		
g	When fear and grief had barred the door								259	

For those who require an Old Testament reading on the Sundays in Eastertide, provision is made in the table on page 60 of *Calendar, Lectionary and Collects*

Year A
The Third Sunday of Easter

Acts **2**: 14a, 36-41; Psalm **116**: 1-4, 12-19; 1 Peter **1**: 17-23; Luke **24**: 13-35

		AMNS	NEH	HTC	HON	MP	H&P	R&S	BPW	CH3
g	Abide with me	13	331	425	6	4	665	336	515	695
s	Alleluia, alleluia, give thanks to the risen Lord			S3	24	30	250	234	31	
s	Alleluia, alleluia, hearts to heaven	80	103	151	25					
g	As we walked home: SS47									
g	Be known to us in breaking bread						597	441		
s	Christ is alive! Let Christians sing						190	260	244	
s	Christ Jesus lay in death's strong bands							235		268
g	Come, risen Lord, and deign to be our guest	349	279		96		605	445		572
e	Come, ye faithful / Alleluia, raise the anthem	145	351	205	99	103	813		269	
g	Hail thee festival day [Easter]		109							
s	I know that my Redeemer lives, what joy			169	232	278	196	278	251	
p	I'll of salvation take the cup							722		565
s	Jesus lives! Thy/Your terrors now	82	112	156	272	373	198	239	253	605
s	Now the green blade rises/riseth	501	115		355		204	243	257	278
g	O thou who this mysterious bread						621			
s	The day of resurrection	75	117	161	474		208	246		267
s	The Lord is risen indeed	84	118		488					265
g	The time was early evening: SS33									
a	We have a gospel to proclaim	431	486	519	532	728	465		585	
p	What shall I render to my God						703			

686

Year B
The Third Sunday of Easter

Acts 3: 12-19; Psalm 4; 1 John 3: 1-7; Luke 24: 36b-48

		AMNS	NEH	HTC	HON	MP	H&P	R&S	BPW	CH3
s	Alleluia, alleluia, give thanks to the risen Lord			S3	24	30	250	234	31	
s	Alleluia, alleluia, hearts to heaven	80	103	151	25					
e	Behold the amazing gift of love						666	587		396
s	Christ is alive! Let Christians sing						190	260	244	
s	Christ Jesus lay in death's strong bands							235		268
s	Come, let us to the Lord our God						33	81		69
g	Come, ye faithful / Alleluia, raise the anthem	145	351	205	99	103	813		269	
s	He is Lord, he is Lord			S7	204	220	256	264	378	
s	I know that my Redeemer lives, what joy			169	232	278	196	278	251	
s	Jesus lives! Thy/Your terrors now	82	112	156	272	373	198	239	253	605
s	Now is eternal life	402	114		351		203	432		
s	Now the green blade rises/riseth	501	115		355		204	243	257	278
g	O sons and daughters, let us sing	74	125				205	244		277
s	The day of resurrection	75	117	161	474		208	246		267
s	The Lord is risen indeed	84	118		488					265
a	To the Name of our / that brings salvation	121	470	222	523		80	291		373

Year C
The Third Sunday of Easter

Acts **9**: 1-6 [7-20]; Psalm **30**; Revelation **5**: 11-14; John **21**: 1-19

		AMNS	NEH	HTC	HON	MP	H&P	R&S	BPW	CH3
s	Alleluia, alleluia, give thanks to the risen Lord			S3	24	30	250	234	31	
s	Alleluia, alleluia, hearts to heaven	80	103	151	25					
e	Awake and sing the song							379		
s	Christ Jesus lay in death's strong bands							235		268
s	Christ the Lord is risen today / Love's redeeming work is done / All creation	83	113	150	324	76	193	232	246	275
e	Come, let us join our cheerful songs	144	349	206	94	93	810	382	6	
s	Come, ye faithful / Alleluia, raise the anthem	145	351	205	99	103	813		269	
s	Easter glory fills the sky									276
e	From all that/who dwell/live beneath	98		580	146		489	723		362
a	God moves in a mysterious way	112	365		173	193	65	59	122	147
e	Hail thou/our once-despisèd/rejected Jesus			175	192	203	222		273	
s	Hark, my soul, it is the Lord / Christian, do you hear the Lord	244		472	197	209	521	348		676
s	He is Lord, he is Lord			S7	204	220	256	264	378	
e	Heavenly hosts in ceaseless worship			570						
s	I know that my Redeemer lives, what joy			169	232	278	196	278	251	
g	James and Andrew, Peter and John				257					
s	Now the green blade rises/riseth	501	115		355		204	243	257	278
s	The day of resurrection	75	117	161	474		208	246		267
s	The Lord is risen indeed	84	118		488					265
p	Through all the changing scenes of life	209	467	46	516	702	73	685	544	
a	We sing the glorious conquest	313	155							
e	Ye/You servants of God, your Master proclaim	149	476	520	565	784	278	293	76	372

Year A
The Fourth Sunday of Easter

Acts **2**: 42-47; Psalm **23**; 1 Peter **2**: 19-25; John **10**: 1-10

		AMNS	NEH	HTC	HON	MP	H&P	R&S	BPW	CH3
pg	Faithful Shepherd, feed me		282	29	117					
e	In heavenly love abiding			458	246	331	678	590	555	681
g	Jesus the Lord said/says, I am the Bread					384	137	199	202	
a	Jesus, where'er thy people meet / Lord Jesus, when your people	162	390	371	282		549	476		
g	Loving Shepherd of thy/your sheep	134		305	325					93
e	Shepherd divine, our wants relieve	228					558			
g	Souls of men / Restless souls / There's a wideness	251	461	443	501	607,683	230	353	573	218
pg	The God of love my shepherd is	110	77		479		43	677		
pg	The King of love my shepherd is	126	457	44	484	649	69	552	394	388
pg	The Lord's my shepherd, I'll not want	426	459	591/45	490	660	70	679	395	387
g	Thou Shepherd of Israel and mine						750			
s	What Adam's disobedience cost	524					430			

For seasonal hymns see those marked s in the lists for the First, Second and Third Sundays of Easter

Year B
The Fourth Sunday of Easter

Acts **4**: 5-12; Psalm **23**; 1 John **3**: 16-24; John **10**: 11-18

		AMNS	NEH	HTC	HON	MP	H&P	R&S	BPW	CH3
e	Almighty Father, who for us thy Son didst give	338					401	621		
a	Christ is our corner-stone	161	206	564	77					
g	Good Christian men / Good Christians all, rejoice		107	154	181	196	104	238	250	183
g	How sweet the name of Jesus sounds	122	374	211	220	251	257	277	339	376
e	I come with joy to meet my Lord	473		408	227		610	447	437	
a	Jesus! the name high over all			213		385	264			
g	Sing we the song of those who stand						821	666		
p	The God of love my shepherd is	110	77		479		43	677		
s	What Adam's disobedience cost	524					430			

For seasonal hymns see those marked s in the lists for the First, Second and Third Sundays of Easter

Year C
The Fourth Sunday of Easter

Acts **9**: 36-43; Psalm **23**; Revelation **7**: 9-17; John **10**: 22-30

		AMNS	NEH	HTC	HON	MP	H&P	R&S	BPW	CH3
g	Christ who knows all his sheep	347						470		672
p	Faithful Shepherd, feed me		282	29	117					
e	How bright these glorious spirits shine	306	227	572						533
s	Jesus, good above all other	378	387	96	269		732	528		111
g	Loving Shepherd of thy/your sheep	134		305	325					93
s	Now is eternal life	402	114		351		203	432		
p	The God of love my shepherd is	110	77		479		43	677		
p	The King of love my shepherd is	126	457	44	484	649	69	552	394	388
p	The Lord's my shepherd, I'll not want	426	459	591/45	490	660	70	679	395	387
g	Thine/Yours for ever	234	463	556	504					
s	What Adam's disobedience cost	524					430			
e	Who are these, like stars appearing	323	231		555					

For seasonal hymns see those marked s in the lists for the First, Second and Third Sundays of Easter

Year A
The Fifth Sunday of Easter

Acts 7: 55-60; Psalm 31: 1-5, 15-16; 1 Peter 2: 2-10; John 14: 1-14

		AMNS	NEH	HTC	HON	MP	H&P	R&S	BPW	CH3
s	A brighter dawn is breaking		102		1					
e	Christ is made the sure foundation / Blessed city, heavenly Salem	283/33 2	204/20 5	559	76		485	559	474	10
e	Christ is our corner-stone	161	206	564	77					
g	Come, my way, my truth, my life						254	352		
s	Creatures, once in safety held: SS5									
a	Head of thy Church triumphant						818			
g	How sweet the name of Jesus sounds	122	374	211	220	251	257	277	339	376
p	Put thou thy trust / Commit thou all thy griefs	223			429		672	550		669
e	See where our great High Priest						622			
a	Stephen, first of Christian martyrs		201							
e	The Church's one foundation	170	484	501	473	640	515	566	393	420
g	Thou art / You are the way	128	464	113	512	695	234	554		121
e	Ye that know the Lord is gracious	175	477							

For seasonal hymns see those marked s in the lists for the First, Second and Third Sundays of Easter

Year B
The Fifth Sunday of Easter

Acts **8**: 26-40; Psalm **22**: 25-31; 1 John **4**: 7-21; John **15**: 1-8

		AMNS	NEH	HTC	HON	MP	H&P	R&S	BPW	CH3
g	Bread of heaven, on thee we feed	271	276	398	67			442		
p	Christ the Lord is risen today / Love's redeeming work is done / All creation	83	113	150	324	76	193	232	246	275
s	Come, let us to the Lord our God						33	81		69
g	Come, we that love the Lord						487	384	525	
s	Creatures, once in safety held: SS5									
s	Lord, teach us how to pray aright	227	406	367	316		551			
e	Love divine, all loves excelling	131	408	217	321	449	267	663	559	437
e	Now the green blade rises/riseth	501	115		355		204	243	257	278
a	O love, how deep, how broad, how high	119	425		383		229	283	207	223

For seasonal hymns see those marked s in the lists for the First, Second and Third Sundays of Easter

Year C
The Fifth Sunday of Easter

Acts **11**: 1-18; Psalm **148**; Revelation **21**: 1-6; John **13**: 31-35

		AMNS	NEH	HTC	HON	MP	H&P	R&S	BPW	CH3
a	All hail the power of Jesus' name	140	332	587/203	13	13	252		29	382
g	Christ from whom all blessings flow			491			764	561		
g	Come down, O Love Divine	156	137	231	90	89	281	294	283	115
s	Come, let us to the Lord our God						33	81		69
e	Come, we that love the Lord						487	384	525	
a	Jesus shall reign where'er the sun	143	388	516	277	379	239	269	313	413
e	Lord God, by whom all change is wrought						39	68		
s	Lord, teach us how to pray aright	227	406	367	316		551			
e	O holy City, seen of/by John	409						628		509
e	O what their joy / What of those sabbaths	186	432					659		535
p	Praise the Lord! ye/you/let heaven(s), adore him	195	437	583	425		15	116	67	37
e	Songs of praise the angels sang	196	451	350			512	667		38
g	The great love of God						45	105		415
p	The Lord of heaven confess									135

For seasonal hymns see those marked s in the lists for the First, Second and Third Sundays of Easter

Year A
The Sixth Sunday of Easter

Acts **17**: 22-31; Psalm **66**: 8-20; 1 Peter **3**: 13-22; John **14**: 15-21

		AMNS	NEH	HTC	HON	MP	H&P	R&S	BPW	CH3
g	Beloved, let us love			468				610		
g	Come down, O Love Divine	156	137	231	90	89	281	294	283	115
e	Come ye faithful, raise the strain / Spring has come	76	106	160	100		194	236	248	269
g	Come, thou everlasting Spirit						298	315		
s	Creatures, once in safety held: SS5									
s	God moves in a mysterious way	112	365		173	193	65	59	122	147
e	God of wilderness and jungle: SS3									
p	Jesus, my Truth, my Way						734			
a	Lord of beauty, thine the splendour	106	265		314					120
e	Lord, thy Church on earth is seeking						774	579		
e	Lord, you give the great commission							580		
p	O God of Bethel / O God of Jacob	216	416	35	364		442	71	599	72
g	Our blest/great Redeemer	151		241	410	548	312	330		336

See also hymns for Rogationtide, page 191

Year B
The Sixth Sunday of Easter

Acts **10**: 44-48; Psalm **98**; 1 John **5**: 1-6; John **15**: 9-17

		AMNS	NEH	HTC	HON	MP	H&P	R&S	BPW	CH3
g	Beloved, let us love			468				610		
g	Come down, O Love Divine	156	137	231	90	89	281	294	283	115
s	God makes his rain to fall: SS96									
a	Holy Spirit, come, confirm us	471	140		214		288	298	289	
g	Lord/Great God, your love has called us here	489		480			500	339	442	
p	New songs of celebration render	498		343	350		491	709		
e	Rock of ages	135	445	593	437	582	273	365	545	83
e	Spirit of faith, come down						325			
s	Spread, O spread, thou mighty word		482							
g	The Son of God proclaim	427		415			627	458	455	
s	Thy ceaseless, unexhausted love						48	106		

See also hymns for Rogationtide, page 191

Acts **16**: 9-15; Psalm **67**; Revelation **21**:10, 22—22:5; John **14**: 23-29 or John **5**: 1-9

		AMNS	NEH	HTC	HON	MP	H&P	R&S	BPW	CH3
g	A charge to keep I have						785			
s	Breathe on me, Breath of God	157	342	226	69	67	280	295	282	103
e	City of God, how broad and far	173	346		85		809			422
g	Dear Lord and Father of mankind	115	353	356	106	111	673	492	84	76
s	God as Fire, send your Spirit: SS52									
p	God of mercy, God of grace	179	366	293	175			575	48	497
g	Grant us your peace: SS14									
g2	Have faith in God, my heart	372		431	201		675	499	336	
e	Jesus calls us: o'er/in the tumult	312	200	104	266	359	141	355		211
e	Light's abode, celestial Salem	185	401		305					
g2	O for a thousand tongues to sing	125	415	219	362	496	744	285	59	371
e	O holy City, seen of/by John	409						628		509
g	Peace, perfect peace, in this dark world of sin			467	413	555			561	
g	Peace, perfect peace, is the gift				414			594	112	
g	Put peace into each other's hands							635	637	
e	The stream of life is flowing here: SS13									

See also hymns for Rogationtide, page 191

Years A, B, C
Ascension Day

Acts **1**: 1-11; Daniel **7**: 9-14; Psalm **47** or **93**; Ephesians **1**: 15-23 or Acts **1**: 1-11; Luke **24**: 44-53

		AMNS	NEH	HTC	HON	MP	H&P	R&S	BPW	CH3
s	All hail the power of Jesus' name	140	332	587/203	13	13	252		29	382
s	Alleluia! sing to Jesus	262	271	170	26	207	592		270	
s	Be still for the presence / Spirit of the Lord				53	50			5	
s	Christ triumphant, ever reigning			173	81	77			306	
s	Come, let us join our cheerful songs	144	349	206	94	93	810	382	6	
s	Crown him with many crowns	147	352	174	103	109	255	262	37	298
s	Eternal Monarch, King most high		128							
s	God is gone up on high							253		
g	God of wilderness and jungle: SS3									
s	Hail the day that sees him rise	87	130	176	191	202	197	252	272	
g	Handed over to be orphaned: SS50									
s	Head of the Church, our risen Lord						547	562		
s	Jesus invites his saints						612	434	438	
s	Join all the glorious names			214		392	78	280	557	304
s	Lord of the worlds above	165								
s	Rejoice! the Lord is King	139	443	180	432	575	243	657	317	296
s	See the Conqueror mounts in triumph	88	132	181	441					
s	The golden gates are lifted up							256		
s	The head that was once crowned with thorns	141	134	182	480	647	209	257	274	286
s	The Lord ascendeth up on high		135				210			287
s	The Lord Jehovah reigns						59			
s	We have a gospel to proclaim	431	486	519	532	728	465		585	

Year A

The Seventh Sunday of Easter (Sunday after Ascension Day)

Acts **1**: 6-14; Psalm **68**: 1-10, 32-35; 1 Peter **4**: 12-14, **5**: 6-11; John **17**: 1-11

		AMNS	NEH	HTC	HON	MP	H&P	R&S	BPW	CH3
ls	All hail the power of Jesus' name	140	332	587/203	13	13	252		29	382
ls	Alleluia! sing to Jesus	262	271	170	26	207	592		270	
o	Breathe on me, Breath of God	157	342	226	69	67	280	295	282	103
g	Christ is the King! O friends rejoice	345	345	492				571	475	474
ls	Christ triumphant, ever reigning			173	81	77			306	
ls	Come, let us join our cheerful songs	144	349	206	94	93	810	382	6	
ls	Crown him with many crowns	147	352	174	103	109	255	262	37	298
ls	Eternal Monarch, King most high		128							
a	Hail the day that sees him rise	87	130	176	191	202	197	252	272	
ls	Jesus shall reign where'er the sun	143	388	516	277	379	239	269	313	413
ls	Lord, enthroned in heavenly splendour	263	296	416	309	431	616			583
g	Lord Christ, the Father's mighty Son	386						568		
o	O for a heart to praise my God	230	74	483	361	495	536	514	538	85
a	O Spirit of the living God			513			322	577	579	496
g	O thou who at thy eucharist / O Christ at your first eucharist	265	302	420	391		779			492
ls	Rejoice! the Lord is King	139	443	180	432	575	243	657	317	296
p	See the Conqueror mounts in triumph	88	132	181	441					
ls	The golden gates are lifted up							256		
e	The head that was once crowned with thorns	141	134	182	480	647	209	257	274	286
ls	The Lord ascendeth up on high		135				210			287

Year B

The Seventh Sunday of Easter (Sunday after Ascension Day)

Acts 1: 15-17, 21-26; Psalm 1; 1 John 5: 9-13; John 17: 6-19

		AMNS	NEH	HTC	HON	MP	H&P	R&S	BPW	CH3
sl	All hail the power of Jesus' name	140	332	587/203	13	13	252		29	382
ls	Alleluia! sing to Jesus	262	271	170	26	207	592		270	
o	Breathe on me, Breath of God	157	342	226	69	67	280	295	282	103
ls	Christ triumphant, ever reigning			173	81	77			306	
ls	Come, let us join our cheerful songs	144	349	206	94	93	810	382	6	
ls	Crown him with many crowns	147	352	174	103	109	255	262	37	298
ls	Hail the day that sees him rise	87	130	176	191	202	197	252	272	
p	Happy are they who walk in God's wise way							669		
ls	Lord, enthroned in heavenly splendour	263	296	416	309	431	616			583
g	Lord Christ, the Father's mighty Son	386						568		
g	Now is eternal life	402	114		351		203	432		
o	O for a heart to praise my God	230	74	483	361	495	536	514	538	85
g	O thou who at thy eucharist / O Christ at your first eucharist	265	302	420	391		779			492
ls	Rejoice! the Lord is King	139	443	180	432	575	243	657	317	296
ls	See the Conqueror mounts in triumph	88	132	181	441					
a	The eternal gifts of Christ the King	297	213		476					540
ls	The golden gates are lifted up							256		
ls	The head that was once crowned with thorns	141	134	182	480	647	209	257	274	286
ls	The Lord ascendeth up on high		135				210			287
a	The Saviour, when to heaven he rose						211			

Year C
The Seventh Sunday of Easter (Sunday after Ascension Day)

Acts **16**: 16-34; Psalm **97**; Revelation **22**: 12-14, 16-17, 20-21; John **17**: 20-26

		AMNS	NEH	HTC	HON	MP	H&P	R&S	BPW	CH3
s	All hail the power of Jesus' name	140	332	587/203	13	13	252		29	382
s	Alleluia! sing to Jesus	262	271	170	26	207	592		270	
s	At the name of Jesus	148	338	172	46	41	74	261	370	300
o	Breathe on me, Breath of God	157	342	226	69	67	280	295	282	103
s	Christ is the King! O friends rejoice	345	345	492				571	475	474
e	Christ is the world's true light	346	494	323	78		456	601	618	505
s	Christ triumphant, ever reigning			173	81	77			306	
e	Come, let us join our cheerful songs	144	349	206	94	93	810	382	6	
e	Crown him with many crowns	147	352	174	103	109	255	262	37	298
s	Eternal Monarch, King most high		128							
s	Hail the day that sees him rise	87	130	176	191	202	197	252	272	
e	Hark what a sound, and too divine for hearing						236	660		
s	Lord, enthroned in heavenly splendour	263	296	416	309	431	616			583
o	O for a heart to praise my God	230	74	483	361	495	536	514	538	85
e	Rejoice! the Lord is King	139	443	180	432	575	243	657	317	296
s	See the Conqueror mounts in triumph	88	132	181	441					
s	Songs of praise the angels sang	196	451	350			512	667		38
s	The golden gates are lifted up							256		
s	The head that was once crowned with thorns	141	134	182	480	647	209	257	274	286
s	The Lord ascendeth up on high		135				210			287
e	Thy/Your kingdom come, O God	177	499	334	519		783	638	644	322

Year A
Day of Pentecost (Whit Sunday)

Acts **2**: 1-21 or Numbers **11**: 24-30; Psalm **104**: 24-34, 35b; 1 Corinthians **12**: 3b-13 or Acts **2**: 1-21;
John **20**: 19-23 or John **7**: 37-39

		AMNS	NEH	HTC	HON	MP	H&P	R&S	BPW	CH3
ls	Away with our fears, our troubles and tears			224			296	323	279	
al	Christians, lift up your hearts ... Praise for the Spirit	444		229						
ls	Come down, O Love Divine	156	137	231	90	89	281	294	283	115
ls	Come, gracious Spirit, heavenly dove	153	347							116
o	Come, Holy Ghost, our hearts inspire (Wesley)	448	348		91		469	312	97	122
g	Come, Holy Ghost, our souls inspire	93	138	589	92	90	283	751		342
ls	Come, Holy Spirit, heavenly dove						297	299		
g	Come, thou/most Holy Spirit, come / Come, thou Holy Paraclete	92	139	227	97		284	297		105
ls	Creator Spirit, by whose aid						285		286	118
a	God as Fire, send your Spirit: SS52									
e	Holy Spirit, ever dwelling/living		141				303	324	290	334
g	Jesus, the gift divine I know						318			
e	Let every Christian pray	478		230			305			
e	Lord God, the Holy Ghost						306			332
e	O Holy Ghost, thy people bless / O Holy Spirit, come to bless	155		238	370					
a	O joy, because the circling year / Rejoice! the year upon its way		136		433					329/330
g	O King enthroned on high	158	421		373		311	296		
p	O worship the King all glorious above	101	433	24	393	528	28	47	63	35
a	On the day of Pentecost	504								
a	Our Lord, his passion ended	91					323	328		
a	Rushing wind that fills: SS51									
ls	Sing to him in whom creation		142				324			
ls	Spirit of God, unseen as the wind								295	
ls	Spirit of God within me			243			294	304	296	
a	Spirit of mercy, truth and love	89	143		453					338
ls	Spirit of the living God, fall afresh on me			S23	454	612	295	308	298	
ls	There's a spirit in the air	515		245			326	329	300	

Year B
Day of Pentecost (Whit Sunday)

Acts **2**: 1-21 or Ezekiel **37**: 1-14; Psalm **104**: 24-34, 35b; Romans **8**: 22-27 or Acts **2**: 1-21;
John **15**: 26-27, **16**: 4b-15

		AMNS	NEH	HTC	HON	MP	H&P	R&S	BPW	CH3
ls	Away with our fears, our troubles and tears			224			296	323	279	
e	Born by the Holy Spirit's breath			225		61	279		281	
o	Breathe on me, Breath of God	157	342	226	69	67	280	295	282	103
al	Christians, lift up your hearts ... Praise for the Spirit	444		229						
ls	Come down, O Love Divine	156	137	231	90	89	281	294	283	115
g	Come, gracious Spirit, heavenly dove	153	347							116
g	Come, Holy Ghost, our souls inspire	93	138	589	92	90	283	751		342
g	Come, Holy Spirit, heavenly dove						297	299		
g	Come, thou/most Holy Spirit, come / Come, thou Holy Paraclete	92	139	227	97		284	297		105
a	Creator Spirit, by whose aid						285		286	118
a	God as Fire, send your Spirit: SS52									
a	Holy Spirit, ever dwelling/living		141				303	324	290	334
e	I will pour out my Spirit						292			
a	Let every Christian pray	478		230			305			
o	O Breath of life, come sweeping / O Breath of love, come breathe			237	356	488	777	302	293	339
a	O Holy Ghost, thy people bless / O Holy Spirit, come to bless	155		238	370					
p	O worship the King all glorious above	101	433	24	393	528	28	47	63	35
a	On the day of Pentecost	504								
a	Our Lord, his passion ended	91					323	328		
a	Rushing wind that fills: SS51									
ls	Sing to him in whom creation		142				324			
a	Spirit of God, unseen as the wind								295	
g	Spirit of God within me			243			294	304	296	
a	Spirit of mercy, truth and love	89	143		453					338
g	Spirit of the living God, fall afresh on me			S23	454	612	295	308	298	
ls	There's a spirit in the air	515		245			326	329	300	
a	Upon the day of Pentecost						328			

Year C
Day of Pentecost (Whit Sunday)

Acts **2**: 1-21 or Genesis **11**: 1-9; Psalm **104**: 24-34, 35b; Romans **8**: 14-17 or Acts **2**: 1-21;

John **14**: 8-17 [25-27]

		AMNS	NEH	HTC	HON	MP	H&P	R&S	BPW	CH3
s	Away with our fears, our troubles and tears			224			296	323	279	
e	Born by the Holy Spirit's breath			225		61	279		281	
al	Christians, lift up your hearts ... Praise for the Spirit	444		229						
s	Come down, O Love Divine	156	137	231	90	89	281	294	283	115
g	Come, gracious Spirit, heavenly dove	153	347							116
a	Come, Holy Ghost, our souls inspire	93	138	589	92	90	283	751		342
g	Come, Holy Spirit, heavenly dove						297	299		
g	Come, thou/most Holy Spirit, come / Come, thou Holy Paraclete	92	139	227	97		284	297		105
p	Creator of the earth and skies	351		320			419	82		
a	Creator Spirit, by whose aid						285		286	118
e	Eternal Spirit of the living Christ							300		
a	God as Fire, send your Spirit: SS52									
g	Holy Spirit, come, confirm us	471	140		214		288	298	289	
e	Holy Spirit, ever dwelling/living		141				303	324	290	334
a	I will pour out my Spirit						292			
a	Let every Christian pray	478		230			305			
s	O Holy Ghost, thy people bless / O Holy Spirit, come to bless	155		238	370					
s	O King enthroned on high	158	421		373		311	296		
a	On the day of Pentecost	504								
a	Our Lord, his passion ended	91					323	328		
a	Rushing wind that fills: SS51									
s	Sing to him in whom creation		142				324			
a	Spirit of God, unseen as the wind								295	
g	Spirit of God within me			243			294	304	296	
a	Spirit of mercy, truth and love	89	143		453					338
g	Spirit of the living God, fall afresh on me			S23	454	612	295	308	298	
s	There's a spirit in the air	515		245			326	329	300	
a	Upon the day of Pentecost						328			

Years A, B, C
Ordinary Time: Trinity Sunday

Year A: Isaiah **40**: 12-17, 27-31; Psalm **8**; 2 Corinthians **13**: 11-13; Matthew **28**: 16-20

Year B: Isaiah **6**: 1-8; Psalm **29**; Romans **8**: 12-17; John **3**: 1-17

Year C: Proverbs **8**: 1-4, 22-31; Psalm **8**; Romans **5**: 1-5; John **16**: 12-15

		AMNS	NEH	HTC	HON	MP	H&P	R&S	BPW	CH3
s	All hail, adored Trinity		145							
e	Born by the Holy Spirit's breath			225		61	279		281	
s	Bright the vision / Round the Lord	96	343	578	70		445	665	71	353
g	Christ is alive! Let Christians sing						190	260	244	
g	Come, Father, Son and Holy Ghost						580			
s	Father all-powerful, thine is the kingdom	355								
s	Father eternal, Lord of the ages		356	1						
s	Father in heaven, grant to your children			2			3	28	38	
s	Father most holy, merciful and loving/tender	94	144	3	123		5			31
s	Father of heaven, whose love profound	97	358	359	124		519			77
s	Father, we adore you			S5	125	139		29	39	
s	Glory be to God the Father									354
gl	Go forth for God		321							
s	God the Father, throned in splendour								50	
g	Holy Spirit, Truth divine			235			289	301	292	106
s	Holy, holy, holy, Lord God almighty	95	146	7/594	212	237	7	34	51	352
ps	How excellent in all the earth									138
s	How shall I sing that majesty	472	373				8	661		
s	I bind unto myself / myself to God today / Christ be with me		159	5	225		695	36		402
g	I will pour out my Spirit						292			
s	May the grace of Christ our Saviour	181		370	333		762		110	634
s	Meekness and majesty				335	465			58	
s	Most ancient of all mysteries		147							
s	O God, by whose almighty plan	406					396	651		
s	O Trinity, O Trinity			6						
s	Praise the Father, God of justice			8						
g	Spirit of God within me			243			294	304	296	
e	Spirit of truth, essential God						480	313		
s	This day God gives me	516						79		
s	Thou/God whose almighty word	180	466	506	514	699	29	38	591	494
s	Three in One and One in Three			12	515					
s	We believe in God almighty, Maker			10						
s	We give immortal praise	520		11			18	37	72	

494

Year A
Proper 4

Continuous: Genesis **6**: 9-22, **7**: 24, **8**: 14-19 and Psalm **46**
or *Related:* Deuteronomy **11**: 18-21, 26-28 and Psalm **31**: 1-5, 19-24;
Romans **1**: 16-17, **3**: 22b-28 [29-31]; Matthew **7**: 21-29

It is intended that churches should follow either the Continuous or Related scheme of readings in any one year.
Hymns selected for the Continuous scheme are marked o1 or p1,
and those for the Related scheme are marked o2 or p2.

		AMNS	NEH	HTC	HON	MP	H&P	R&S	BPW	CH3
p1	A safe stronghold/fortress/refuge	114		523		2	661	585	375	406/7
e	And can it be			452/588	30	33	216	366	328	409
p1	Be still and know that I am God				52	48			280	
g	Christ be my leader by night as by day						709			
g	City of God, how broad and far	173	346		85		809			422
g	Come, let us to the Lord our God						33	81		69
e	Come, ye faithful / Alleluia, raise the anthem	145	351	205	99	103	813		269	
o1	Creatures, once in safety held: SS5									
e	Father, whose everlasting love						520			
p1	God is our refuge and our strength							691		24
p1	God is our strength and refuge			527		188			308	
g	How firm a foundation			430	216	243		589	380	
e	I'm not ashamed to own/name my Lord			448	240	323	677	428	343	591
e	Jesus, our Lord and King							429		
o1	Lord of our life, and God of our salvation		404	529	315	441				491
g	My hope is built on nothing less			462		473				411
o1	Now in the name of him who sent						590	425		
p2	Open, Lord, my inward ear						540			
p2g	Rock of ages	135	445	593	437	582	273	365	545	83
g	The right hand of God						408	91		
o1	What Adam's disobedience cost	524					430			

Year B
Proper 4

Continuous: 1 Samuel **3**: 1-10 [11-20] and Psalm **139**: 1-6, 13-18

or *Related:* Deuteronomy **5**: 12-15 and Psalm **81**: 1-10; 2 Corinthians **4**: 5-12; Mark 2:23 — 3:6

It is intended that churches should follow either the Continuous or Related scheme of readings in any one year.
Hymns selected for the Continuous scheme are marked o1 or p1,
and those for the Related scheme are marked o2 or p2.

		AMNS	NEH	HTC	HON	MP	H&P	R&S	BPW	CH3
o2	Can we/man by searching find out God	438					76	80		
e1	Christ, whose glory fills the skies	4	234	266	82	79	457	380		114
o2	Come, divine interpreter						468			
g	Come, let us with our Lord arise	449	254	375			575	383		
o2	Father of all, whose laws have stood			539					335	
g	First of the week and finest day			376						
o2	Help us, O Lord, to learn	373	370	493			474			
o1	Hushed was the evening hymn					253	523	526		123
p2	I sing the almighty power of God					293	334	43		
p1	In all my vast concerns with thee						72			
o2	Lord, be thy word my rule / Lord, make your word	232		250						
o1p1	Lord, speak to me, that I may speak			510		444	553	613	611	485
e	Lord, the light of your love [Shine, Jesus, shine]				317	445			347	
p1	Lord, you have searched and known my ways						71	70	564	
o1	Master, speak! Thy servant heareth / Your servant's listening					459	535		536	
e	O splendour of God's glory						461	537		
e	Out of darkness let light shine			447						
o2	Powerful in making us wise to salvation			252			479			
o1	Speak, Lord, in the stillness			253		608			105	
g	Sweet is the work, my God, my King			377		620	514			
g	The first day of the week	424					576			
p1	There is no moment of my life						428		133	
g	This is the day the Lord hath/has made	22	257	379			577	376		
p1	Thou art / You are before me, Lord, thou art behind						543	731		68
o1	When heaven's voice was still: SS71									

Year C
Proper 4

Continuous: 1 Kings **18**: 20-21 [22-29] 30-39 and Psalm **96**

or *Related:* 1 Kings **8**: 22-23, 41-43 and Psalm **96**: 1-9; Galatians **1**: 1-12; Luke **7**: 1-10

It is intended that churches should follow either the Continuous or Related scheme of readings in any one year.
Hymns selected for the Continuous scheme are marked o1 or p1,
and those for the Related scheme are marked o2 or p2.

		AMNS	NEH	HTC	HON	MP	H&P	R&S	BPW	CH3
g	At even[ing], ere/when the sun was/had set	9	243	315	43	43	142	644	616	52
e	Come, Holy Ghost, our hearts inspire (Wesley)	448	348		91		469	312	97	122
o2	God of light and life's creation			561						
g	I am not worthy, holy Lord			407						570
p	In beauty of his holiness									311
g	Into our world from God he came: SS78									
g	Jesus, my Lord, how rich thy grace / Fountain of good	381					147			459
g	Jesus, thy far-extended fame						148			
p	Let all the world in every corner sing	202	394	342	296	404	10	114	54	361
g	O changeless Christ, for ever new			108					206	
o2	O God, in whom we live and move							409		
p	O sing a new song to the Lord									22
p	O worship / Worship the Lord in the beauty of holiness	49	52	344	394	529	505	187	22	40
o2	Saviour, and can it be						541			
o1	The God of Abraham praise	331	148	9	478	645	452	121	131	358
o2	The heaven of heavens / Where the appointed		312					78		

Year A
Proper 5

Continuous: Genesis **12**: 1-9 and Psalm **33**: 1-12 or *Related:* Hosea **5**:15 — **6**:6 and Psalm **50**: 7-15; Romans **4**: 13-25; Matthew **9**: 9-13, 18-26

		AMNS	NEH	HTC	HON	MP	H&P	R&S	BPW	CH3
g	At the name of Jesus	148	338	172	46	41	74	261	370	300
o2	Brightest and best of the sons of the morning	47	49	338	71	65	123	183	190	201
o2	Come, let us to the Lord our God						33	81		69
o1	Deep in the shadows of the past						447			
e	Father of Jesus Christ, my Lord						693	351		
g	He gave his life in selfless love			405		214			435	
g	He sat to watch o'er customs paid		189							
g	Heal us, Immanuel! Hear our prayer						390	335		
g	Immortal Love, for ever full	133	378	105	243	328	392	267	198	306
g	Jesus calls us: o'er/in the tumult	312	200	104	266	359	141	355		211
g	Jesus came — the heavens adoring			195						
g	Jesus' hands were kind hands						393	197		228
g	Jesus, my Lord, how rich thy grace / Fountain of good	381					147			459
p1	Lift up your heads, ye/you mighty gates	483	8				240			12
g	Lord, I was blind			437		433	423	358	558	
g	O Christ the healer, we have come						395			
op1	O God, thou art the Father						52	73		397
o2	O worship / Worship the Lord in the beauty of holiness	49	52	344	394	529	505	187	22	40
p1	Rejoice, O land, in God thy might / your Lord	296	493	331	431					
e	See how great a flame aspires						781			
g	Shout for joy, loud and long			348						
p1	Songs of praise the angels sang	196	451	350			512	667		38
p1	Thanks/Praise to God whose word	423	438	255			483	319	106	
o1	The God of Abraham praise	331	148	9	478	645	452	121	131	358
g	The Kingdom of God is justice and joy			333		651	139	200	321	
o1	Through all the changing scenes of life	209	467	46	516	702	73	685	544	
o1	Thy/Your way, not mine			555	521					
o1	To Abraham and Sarah							553		
g	We give God thanks for those who knew			318						
g	Where shall my wondering soul begin						706			

Year B
Proper 5

Continuous: 1 Samuel **8**: 4-11 [12-15] 16-20 [**11**: 14-15] and Psalm **138**

or *Related:* Genesis **3**: 8-15 and Psalm **130**; 2 Corinthians **4**:13 — **5**:1; Mark **3**: 20-35

		AMNS	NEH	HTC	HON	MP	H&P	R&S	BPW	CH3
o2p1	All hail the power of Jesus' name	140	332	587/203	13	13	252		29	382
e	Behold the temple of the Lord						808			
e	Fight the good fight	220	359	526	128	143	710	496	524	442
g	God is love: his the care			311	169		220	274	45	416
e1	Here, O my Lord, I see thee/you	274		406		230	608		436	573
o2	In Adam we have all been one	474					420			
g	In Christ there is no east or west	376	480	322	244	329	758	647	482	425
o1	It is God who holds the nations						404			
o2	Jesus, the name high over all			213		385	264			
o2	Join all the glorious names			214		392	78	280	557	304
o2	Lift high the cross	72		508	303	417	170	422	575	550
o1	Lift up your heads, ye/you mighty gates	483	8				240			12
o1	Lord of lords and King eternal	396								
g	Love is his word			481	322				445	
o1	O day of God, draw near/nigh In beauty	405						632	635	511
g	O God, by whose almighty plan	406					396	651		
o2	O lift us up, strong Son of God						427	337		
p2	Out of our failure to create							88		
p2	Out of the depths I cry to thee						429	331		
o2	Praise to the Holiest in the height	117	439	140	426	563	231	103	562	238
p2	Souls of men / Restless souls / There's a wideness	251	461	443	501	607,683	230	353	573	218
e	Spirit of faith, come down						325			
o2	The Lord made man, the Scriptures tell			143						
p1	Thy/Your hand, O God, has guided	171	485	536	518	705	784	567	398	424
o2	Walking in a garden	518	123					334		
o2	What Adam's disobedience cost	524					430			
p2	What is our calling's glorious hope						749			
g	When Jesus walked upon this earth			317						
g	Who would true valour / He who would valiant / Who honours courage	212	372	537/590	205	224	688	557	362	443

Year C
Proper 5

Continuous: 1 Kings **17**: 8-16 [17-24] and Psalm **146** or *Related:* 1 Kings **17**: 17-24 and Psalm **30**;
Galatians **1**: 11-24; Luke **7**: 11-17

		AMNS	NEH	HTC	HON	MP	H&P	R&S	BPW	CH3
e	A heavenly splendour from on high		154							
op2g	All shall be well			149					243	
e	Captains of the saintly band / Christian soldiers	299	215							539
e	Disposer supreme and judge of the earth	298	216		110					
og	Eternal light, shine in my heart			339						
o	Guide me, O thou/my great Redeemer/Jehovah	214	368	528	188	201	437	345	593	89
e	How beauteous/gracious are their feet	301					449	133		
p1	I'll praise my Maker while I've breath			20		320	439	734	127	
op1g	Jesus, the name high over all			213		385	264			
g	Join all the glorious names			214		392	78	280	557	304
p1	Judge eternal, throned in splendour		490	329	285	395	409	626	627	519
p2	Lord Jesus, think on/of me	129	70	316	312		533	363		80
op1g	Lord, I was blind			437		433	423	358	558	
g	O bless the God of Israel			599						
op1	O Father, whose creating hand						349			
op1g	O for a thousand tongues to sing	125	415	219	362	496	744	285	59	371
p2	O love that will/wilt not let me go			486	384	515	685	511	541	677
p2	O worship / Worship the Lord in the beauty of holiness	49	52	344	394	529	505	187	22	40
p1	Sing praise to God who reigns above	193	447				511	75		142
o	Sometimes a light surprises	108					571	595		
p2	The Church's one foundation	170	484	501	473	640	515	566	393	420
e	The eternal gifts of Christ the King	297	213		476					540
p1	The Lord is King! lift up thy/your voice	107		183	485	656	58	76	322	36
og	Thine arm, O Lord, in days of old	285	324		502		397			214
oe	Thou art / You are the way	128	464	113	512	695	234	554		121
e	We have a gospel to proclaim	431	486	519	532	728	465		585	

Year A
Proper 6

Continuous: Genesis **18:** 1-15 [**21:** 1-7] and Psalm **116:** 1-2, 12-19 or *Related:* Exodus **19:** 2-8a and Psalm **100;**
Romans **5:** 1-8; Matthew **9:**35 — **10:**8 [9-23]

		AMNS	NEH	HTC	HON	MP	H&P	R&S	BPW	CH3
p1	All my hope on God is founded	336	333	451	15	16	63	586	327	405
p2	All praise to thee/Christ, for thou / our Lord and King divine	337	335	204	18		253	750		297
p1	Awake, my soul, and with the sun	1	232	264	50		632	378		42
p2	Before Jehovah's aweful/awesome throne / Sing to the Lord	197		15			61	119		2
p1e	Being of beings, God of love						690			
p2e	Born in song						486			
o2	Church of God, elect and glorious			504					406	
e	Come down, O Love Divine	156	137	231	90	89	281	294	283	115
p2	Come, rejoice before your Maker			17					35	
p1e1	Draw nigh and take / Draw near and take		281	401						
o2	Forth in the peace of Christ we go	458	361	542	142			602	607	589
e	Hail thou/our once-despisèd/rejected Jesus			175	192	203	222		273	
g	How shall they hear the word of God			507						
e	I hear the words of love			436						
e	Jesus, thine all-victorious love / My God, I know, I feel thee mine						740			
g	Jesus, thy wandering sheep behold						772			
g	Lord, you give the great commission							580		
eg	Love divine, all loves excelling	131	408	217	321	449	267	663	559	437
e	Morning glory, starlit sky	496						99		
e	Not what these hands / I bless the Christ of God			435		487				410
p1	O God beyond all praising			36	363					
e	O Love divine, how sweet thou art	124	424					372		
e	O thou/Lord who came[st]	233	431	552/596	392	525	745	433	355	110
e	One there is above all others					542	149		560	
g	Send out/forth the gospel			517		593			584	
o	The God of Abraham praise	331	148	9	478	645	452	121	131	358
eg	The Kingdom of God is justice and joy			333		651	139	200	321	
e	We give immortal praise	520		11			18	37	72	
p1	What shall I render to my God						703			
o2	Ye that know the Lord is gracious	175	477							

Year B
Proper 6

Continuous: 1 Samuel **15**:34 — **16**:13 and Psalm **20** or *Related:* Ezekiel **17**: 22-24 and Psalm **92**: 1-4, 12-15; 2 Corinthians **5**: 6-10 [11-13] 14-17; Mark **4**: 26-34

		AMNS	NEH	HTC	HON	MP	H&P	R&S	BPW	CH3
e	All who believe and are baptized							421	402	
g	Almighty God, thy word is cast						466			635
p1	Be thou my vision / Lord be my vision	343	339	545	56	51	378	489	521	87
o1	Blest are the pure in heart	238	341	110	63		724		588	113
e	Christ on whom the Spirit rested			228						
e	Come, thou/O fount of every blessing			337			517	360		
g	For the fruits of his/all creation	457		286	138	153	342	42	123	
e	For the might of thine/your arm we bless thee/you				154		435		479	365
e	Great God, what do I see and hear			189						
o1g	Hail to the Lord's anointed	142	55	190	193	204	125	127	142	317
e	How can we sinners know						728			
e	Lord Christ, when first thou cam'st to men	387						270		255
gl	Lord Jesus, once you spoke	392		112					598	
p1	Lord of our life, and God of our salvation		404	529	315	441				491
e	Lord/Great God, your love has called us here	489		480			500	339	442	
e	Love divine, all loves excelling	131	408	217	321	449	267	663	559	437
e	My God, I love thee/you; not because	65	73	479	344		171	357		379
e	No weight of gold or silver			138						
o1	O Spirit of the living God			513			322	577	579	496
p1	Onward, Christian soldiers/pilgrims	333	435	532	(408)	543	718			480
o1	Rejoice, O people, in the mounting years						657			
gl	Rise and hear! the Lord is speaking	509								
p1	Soldiers of Christ, arise	219	449	533	449	604	719	370	580	441
p1	Stand up, stand up for Jesus	221	453	535	457	617	721			481
p2	Sweet is the work, my God, my King			377		620	514			
e	The Church's one foundation	170	484	501	473	640	515	566	393	420
g	The Kingdom of God is justice and joy			333		651	139	200	321	
p1	The royal banners forward go / As royal banners are unfurled	58	79		492		179	216	228	257
e	We give immortal praise	520		11			18	37	72	
e	We were not there to see you come			121						
o1	What does the Lord require	432					414			

Year C
Proper 6

Continuous: 1 Kings **21:** 1-10 [11-14] 15-21a and Psalm **5:** 1-8

or *Related:* 2 Samuel **11:**26 — **12:**10, **12:** 13-15 and Psalm **32;** Galatians **2:** 15-21; Luke **7:**36 — **8:**3

		AMNS	NEH	HTC	HON	MP	H&P	R&S	BPW	CH3
o	Almighty Father, who for us thy Son didst give	338					401	621		
e	And can it be			452/588	30	33	216	366	328	409
l	Awake, my soul, and with the sun	1	232	264	50		632	378		42
o	Come, O thou all-victorious Lord / O come, our all-victorious			441			418			
e	Come, O thou traveller unknown	243	350				434			
o	Drop, drop, slow tears		82		112					
o	Father of all, whose laws have stood			539					335	
o	Forgive our sins as we forgive	362	66	111	141		134	84	83	
o	Give praise for famous men			568						
e	God made me for himself			361						
e	Great is thy/your faithfulness			260	186	200	66	96	553	
e	Hail thou/our once-despisèd/rejected Jesus			175	192	203	222		273	
g	How sweet the name of Jesus sounds	122	374	211	220	251	257	277	339	376
g	I bind unto myself / myself to God today / Christ be with me		159	5	225		695	36		402
g	Jesus, Lord of life and glory		68							
g	Jesus, lover of my soul	123	383	438	261	372	528	332	345	78
g	Jesus loves me, this I know			303						418
o	Lead us, heavenly Father, lead us	224	393	595	293	400	68	543	597	90
e	Lord, as I wake I turn to you	485	236	267			634	534		
e	No weight of gold or silver			138						
e	None other Lamb						271			
l	Now let us from this table rise	403		419	352		619	463	451	
o	O Christ the Lord, O Christ the King		496				406	630		
g	Rock of ages	135	445	593	437	582	273	365	545	83
e	These are the facts			162		687				
g	Thou hidden love of God, whose height						544			96
g	Ye that know the Lord is gracious	175	477							

Year A
Proper 7

Continuous: Genesis **21**: 8-21 and Psalm **86**: 1-10, 16-17

or *Related:* Jeremiah **20**: 7-13 and Psalm **69**: 7-10 [11-15] 16-18; Romans **6**: 1b-11; Matthew **10**: 24-39

		AMNS	NEH	HTC	HON	MP	H&P	R&S	BPW	CH3
e	A mighty mystery we set forth						579		403	
e	All shall be well			149					243	
e	Baptized in water			381						
e	Born of the water			382						
el	Bread of the world in mercy broken	270	277	396	68		599	443	428	574
g	Christ for the world we sing	344					789	599		500
e	Christians, lift up your hearts ... Here God's life-giving word	446		383						
e	Come, ye faithful / Alleluia, raise the anthem	145	351	205	99	103	813		269	
g	Go, labour on						794			483
e	Have you not heard?			386						
p2	How firm a foundation			430	216	243		589	380	
g	I'm not ashamed to own/name my Lord			448	240	323	677	428	343	591
o2	My God, I know, I feel thee mine						740			
e	Jesus, we follow thee						583			
g	Light of the minds that know him		400	477				529		
e	Lord, for the years			328	310	428		603	535	
e	My God, accept my heart this day	279	318	551	341		701			429
e	Now is eternal life	402	114		351		203	432		
el	Now let us from this table rise	403		419	352		619	463	451	
e	Now lives the Lamb of God			159					255	
e	O for a heart to praise my God	230	74	483	361	495	536	514	538	85
p1	O Lord, hear my prayer				379			398	600	
e	Praise to God, almighty Maker						582	430	414	
g	Take up thy/your cross	237	76	114	465					430
p1	The Lord will come and not be slow	29	15		489		245	128		321
e	The strife is o'er/past	78	119	163	495	670	214	250	261	266
e	This day above all days			164						
e	We know that Christ is raised and dies no more			389				426		
e	With Christ we share a mystic grave		317							

Year B
Proper 7

Continuous: 1 Samuel **17**: [1a, 4-11, 19-23] 32-49 and Psalm **9**: 9-20 or 1 Samuel **17**:57 — **18**:5, **18**: 10-16 and Psalm **133** or *Related:* Job **38**: 1-11 and Psalm **107**: 1-3, 23-32; 2 Corinthians **6**: 1-13; Mark **4**: 35-41

		AMNS	NEH	HTC	HON	MP	H&P	R&S	BPW	CH3
o1e	Be thou my vision / Lord be my vision	343	339	545	56	51	378	489	521	87
g	Begone, unbelief						667			
g	Bless the Lord, creation sings			604						
o1e	Christian, seek not yet repose			355						
g	Commit thou all thy griefs / Put thou thy trust / Give to the winds						672	550		
op2g	Eternal Father, strong to save	292	354	285	114	122	379	58	587	527
p2g	Fierce raged the tempest	225					144			
o1e	Fight the good fight	220	359	526	128	143	710	496	524	442
g	Holy Spirit, Truth divine			235			289	301	292	106
e	I bind unto myself / myself to God today / Christ be with me		159	5	225		695	36		402
p2g	I cannot tell why/how he			194	226	266	238	265	381	
p2g	Jesus calls us: o'er/in the tumult	312	200	104	266	359	141	355		211
g	Jesus, Saviour of the world			607						
o1	Lift up your heads, ye gates of brass						227			471
g	Light of the minds that know him		400	477				529		
p2	Lord, thy word abideth / Lord, your word	166	407	251	318	446	476	317	102	130
p2g	O changeless Christ, for ever new			108					206	
p2g	O Jesus, I have promised	235	420	531	372	501	704	509	352	434
g	O sing a song of Bethlehem	413						201		220
e	Oft in danger, oft in woe / Christian soldiers, onward go	210	434	524	396	533	715			
g	Seed, secret sown in the earth: SS26									
o1e	Soldiers of Christ, arise	219	449	533	449	604	719	370	580	441
p2g	Son of God, eternal Saviour	132	498	102				605	639	454
o2	Songs of praise the angels sang	196	451	350			512	667		38
o1e	Stand up, stand up for Jesus	221	453	535	457	617	721			481
e	This day God gives me	516						79		
g1	This is the day of light	21		380						46
o1	Through all the changing scenes of life	209	467	46	516	702	73	685	544	
p2g	Timeless love! we sing the story			47		707	60			
o1	Who can bind the raging sea: STG 181									
o1	Who would true valour / He who would valiant / Who honours courage	212	372	537/590	205	224	688	557	362	443

Year C
Proper 7

Continuous: 1 Kings **19**: 1-4 [5-7] 8-15a and Psalms **42, 43** or *Related:* Isaiah **65**: 1-9 and Psalm **22**: 19-28; Galatians **3**: 23-29; Luke **8**: 26-39

		AMNS	NEH	HTC	HON	MP	H&P	R&S	BPW	CH3
p1	As pants the hart	226	337		38		416	689		
p1	As the deer pants for the water				39	37				
o1	Be still for the presence / Spirit of the Lord				53	50			5	
o1	Come, living God, when least expected							354		
o1g	Dear Lord and Father of mankind	115	353	356	106	111	673	492	84	76
p1	Father of mercies, in thy/your word	167		247					99	
e	For the healing of the nations	361			139		402	620	621	
e	He went to the top of a mountain: SS63									
p1	I hunger and I thirst			409			730	449		
o1	I searched so long and hard: SS58									
p1	If thou but trust in God / suffer God to guide thee						713			668
e	In Christ there is no east or west	376	480	322	244	329	758	647	482	425
e	Jesus is the Lord of living			309						
p1	Jesus, priceless treasure			461	262		259			
e	Jesus, the very thought of thee/you is sweet	120	291,385	478	264	386	265	509	352	377
p1	Jesus, thou/the joy of loving hearts	255	292	413	265	383	258	389	439	571
o1	Lord Jesus, let these eyes of mine			549						
g	Lord Jesus, think on/of me	129	70	316	312		533	363		80
o1	Lord, you sometimes speak in wonders								101	
o1	My Lord, I did not choose you			107						
o1	O Jesus, I have promised	235	420	531	372	501	704	509	352	434
p1	O send thy/your light forth						537	690	18	7
o1	Open, Lord, my inward ear						540			
o1	Speak, Lord, in the stillness			253		608			105	
o1	Thanks/Praise to God whose word	423	438	255			483	319	106	
e	The great love of God						45	105		415
o1	There is a name I love to hear					672				
g	To God be the glory			584	522	708	463	289	566	374
e	To him we come			518		709			547	
g	When Jesus walked upon this earth			317						
p2	Ye/You servants of God, your Master proclaim	149	476	520	565	784	278	293	76	372

Year A
Proper 8

Continuous: Genesis **22**: 1-14 and Psalm **13** or *Related:* Jeremiah **28**: 5-9 and Psalm **89**: 1-4, 15-18; Romans **6**: 12-23; Matthew **10**: 40-42

		AMNS	NEH	HTC	HON	MP	H&P	R&S	BPW	CH3
e1	And now, O Father, mindful of the love	260	273	392	32		593			580
o1	Begone, unbelief						667			
e	Father, Son, and Holy Ghost						791			
e	Freedom and life are ours			544					528	
o2	God has spoken — by his prophets			248			64		100	
o1	God moves in a mysterious way	112	365		173	193	65	59	122	147
p1	How long, O Lord, will you quite forget me?							671		
e	In full and glad surrender			557	245	330				
e	Jesus, Master, whose I am									431
e	Make me a captive, Lord					455	714	505		445
e	Now lives the Lamb of God			159					255	
e	O for a heart to praise my God	230	74	483	361	495	536	514	538	85
e	Take my life, and let it be	249		554	464	624	705	371	358	462
o1	Teach me thy way, O Lord					626				
o1	The God of Abraham praise	331	148	9	478	645	452	121	131	358
o1	Though troubles assail and dangers affright: BHB 588; HF 397									
p1	Timeless love! we sing the story			47		707	60			
g	Where cross the crowded ways of life						431	606	626	512
e	Who is on the Lord's side?					769	722		615	479
e	Ye/You servants of God, your Master proclaim	149	476	520	565	784	278	293	76	372

Year B
Proper 8

Continuous: 2 Samuel **1**: 1, 17-27 and Psalm **130** or *Related:* Wisdom **1**: 13-15, **2**: 23-24;
(Canticle or substitute OT reading) Lamentations **3**: 23-33; or Psalm **30**; 2 Corinthians **8**: 7-15; Mark **5**: 21-43

		AMNS	NEH	HTC	HON	MP	H&P	R&S	BPW	CH3
g	A stranger once did bless the earth	335						198		
e	Before the heaven and earth			612						
p2g	Father of Jesus Christ, my Lord						693	351		
g	Heal me, hands of Jesus			319						
g	Heal us, Immanuel! Hear our prayer						390	335		
o2	Immortal honours rest: CHH 125; GH 152									
g	Immortal Love, for ever full	133	378	105	243	328	392	267	198	306
g	Jesus' hands were kind hands						393	197		228
p2e	Jesus, if still the same thou art						529			
o2	Jesus, thou/the joy of loving hearts	255	292	413	265	383	258	389	439	571
e	Jesus, the very thought of thee/you is sweet	120	291,385	478	264	386	265	509	352	377
g	Lord of all, to whom alone	492								
g	Lord, I was blind			437		433	423	358	558	
e	My Lord, you wore no royal crown			118						
o2l	New every morning is the love	2	238	270	349	480	636	536		47
g	O Christ the healer, we have come						395			
g	O for a thousand tongues to sing	125	415	219	362	496	744	285	59	371
p2	O love that will/wilt not let me go			486	384	515	685	511	541	677
p1	Out of our failure to create							88		
p1	Out of the depths I cry to thee						429	331		
g	She was made in God's image: SS92									
p2	Souls of men / Restless souls / There's a wideness	251	461	443	501	607,683	230	353	573	218
p2	The Church's one foundation	170	484	501	473	640	515	566	393	420
g	Thine arm, O Lord, in days of old	285	324		502		397			214
e	Thou didst leave thy throne	250	465		513	697	154	192	179	
g	Thou to whom the sick and dying		325							
e	Thou who wast rich / Lord, you were rich			63		700				
g	We give God thanks for those who knew		318							
g	Woman in the night: SS76									
o2	You can't stop rain from falling down								567	

Year C
Proper 8

Continuous: 2 Kings **2**: 1-2, 6-14 and Psalm **77**: 1-2, 11-20 or *Related:* 1 Kings **19**: 15-16, 19-21 and Psalm **16**; Galatians **5**: 1, 13-25; Luke **9**: 51-62

		AMNS	NEH	HTC	HON	MP	H&P	R&S	BPW	CH3
o1	Children of the heavenly King	213	344	566	63					
o1	Christians, lift up your hearts … Praise for the Spirit	444		229						
o1	Come, thou/most Holy Spirit, come / Come, thou Holy Paraclete	92	139	227	97		284	297		105
e	Dost thou truly seek renown		81							
g	Filled with the Spirit's power	359		233	131		314			
e	For the fruits of his/all creation	457		286	138	153	342	42	123	
e	Freedom and life are ours			544					528	
e	Give me joy in my heart / oil in my lamp	459		S11	153	167	492	523	530	
e	Give me/us the wings of faith	324	225		156		815	664		
p1	God moves in a mysterious way	112	365		173	193	65	59	122	147
e	Here within this house of prayer			563						
p2e	Holy Spirit, Truth divine			235			289	301	292	106
p1	How firm a foundation			430	216	243		589	380	
o1	Jerusalem on high			565						
g	Jesus, good above all other	378	387	96	269		732	528		111
e	Jesus, the very thought of thee/you is sweet	120	291,385	478	264	386	265	509	352	377
p2	Jesus, thou/the joy of loving hearts	255	292	413	265	383	258	389	439	571
p2e	Lead us, heavenly Father, lead us	224	393	595	293	400	68	543	597	90
e	Let saints on earth / Come let us join our friends above	182	396	574	297	409	812	472		543
g	Lord, who left the highest heaven			97						
e	May we, O Holy Spirit, bear your fruit			236						
g	My song is love unknown	63	86	136	346	478	173	207	204	224
o1g	O happy band of pilgrims	208	418	530	368					
e	O Holy Spirit, giver of life			239						
e	Of all the Spirit's gifts to me	503					320			
e	Spirit of holiness, wisdom and faithfulness			246		611				
o1e	The prophets spoke in days of old	513								
g	Thou didst leave thy throne	250	465		513	697	154	192	179	
p1	Through all the changing scenes of life	209	467	46	516	702	73	685	544	
o1	Ye/You holy angels bright	198	475	353	564	783	20	125	23	363

Year A
Proper 9

Continuous: Genesis **24**: 34-38, 42-49, 58-67 and Psalm **45**: 10-17 or (Canticle) Song of Solomon **2**: 8-13 or
Related: Zechariah **9**: 9-12 and Psalm **145**: 8-14; Romans **7**: 15-25a; Matthew **11**: 16-19, 25-30

		AMNS	NEH	HTC	HON	MP	H&P	R&S	BPW	CH3
p2	All glory, honour, blessing and power: SS2									
g	All ye who seek a comfort / for sure relief	64	63		22					
g	Alleluia! sing to Jesus	262	271	170	26	207	592		270	
o1	Be thou my vision / Lord be my vision	343	339	545	56	51	378	489	521	87
e	Dear Master, in whose life I see						522	493	337	691
g	Father in heaven, grant to your children			2			3	28	38	
g	Father of mercy, God of consolation		323					645		
g	Forth in thy/your name, O Lord	239	235	306	143	159	381	521	526	463
op2	Hail to the Lord's anointed	142	55	190	193	204	125	127	142	317
g	Hark what a sound, and too divine for hearing						236	660		314
o1	Have faith in God, my heart	372		431	201		675	499	336	
g	Here, O my Lord, I see thee/you	274		406		230	608		436	573
g	Here within this house of prayer			563						
g	How sweet the name of Jesus sounds	122	374	211	220	251	257	277	339	376
g	I cannot tell why/how he			194	226	266	238	265	381	
g	I heard the voice of Jesus say	247	376		231	275	136	349		212
c	Jesus, lover of my soul	123	383	438	261	372	528	332	345	78
g	Jesus shall reign where'er the sun	143	388	516	277	379	239	269	313	413
g	Just as I am, without one plea	246	294	440	287	396	697	364	346	79
o1	Lord, be thy word my rule / Lord, make your word	232		250						
c	Loved with everlasting love			482		452				
p2	My God, my King, thy various praise						12	115		
g	O Christ the same		258	263						
e	O lift us up, strong Son of God						427	337		
g	One there is above all others				542	149			560	
g	So dies this man, this carpenter: SS41									
lp2	The day thou gavest / you gave us, Lord, is ended	16	252	280	475	641	648	584	319	646
p2e	The strife is o'er/past	78	119	163	495	670	214	250	261	266
o2	There's a light upon the mountains					679	246		149	
g	Thou art / You are the way	128	464	113	512	695	234	554		121
p1	Wake, O wake / Sleepers, wake	32	16	199	529		249	132		315
g	What a friend we have in Jesus			373	541	746	559	413	603	
g	When the Son of Mary: SS80 HSN82									

Year B
Proper 9

Continuous: 2 Samuel **5**: 1-5, 9-10 and Psalm **48** or *Related:* Ezekiel **2**: 1-5 and Psalm **123**;
2 Corinthians **12**: 2-10; Mark **6**: 1-13

		AMNS	NEH	HTC	HON	MP	H&P	R&S	BPW	CH3
e	Captain of Israel's host						62			
p1	City of God, Jerusalem			187						
o2	Come with all joy to sing to God			16						
e	Dear Lord, for all in pain: AHB 396									
e	Enthrone thy God within thy heart						692			
e	Father, hear the prayer we offer	113	357	360	120	132	436	495	523	
p1	Glorious things of thee/you are spoken	172	362	494	158	173	817	560	480	421
o2	God has spoken — by his prophets			248			64		100	
o1	God is our strength and refuge			527		188			308	
e	God of almighty love						793			
o1	God save and bless our nation			325						
p1	Great is our redeeming Lord						438			
e	I could not do without thee: AMR353									
p1e	Jesus, thy boundless love to me						696	506		
g	Join all the glorious names			214		392	78	280	557	304
g	Lord of all hopefulness	394	239	101	313		552	531	517	92
e	Lord of all power, I give you my will / Lord of creation, to you be all praise	395		547		440	699	532		428
p1	Now thank we all our God	205	413	33	354	486	566	72	128	368
g	O Christ, the master carpenter			135						
g	Songs of thankfulness and praise	53	56	98	451			191		
e	Still near me, O my Saviour			464						
o2e	Thanks/Praise to God whose word	423	438	255			483	319	106	
o2l	The prophets spoke in days of old	513								
o1	Thy/Your hand, O God, has guided	171	485	536	518	705	784	567	398	424
g	When the Lord in glory comes			201		758				

Year C
Proper 9

Continuous: 2 Kings **5**: 1-14 and Psalm **30** or *Related:* Isaiah **66**: 10-14 and Psalm **66**: 1-9; Galatians **6**: [1-6] 7-16; Luke **10**: 1-11, 16-20

		AMNS	NEH	HTC	HON	MP	H&P	R&S	BPW	CH3
e	As now the sun's declining rays		242		37					
e	Beneath the cross of Jesus				59	55	165			684
p2	By every nation, race and tongue			579						
gl	Christ is risen! Alleluia					74			245	
g	Glorious things of thee/you are spoken	172	362	494	158	173	817	560	480	421
g	Go forth and tell			505	164	178	770	574	570	
ge	Go, labour on						794			483
g	He that is down need fear no fall	218					676			
e	Help us to help each other / Jesus, united by thy grace	374		540	208		773	500		
g	How can we sinners know						728			
p2	How firm a foundation			430	216	243		589	380	
g	I cannot forget them: SS82									
e	I'm not ashamed to own/name my Lord			448	240	323	677	428	343	591
e	In the Cross of Christ I glory		379		249	338	167	224	344	259
e	Jesus, Lord, we look to thee	380	481				759	564		
g	Join all the glorious names			214		392	78	280	557	304
o1	Just as I am, without one plea	246	294	440	287	396	697	364	346	79
p2	Let all the world in every corner sing	202	394	342	296	404	10	114	54	361
o2	Like a mighty river flowing			32		419			632	
o2	Like a river glorious			463		421				
g	Lord, you give the great commission							580		
g	Love divine, all loves excelling	131	408	217	321	449	267	663	559	437
e	No weight of gold or silver			138						
o2	Sing praise to God who reigns above	193	447				511	75		142
g	The Kingdom of God is justice and joy			333		651	139	200	321	
o1	There is a fountain			144		671				
e	We sing the praise of him who died	138	94	146	536	738	182	229	231	258
e	When I survey the wondrous cross	67	95	147	549	755	180	217	233	254
op2e	When peace like a river					757				

Year A
Proper 10

Continuous: Genesis **25**: 19-34 and Psalm **119**: 105-112 or *Related:* Isaiah **55**: 10-13 and Psalm **65**: [1-8] 9-13; Romans **8**: 1-11; Matthew **13**: 1-9, 18-23

		AMNS	NEH	HTC	HON	MP	H&P	R&S	BPW	CH3
g	Almighty God, thy word is cast						466			635
e	And can it be		`	452/588	30	33	216	366	328	409
o2l	At even[ing], ere/when the sun was/had set	9	243	315	43	43	142	644	616	52
e	Born by the Holy Spirit's breath			225		61	279		281	
o2g	Christ's Church shall glory in his power			522						
p1e	Come down, O Love Divine	156	137	231	90	89	281	294	283	115
e	Father of heaven, whose love profound	97	358	359	124		519			77
p1	Father of mercies, in thy/your word	167		247					99	
e	Give to our God immortal praise	460		31	155	171	22	94	47	
e	He lives in us, the Christ of God			457					554	
e	He stood before the court			129						
p1	Help us, O Lord, to learn	373	370	493			474			
e	Holy Spirit, Truth divine			235			289	301	292	106
p1	Lamp of our feet: AHB 302									
p1	Lord, I have made thy word my choice	490					475	316		
p1	Lord, thy word abideth / Lord, your word shall guide us	166	407	251	318	446	476	317	102	130
p1	O Word of God incarnate					527	478			
p1	Powerful in making us wise to salvation			252			479			
g	Rise and hear! the Lord is speaking	509								
g	Seed, secret sown in the earth: SS26									
e	Spirit of faith, by faith be mine: WAM 75									
e	Spirit of God within me			243			294	304	296	
p2	The earth is yours, O God			290						
g	The sower went forth sowing: AMR 486; AHB 652									
p1	The will of God to mark my way: CFW 607									
e	These are the facts			162		687				
o2	To God be the glory			584	522	708	463	289	566	374
e	We give immortal praise	520		11			18	37	72	
p1	When we walk with the Lord				553	760	687		548	
o2	You shall go out with joy				571	796		415		

Year B
Proper 10

Continuous: 2 Samuel **6**: 1-5, 12b-19 and Psalm **24** or *Related:* Amos **7**: 7-15 and Psalm **85**: 8-13; Ephesians **1**: 3-14; Mark **6**: 14-29

		AMNS	NEH	HTC	HON	MP	H&P	R&S	BPW	CH3
el	Again the Lord's own day is here	20								
p1el	All-holy Father, King of endless glory			391						
p1	At the name of Jesus	148	338	172	46	41	74	261	370	300
o1	Bless the Lord, our fathers' God			610						
e	Come, thou/O fount of every blessing			337			517	360		
e	Come, ye faithful / Alleluia, raise the anthem	145	351	205	99	103	813		269	
p1	Crown him with many crowns	147	352	174	103	109	255	262	37	298
e	Eternal Light! Eternal Light!			454			458	83	85	357
e	Father in heaven, grant to your children			2			3	28	38	
o2g	Give praise for famous men			568						
o2	God has spoken — by his prophets			248			64		100	
p1	God in his love for us lent us this planet						343	85		
e	Great God of wonders! All thy ways					197	38			
e	Jesus my Lord, my God, my all		384	476						
e	Lead us, heavenly Father, lead us	224	393	595	293	400	68	543	597	90
p1	Lift up your heads, ye gates of brass						227			471
p1	Lift up your heads, ye/you mighty gates	483	8				240			12
g	Lo, in the wilderness a voice	384	170							
p2	Lord, thine heart in love hath yearned							704		75
p1	Make way, make way, for Christ the King				329	457		141		
e	My Lord, I did not choose you			107						
p1	Our Lord is risen from the dead						206			
e	Praise be to Christ in whom we see			220						
p1e	Souls of men / Restless souls / There's a wideness	251	461	443	501	607,683	230	353	573	218
p1	The earth belongs unto the Lord									566
p1	The eternal gates lift up their heads / are lifted up		133							288
p1	The golden gates are lifted up							256		
o1e	Thy/Your hand, O God, has guided	171	485	536	518	705	784	567	398	424
e	To God be the glory			584	522	708	463	289	566	374
p1	Ye/You gates, lift up your heads on high						516	681	276	566

Year C
Proper 10

Continuous: Amos 7: 7-17 and Psalm 82 or *Related:* Deuteronomy 30: 9-14 and Psalm 25: 1-10; Colossians 1: 1-14; Luke 10: 25-37

		AMNS	NEH	HTC	HON	MP	H&P	R&S	BPW	CH3
e	All-holy Father, King of endless glory			391						
g	Almighty Father, who for us thy Son didst give	338					401	621		
e	Come, ye faithful / Alleluia, raise the anthem	145	351	205	99	103	813		269	
eg	Father in heaven, grant to your children			2			3	28	38	
g	Father of all, whose laws have stood			539					335	
eg	Gracious Spirit, dwell with me						286			
e	Gracious Spirit, Holy Ghost / Holy Spirit, gracious Guest	154	367	474	184	198	301	310	288	438
g	Hark, my soul, it is the Lord / Christian, do you hear the Lord	244		472	197	209	521	348		676
eg	Help us to help each other / Jesus, united by thy grace	374		540	208		773	500		
g	I was lying in the roadway: SS98									
o2	Immortal Love, for ever full	133	378	105	243	328	392	267	198	306
g	Jesus, Lord, we look to thee	380	481				759	564		
p2g	Lord Christ, who on thy heart didst bear	388			308		394			
e	Lord, teach us how to pray aright	227	406	367	316		551			
g	My God, accept my heart this day	279	318	551	341		701			429
o2	Not far beyond the sea	401					477	318		
eg	O God of mercy, God of might							615		461
p2	Show me thy ways, O Lord									74
e	Soldiers of Christ, arise	219	449	533	449	604	719	370	580	441
e	Speak, Lord, in the stillness			253		608			105	
p2	Teach me thy way, O Lord					626				
p1g	The God who rules this earth	425								
p1	The Lord will come and not be slow	29	15		489		245	128		321
g	Thou to whom the sick and dying		325							
p1	Thy/Your kingdom come, O God	177	499	334	519		783	638	644	322
p2	Thy/Your way, not mine			555	521					
gl	Welcome to another day			272						
el	When morning gilds the skies	146	473	223	551	756	276	292	73	370
p1g	Who can sound the depths of sorrow					766				
e	Ye that know the Lord is gracious	175	477							

Year A
Proper 11

Continuous: Genesis **28**: 10-19a and Psalm **139**: 1-12, 23-24 or *Related:* Wisdom **12**: 13, 16-19 or Isaiah **44**: 6-8 and Psalm **86**: 11-17; Romans **8**: 12-25; Matthew **13**: 24-30, 36-43

		AMNS	NEH	HTC	HON	MP	H&P	R&S	BPW	CH3
g	Almighty God, thy word is cast						466			635
e	Arise, my soul, arise						217			
o1	As Jacob with travel was weary one day	435			36		444			
p1	Awake, my soul, and with the sun	1	232	264	50		632	378		42
o1	Beneath the cross of Jesus				59	55	165			684
o1	Blessed assurance				62	59	668		329	
e	Born by the Holy Spirit's breath			225		61	279		281	
o1	God has spoken — by his prophets			248			64		100	
o1l	God, that madest earth and heaven	12	245		178		641			
g	Happy are they, they that/who love God	176	369	473	195		711			408
e	He lives in us, the Christ of God			457					554	
e	Holy Spirit, come, confirm us	471	140		214		288	298	289	
o2	How good is the God we adore / This, this is the God			450	217	244	277	542	338	
o1	Lo, God is here! let us adore		209				531			
e	Lord God, the Holy Ghost						306			332
g	Lord Jesus, once you spoke to men	392		112					598	
p2	Lord of all, to whom alone	492								
p1	Lord, you have searched and known my ways						71	70	564	
o1	Nearer, my God, to thee				348	482	451			689
o2	None other Lamb						271			
p2	Not the grandeur of the mountains: CFW382									
o1	O God of Bethel / O God of Jacob	216	416	35	364		442	71	599	72
o1	O happy band of pilgrims	208	418	530	368					
p1l	Saviour, again to thy/your dear name	15	250	281	438	584	643	640		649
p1	Search me, O God, my actions try: AHB 148									
p2	Teach me thy way, O Lord					626				
p1	There is no moment of my life						428		133	
p1	Thou art / You are before me, Lord, thou art behind						543	731		68
o1	Timeless love! we sing the story			47		707	60			
p1	When I watch a child at play: SS9									

Year B
Proper 11

Continuous: 2 Samuel **7**: 1-14a and Psalm **89**: 20-37 or *Related:* Jeremiah **23**: 1-6 and Psalm **23**; Ephesians **2**: 11-22; Mark **6**: 30-34, 53-56

		AMNS	NEH	HTC	HON	MP	H&P	R&S	BPW	CH3
o2	All hail the power of Jesus' name	140	332	587/203	13	13	252		29	382
g	Behold us, Lord, a little space						376			453
e	Christ is made the sure foundation / Blessed city, heavenly Salem	283/332	204/205	559	76		485	559	474	10
e	Christ is our corner-stone	161	206	564	77					
e	Christ is the world's light	440		321			455	600	34	
e	Christ is the world's true light	346	494	323	78		456	601	618	505
e	Church of God, elect and glorious			504					406	
g	Come ye yourselves apart: AHB375									
p2	Faithful Shepherd, feed me		282	29	117					
e	He/they want/lack not friends	183	371				495	481		
el	I come with joy to meet my Lord	473		408	227		610	447	437	
g	Immortal Love, for ever full	133	378	105	243	328	392	267	198	306
e	In Christ there is no east or west	376	480	322	244	329	758	647	482	425
01	Lord, you need no house			546					349	
p2	My God, and/now is thy table spread	259		418	342					
e	Peace, perfect peace, in this dark world of sin			467	413	555			561	
e	The Church's one foundation	170	484	501	473	640	515	566	393	420
o1l	The day thou gavest / you gave us, Lord, is ended	16	252	280	475	641	648	584	319	646
o2	The God of Abraham praise	331	148	9	478	645	452	121	131	358
p2	The God of love my shepherd is	110	77		479		43	677		
p2	The King of love my shepherd is	126	457	44	484	649	69	552	394	388
p2	The Lord is King! lift up thy/your voice	107		183	485	656	58	76	322	36
o1	The Lord, my shepherd, rules my life			45						
p2	The Lord's my shepherd, I'll not want	426	459	591/45	490	660	70	679	395	387
e	The Spirit came, as promised			244					297	
g	Thine arm, O Lord, in days of old	285	324		502		397			214
o2	Thy/Your kingdom come, O God	177	499	334	519		783	638	644	322
e	To God be the glory			584	522	708	463	289	566	374

Year C
Proper 11

Continuous: Amos 8: 1-12 and Psalm 52 or *Related:* Genesis 18: 1-10a and Psalm 15; Colossians 1: 15-28; Luke 10: 38-42

		AMNS	NEH	HTC	HON	MP	H&P	R&S	BPW	CH3
e	At the name of Jesus	148	338	172	46	41	74	261	370	300
e	Come, let us worship the Christ of creation			207						
o1	Father of mercies, in thy/your word	167		247					99	
p2	God be in my head	236	328	543	166		694	498	592	433
e	God's glory fills the universe							275		
g	Hail thou/our once-despisèd/rejected Jesus			175	192	203	222		273	
o1	Hail to the Lord's anointed	142	55	190	193	204	125	127	142	317
o1e	How firm a foundation			430	216	243		589	380	
el	I come with joy to meet my Lord	473		408	227		610	447	437	
e	Jesus, our hope, our hearts' desire			178						302
el	Lord, enthroned in heavenly splendour	263	296	416	309	431	616			583
e	Lord of the Church, we pray for our renewing			499		442			486	
o2e	My God, how wonderful thou art / you are	102	410	369	343	468	51	408		356
e	Nature with open volume stands	497	87				174	219		
e	O Christ the same, through all our story's pages		258	263						
g	O Lord of life, thy quickening voice						637			48
e	O Spirit of the living God			513			322	577	579	496
e	Of the Father's love/heart begotten / God of God	33	33	56	395		79	181	145	198
e	Peace, perfect peace, in this dark world of sin			467	413	555			561	
e	Praise be to Christ in whom we see			220						
p1e	Praise to the Lord, the Almighty	207	440	40	427	564	16	74	68	9
g	Seek ye first the Kingdom of God				442	590	138	512	357	
e	The brightness of God's glory			221						
o2	The God of Abraham praise	331	148	9	478	645	452	121	131	358
el	The Son of God proclaim	427		415			627	458	455	
g	When we walk with the Lord				553	760	687		548	
e	With glorious clouds encompassed round						184			
p2	Within thy tabernacle, Lord									5
g	Woman in the night: SS76									

Year A
Proper 12

Continuous: Genesis **29**: 15-28 and Psalm **105**: 1-11, 45b or Psalm **128**

or *Related:* 1 Kings **3**: 5-12 and Psalm **119**: 129-136; Romans **8**: 26-39; Matthew **13**: 31-33, 44-52

		AMNS	NEH	HTC	HON	MP	H&P	R&S	BPW	CH3
p	As man and woman we were made						364	466	506	
o2	Be it my only wisdom here						786			
o	Be thou my vision / Lord be my vision	343	339	545	56	51	378	489	521	87
e	Born by the Holy Spirit's breath			225		61	279		281	
e	Eternal Spirit of the living Christ							300		
e	God moves in a mysterious way	112	365		173	193	65	59	122	147
o	God of grace and God of glory	367		324	174	192	712	344	572	88
o	God, you have / who hast given us power	469					345			452
o	Happy the man that finds the grace						674			
e	Have faith in God, my heart	372		431	201		675	499	336	
e	He lives in us, the Christ of God			457					554	
g	Jesus, priceless treasure			461	262		259			
gl	Lord, thy word abideth / Lord, your word shall guide us	166	407	251	318	446	476	317	102	130
e	Now is eternal life	402	114		351		203	432		
g	Now let us learn of Christ			503						
p	O God of Bethel / O God of Jacob	216	416	35	364		442	71	599	72
g	Seed, secret sown in the earth: SS26									
e	Shepherd divine, our wants relieve	228					558			
e	Spirit of God within me			243			294	304	296	
e	Spread, O spread, thou mighty word		482							
p	The God of Abraham praise	331	148	9	478	645	452	121	131	358
g	'The Kingdom is upon you!'	512								
g	The Kingdom of God is justice and joy			333		651	139	200	321	
e	The Saviour died, but rose again						233	597		293
e	We do not know how to pray as we ought						545	400		

Year B
Proper 12

Continuous: 2 Samuel 11: 1-15 and Psalm 14 or Related: 2 Kings 4: 42-44 and Psalm 145: 10-18; Ephesians 3: 14-21; John 6: 1-21

		AMNS	NEH	HTC	HON	MP	H&P	R&S	BPW	CH3
p2	All glory, honour, blessing and power: SS2									
p1	As if you were not there: LFB 72									
g	Bread of heaven, on thee we feed	271	276	398	67			442		
e	Come dearest Lord, descend and dwell						725	381	284	637
o1	Creator of the earth and skies	351		320			419	82		
g	Eternal Father, strong to save	292	354	285	114	122	379	58	587	527
e	Father and God, from whom our world derives			357						
g	For the fruits of his/all creation	457		286	138	153	342	42	123	
g	Guide me, O thou/my great Redeemer/Jehovah	214	368	528	188	201	437	345	593	89
g	Here comes Jesus: SS79									
o1	How can we sing with joy to God			362					86	
g	I saw the man from Galilee: SS88									
g	I sought the Lord, and afterward							368		
o1	I want a principle within						422			
e	It passeth / Beyond all knowledge, that dear love of thine			471		349	526			
g	Just as I am, without one plea	246	294	440	287	396	697	364	346	79
g	Let us break bread together	480			299	414	615	452	443	
g	Let us talents and tongues employ	481		414	301			453		
p2	Let us, with a gladsome mind / Let us gladly with one mind	204	397	23	302	415	27		56	33
e	Not far beyond the sea	401					477	318		
g	O bread to pilgrims given / O food of men wayfaring		300				620	456		
e	O Love divine, how sweet thou art	124	424					372		
o2	Praise and thanksgiving be to our creator	506								
p2	Sing to the Lord a joyful song						17	77		366
o2	The Church of Christ in every age						804	636	613	
g	When the Son of Mary: SS80 HSN82									

Year C
Proper 12

Continuous: Hosea **1**: 2-10 and Psalm **85** or *Related:* Genesis **18**: 20-32 and Psalm **138**;
Colossians **2**: 6-15 [16-19]; Luke **11**: 1-13

		AMNS	NEH	HTC	HON	MP	H&P	R&S	BPW	CH3
e	All who believe and are baptized							421	402	
e	At the name of Jesus	148	338	172	46	41	74	261	370	300
g	Beyond the mist and doubt							490		
e	Christ above all glory seated						189			
g	Father God in heaven, hallowed						518			
g	Father God in heaven, Lord			358						
o1	Father of heaven, whose love profound	97	358	359	124		519			77
g	Forgive our sins as we forgive	362	66	111	141		134	84	83	
p2	God is in his temple					186	494	32	7	
o1	Hark, my soul, it is the Lord / Christian, do you hear the Lord	244		472	197	209	521	348		676
e	Head of the Church, our risen Lord						547	562		
p2	Jesus, where'er thy people meet / Lord Jesus, when your people	162	390	371	282		549	476		
e	Lift high the cross	72		508	303	417	170	422	575	550
o2	Lord, save thy world; in bitter need	397					425			
o2	Lord, teach us how to pray aright	227	406	367	316		551			
p1	Lord, thine heart in love hath yearned							704		75
g	Now let us learn of Christ		503							
o1	O lift us up, strong Son of God						427	337		
p1	O Spirit of the living God			513			322	577	579	496
g	Prayer is the soul's sincere/supreme desire		442	372		567	557			
o2	The God who sent the prophets						454			
p1	The Lord will come and not be slow	29	15		489		245	128		321
g	Thy/Your kingdom come, O God	177	499	334	519		783	638	644	322
g	Who's that knocking?: SS99									

Year A
Proper 13

Continuous: Genesis **32**: 22-31 and Psalm **17**: 1-7, 15 or *Related:* Isaiah **55**: 1-5 and Psalm **145**: 8-9, 14-21; Romans **9**: 1-5; Matthew **14**: 13-21

		AMNS	NEH	HTC	HON	MP	H&P	R&S	BPW	CH3
p2	All glory, honour, blessing and power: SS2									
p1	Be thou / O Lord, my/our guardian	217	64	374	55					
g	Bread of heaven, on thee we feed	271	276	398	67			442		
o1	Come, O thou traveller unknown	243	350				434			
o2	Glorious things of thee/you are spoken	172	362	494	158	173	817	560	480	421
p2	Good unto all men is the Lord									617
g	Guide me, O thou/my great Redeemer/Jehovah	214	368	528	188	201	437	345	593	89
g	How lovely is thy dwelling place — my soul					247				
g	How lovely is thy dwelling place — tabernacles							703		4
o2	I hunger and I thirst			409			730	449		
g	I saw the man from Galilee: SS88									
o1	My name was Jacob: SS65									
g	O bread to pilgrims given / O food of men wayfaring		300				620	456		
g	O Father, whose creating hand						349			
g	O God, unseen yet ever near	272		421	367					
p2	Praise to the Lord, the Almighty	207	440	40	427	564	16	74	68	9
o1	Shepherd divine, our wants relieve	228					558			
e	The God of Abraham praise	331	148	9	478	645	452	121	131	358
e	To Abraham and Sarah							553		
p2	We would extol thee	206								
l	When morning gilds the skies	146	473	223	551	756	276	292	73	370

Year B
Proper 13

Continuous: 2 Samuel **11**:26 — **12**:13a and Psalm **51**: 1-12

or *Related:* Exodus **16**: 2-4, 9-15 and Psalm **78**: 23-29; Ephesians **4**: 1-16; John **6**: 24-35

		AMNS	NEH	HTC	HON	MP	H&P	R&S	BPW	CH3
g	As we break the bread			393				439		
g	Bread of heaven, on thee we feed	271	276	398	67			442		
g	Bread of the world in mercy broken	270	277	396	68		599	443	428	574
e	Christ from whom all blessings flow			491			764	561		
e	Christ is the King! O friends rejoice	345	345	492				571	475	474
o1	Come, O thou all-victorious Lord / O come, our all-victorious			441			418			
el	Come, risen Lord, and deign to be our guest	349	279		96		605	445		572
e	Father, Lord of all creation	356			122				620	
o2	Guide me, O thou/my great Redeemer/Jehovah	214	368	528	188	201	437	345	593	89
e	He went to the top of a mountain: SS63									
e	Head of the Church, our risen Lord						547	562		
g	I am the bread of life			S10	222	261	611			
o2	I hunger and I thirst			409			730	449		
e	In Christ there is no east or west	376	480	322	244	329	758	647	482	425
g	Jesus the Lord said/says, I am the Bread					384	137	199	202	
g	Jesus, thou/the joy of loving hearts	255	292	413	265	383	258	389	439	571
e	Jesus, the very thought of thee/you is sweet	120	291,385	478	264	386	265	509	352	377
p1	Just as I am, without one plea	246	294	440	287	396	697	364	346	79
g	Lord Jesus Christ, you have come to us	391	297	417	311	435	617	373	444	
p2	O bread to pilgrims given / O food of men wayfaring		300				620	456		
p1	O for a heart to praise my God	230	74	483	361	495	536	514	538	85
p1	O God, be gracious to me in thy/your love							695		64
p2	O God, unseen yet ever near	272		421	367					
p2	O praise our great and glorious Lord		116							
eg	O thou who at thy eucharist / O Christ at your first eucharist	265	302	420	391		779			492
o1	Rise and hear! the Lord is speaking	509								
p1	Rock of ages	135	445	593	437	582	273	365	545	83
e	The Saviour, when to heaven he rose						211			
e	Through the night of doubt and sorrow	211	468	466	517		441		546	423
e	Thy/Your hand, O God, has guided	171	485	536	518	705	784	567	398	424

Year C
Proper 13

Continuous: Hosea **11**: 1-11 and Psalm **107**: 1-9, 43

or *Related:* Ecclesiastes **1**: 2, 12-14, **2**: 18-23 and Psalm **49**: 1-12; Colossians **3**: 1-11; Luke **12**: 13-21

		AMNS	NEH	HTC	HON	MP	H&P	R&S	BPW	CH3
p2	All my hope on God is founded	336	333	451	15	16	63	586	327	405
o2	As if you were not there: LFB72									
g	Be thou my vision / Lord be my vision	343	339	545	56	51	378	489	521	87
o2	Blest are the saints/is the man / How blest are they						670	541		324
e	Christ is alive! Let Christians sing						190	260	244	
e	Christ is the world's true light	346	494	323	78		456	601	618	505
e	Come, let us with our Lord arise	449	254	375			575	383		
o1	God is love: let heaven adore him	365	364		170	187	36	95	374	
p2	God of grace and God of glory	367		324	174	192	712	344	572	88
p2	Hast thou not known						446	61		
g	He that is down need fear no fall	218					676			
o	How long, O Lord, will you quite forget me?							671		
e	In Christ there is no east or west	376	480	322	244	329	758	647	482	425
g	Jesus, priceless treasure			461	262		259			
o1	My God, how wonderful thou art / you are	102	410	369	343	468	51	408		356
p1	Now thank we all our God	205	413	33	354	486	566	72	128	368
g	O worship / Worship the Lord in the beauty of holiness	49	52	344	394	529	505	187	22	40
o2	Put thou thy trust / Commit thou all thy griefs	223			429		672	550		669
o1	Sing praise to God who reigns above	193	447				511	75		142
e	Sing we the song of those who stand						821	666		
o2	Stay with us, God							338		
g	Take my life, and let it be	249		554	464	624	705	371	358	462
o1	Thy ceaseless, unexhausted love						48	106		
p1	When all thy/your mercies	109	472	39	544	751	573	109		150
e	Ye faithful souls who Jesus know						751			

Year A
Proper 14

Continuous: Genesis **37**: 1-4, 12-28 and Psalm **105**: 1-6, 16-22, 45b
or *Related:* 1 Kings **19**: 9-18 and Psalm **85**: 8-13; Romans **10**: 5-15; Matthew **14**: 22-33

		AMNS	NEH	HTC	HON	MP	H&P	R&S	BPW	CH3
e	At the name of Jesus	148	338	172	46	41	74	261	370	300
g	Blest are thy saints									
e	Christ is the world's true light	346	494	323	78		456	601	618	505
o1	Creator of the earth and stars									
o2	Dear Lord and Father of mankind	115	353	356	106	111	673	492	84	76
e	Go forth and tell			505	164	178	770	574	570	
g	Have faith in God, my heart	372		431	201		675	499	336	
e	How beauteous/gracious are their feet	301					449	133		
e	How shall they hear the word of God			507						
e	How sweet the name of Jesus sounds	122	374	211	220	251	257	277	339	376
o2	I searched so long and hard: SS58									
g	I sought the Lord, and afterward							368		
e	I'm not ashamed to own/name my Lord			448	240	323	677	428	343	591
g	Light of the minds that know him		400	477				529		
g	My dear Redeemer and my Lord							205	205	
e	Name of all majesty		218		481					
e	Not far beyond the sea	401					477	318		
o1	O crucified Redeemer	404					424	604		
p1	O God of Bethel / O God of Jacob	216	416	35	364		442	71	599	72
o2	Open, Lord, my inward ear						540			
g	Pray when the morn is breaking: EH473									
p1	The God of Abraham praise	331	148	9	478	645	452	121	131	358
p	The Lord will come and not be slow	29	15		489		245	128		321
e	To the Name of our / that brings salvation	121	470	222	523		80	291		373

Year B
Proper 14

Continuous: 2 Samuel **18**: 5-9, 15, 31-33 and Psalm **130** or *Related:* 1 Kings **19**: 4-8 and Psalm **34**: 1-8; Ephesians **4**:25 — **5**:2; John **6**: 35, 41-51

		AMNS	NEH	HTC	HON	MP	H&P	R&S	BPW	CH3
o1	Abide with me	13	331	425	6	4	665	336	515	695
g	Author of life divine	258	274	395	48		596	440		587
g	Bread of heaven, on thee we feed	271	276	398	67			442		
g	Bread of the world in mercy broken	270	277	396	68		599	443	428	574
g	Father, we thank thee, who hast planted / you now for planting	357	284				*603*	444	434	586
e	God is love, and where true love is / Here in Christ we gather	465	513				757	473		
p2	God will I bless at all times									391
g	I am the bread of life			S10	222	261	611			
e	Jesus, Lord, we look to thee	380	481				759	564		
p1	Lord, from the depths to thee I cried									65
e	Make me a channel of your peace			S19	328	456	776	629	634	
e	May the mind of Christ my Saviour			550	334	463	739		537	432
o1	My faith looks up to thee		72		339	469	683			81
g	O bread to pilgrims given / O food of men wayfaring		300				620	456		
e	O Jesus, King most wonderful	120	386	484			269	356	353	378
o1	O love that will/wilt not let me go			486	384	515	685	511	541	677
p1	Out of our failure to create							88		
p1	Out of the depths I cry to thee						429	331		
o2	Put thou thy trust / Commit thou all thy griefs	223			429		672	550		669
p1	Souls of men / Restless souls / There's a wideness	251	461	443	501	607,683	230	353	573	218
p2	Through the night of doubt and sorrow	211	468	466	517		441		546	423
o2	When our confidence is shaken						686			
o2	When, O God, our faith is tested							343		
e	Where love and loving-kindness dwell	528								

Year C
Proper 14

Continuous: Isaiah 1: 1, 10-20 and Psalm 50: 1-8, 22-23 or Related: Genesis 15: 1-6 and Psalm 33: 12-22; Hebrews 11: 1-3, 8-16; Luke 12: 32-40

		AMNS	NEH	HTC	HON	MP	H&P	R&S	BPW	CH3
e	Author of faith, eternal Word						662			
g	Children of the heavenly King	213	344	566	63					
o2	Creatures, once in safety held: SS5									
o2	Father of Jesus Christ, my Lord						693	351		
p2	God of love and truth and beauty	368					403			
g	He that is down need fear no fall	218					676			
e	How beauteous/gracious are their feet	301					449	133		
e	Jerusalem the golden	184	381	573	259			662	312	537
e	Jerusalem, my happy home / thou city blest	187	225	569	258					
o1	Jesus, lover of my soul	123	383	438	261	372	528	332	345	78
o1	Jesus, thou soul of all our joys						761			
o1	Just as I am, without one plea	246	294	440	287	396	697	364	346	79
e	Leader of faithful souls and guide						819			
p1	Lift up your heads, ye/you mighty gates	483	8				240			12
p2	Lord, for the years			328	310	428		603	535	
e	My soul, there is a country	191	412							693
o1	Not for our sins alone	229								
e	O what their joy / What of those sabbaths	186	432					659		535
e	One more step along the world I go				405		746	549	356	
p2	Rejoice, O land, in God thy might / your Lord	296	493	331	431					
o2	The God of Abraham praise	331	148	9	478	645	452	121	131	358
p1	The Lord will come and not be slow	29	15		489		245	128		321
e	To Abraham and Sarah							553		
g	Wake, O wake / Sleepers, wake	32	16	199	529		249	132		315
g	Ye/You servants of the Lord	150	18	598	566		248			319

Year A
Proper 15

Continuous: Genesis 45: 1-15 and Psalm 133 or Related: Isaiah 56: 1, 6-8 and Psalm 67;
Romans 11: 1-2a, 29-32; Matthew 15: [10-20] 21-28

		AMNS	NEH	HTC	HON	MP	H&P	R&S	BPW	CH3
g	All hail the power of Jesus' name	140	332	587/203	13	13	252		29	382
e	And can it be			452/588	30	33	216	366	328	409
e	Come, O thou all-victorious Lord / O come, our all-victorious			441			418			
e	Father of everlasting grace						300			
e	Father, whose everlasting love						520			
p2	God of mercy, God of grace	179	366	293	175			575	48	497
p1	Happy are they, they that/who love God	176	369	473	195		711			408
p1	How good a thing it is			497						
o2	I cannot tell why/how he whom angels worship			194	226	266	238	265	381	
o1g	In Christ there is no east or west	376	480	322	244	329	758	647	482	425
o1	Jesus, Lord, we look to thee	380	481				759	564		
g	Jesus shall reign where'er the sun	143	388	516	277	379	239	269	313	413
p2	Lord, bless us and pity us									493
o1	O Holy Spirit, Lord of grace	152	419		371		310			
p1	Pray that Jerusalem may have		441				510	727		
e	Souls of men / Restless souls / There's a wideness	251	461	443	501	607,683	230	353	573	218
e	We have a gospel to proclaim	431	486	519	532	728	465		585	
e	When Christ was lifted from the earth	525		335				655		
o1	Where love and loving-kindness dwell	528								

Year B
Proper 15

Continuous: 1 Kings **2:** 10-12, **3: 3-14** and Psalm **111** or *Related:* Proverbs **9:** 1-6 and Psalm **34:** 9-14; Ephesians **5:** 15-20; John **6:** 51-58

		AMNS	NEH	HTC	HON	MP	H&P	R&S	BPW	CH3
e	Angel-voices ever singing	163	336	307	33	34	484	405	1	455
e	Awake, awake, fling off the night	342			49				404	
o1	Be it my only wisdom here						786			
o1	Be thou my vision / Lord be my vision	343	339	545	56	51	378	489	521	87
g	Bread of heaven, on thee we feed	271	276	398	67			442		
g	Bread of the world in mercy broken	270	277	396	68		599	443	428	574
g	Draw nigh and take / Draw near and take		281	401						
p2	Father, who on man dost shower						341			515
o1	Give to me, Lord, a thankful heart						548	497	531	
e	Glory in highest heaven	277								
e	Glory to thee who safe hast kept (*See also* Awake, my soul)	1	233		550					
e	Glory, love, and praise, and honour	461	287		160		35			
p2	God of love and truth and beauty	368					403			
o2	Happy the man that finds the grace						674			
g	Here, Lord, we take the broken bread			404			604	448	440	
g	I am the bread of life			S10	222	261	611			
p1	Lord, as I wake I turn to you	485	236	267			634	534		
o1	Lord of all power, I give you my will / Lord of creation, to you be all praise	395		547		440	699	532		428
o2	My God, and/now is thy table spread	259		418	342					
g	O bread to pilgrims given / O food of men wayfaring		300				620	456		
p2	Put peace into each other's hands							635	637	
e	Now / Sing, my tongue / Of the glorious body	252	268		352		624	457	449	578
e	Songs of praise the angels sang	196	451	350			512	667		38
p2	Tell his praise in song and story			41					563	
p1	We praise you, Lord, for all that's true and pure							516		
e	When, in our music, God is glorified				550		388	414		
e	When morning gilds the skies	146	473	223	551	756	276	292	73	370
o	Who can measure heaven and earth			27						

Continuous: Isaiah **5**: 1-7 and Psalm **80**: 1-2, 8-19 or *Related:* Jeremiah **23**: 23-29 and Psalm **82**; Hebrews **11**:29 — **12**:2; Luke **12**: 49-56

		AMNS	NEH	HTC	HON	MP	H&P	R&S	BPW	CH3
e	A cloud of witnesses: BWF72									
e	A glorious company we sing						787	570		426
o1	Awake, awake, fling off the night	342			49				404	
o1	Awake, my soul, and with the sun	1	232	264	50		632	378		42
e	Awake, my soul, stretch every nerve							487		
e	Behold what witnesses unseen									531
o2	Come, Holy Ghost, our hearts inspire (Wesley)	448	348		91		469	312	97	122
o2	Come, O thou all-victorious Lord / O come, our all-victorious			441			418			
e	Fight the good fight	220	359	526	128	143	710	496	524	442
p1	For the might of thine/your arm we bless thee/you					154	435		479	365
g	Forgive our sins as we forgive	362	66	111	141		134	84	83	
e	Give me/us the wings of faith	324	225		156		815	664		
g	Help us to help each other / Jesus, united by thy grace	374		540	208		773	500		
p2	Judge eternal, throned in splendour		490	329	285	395	409	626	627	519
p1	O God of Bethel / O God of Jacob	216	416	35	364		442	71	599	72
g	O God, your love's undying flame							327		
g	O thou/Lord who came[st]	233	431	552/596	392	525	745	433	355	110
g	See how great a flame aspires						781			
e	The head that was once crowned with thorns	141	134	182	480	647	209	257	274	286
p2	The Lord will come and not be slow	29	15		489		245	128		321
p2	What Adam's disobedience cost	524					430			

Year A
Proper 16

Continuous: Exodus 1:8 — 2:10 and Psalm 124 or *Related:* Isaiah 51: 1-6 and Psalm 138; Romans 12: 1-8; Matthew 16: 13-20

		AMNS	NEH	HTC	HON	MP	H&P	R&S	BPW	CH3
e	Almighty Father of all things that be						375	485		451
e	Born in song						486			
e	Christ from whom all blessings flow			491			764	561		
p2	God is in his temple					186	494	32	7	
e	God is love, and where true love is / Here in Christ we gather	465	513				757	473		
o2	God is the refuge of his saints						53			
o1	God moves in a mysterious way	112	365		173	193	65	59	122	147
g	God, your glory we have seen in your Son						459	746		469
e	Help us to help each other / Jesus, united by thy grace	374		540	208		773	500		
g	It was easy up to Caesarea Philippi: SS27									
p2	Jesus, where'er thy people meet / Lord Jesus, when your people	162	390	371	282		549	476		
g	Join all the glorious names		214			392	78	280	557	304
e	Let him to whom we now belong						698			
e	Lord of all good, our gifts we bring to thee	393					797	404		458
o1	'Moses, I know you're the man'				338		450	547	489	
p1	Now Israel may say and that truly									392
e	O thou who at thy eucharist / O Christ at your first eucharist	265	302	420	391		779			492
e	Take my life, and let it be	249		554	464	624	705	371	358	462
g	The Church's one foundation	170	484	501	473	640	515	566	393	420
g	Thou art the Christ, O Lord	317	172							
o2	To Abraham and Sarah							553		
o1	When Israel was in Egypt's land							643		
e	Where love and loving-kindness dwell	528								

Year B
Proper 16

Continuous: 1 Kings 8: [1, 6, 10-11] 22-30, 41-43 and Psalm 84
or Related: Joshua 24: 1-2a, 14-18 and Psalm 34: 15-22; Ephesians 6: 10-20; John 6: 56-69

		AMNS	NEH	HTC	HON	MP	H&P	R&S	BPW	CH3
g	As we break the bread			393				439		
g	Bread of the world in mercy broken	270	277	396	68		599	443	428	574
o1	Christ is made the sure foundation / Blessed city, heavenly Salem	283/332	204/205	559	76		485	559	474	10
o1	Christ is our corner-stone	161	206	564	77					
p2	Come, we that love the Lord						487	384	525	
e	Give me, O Christ, the strength							524		
p2	God will I bless at all times, his praise									391
o1	Great Shepherd of thy/your people, hear	164		363			490	387		
p1	How lovely is thy dwelling place — tabernacles							703		4
g	How sweet the name of Jesus sounds	122	374	211	220	251	257	277	339	376
g	I am the bread of life			S10	222	261	611			
o2	Jesus calls us: o'er/in the tumult	312	200	104	266	359	141	355		211
g	Jesus the Lord said/says, I am the Bread					384	137	199	202	
g	Lord Jesus, once you spoke to men	392		112					598	
p1	Lord of the worlds above	165								
g	O bread to pilgrims given / O food of men wayfaring		300				620	456		
p2	O God of Bethel / O God of Jacob	216	416	35	364		442	71	599	72
e	Oft in danger, oft in woe / Christian soldiers, onward go	210	434	524	396	533	715			
o1	Open now the gates of beauty							390		
e	Soldiers of Christ, arise	219	449	533	449	604	719	370	580	441
e	Stand up, stand up for Jesus	221	453	535	457	617	721			481
p2	Thee will I praise with all my heart						41			
o2	Thine/Yours for ever	234	463	556	504					
o2	Who is on the Lord's side?					769	722		615	479
g	Your words to me are life and health						482	321		

Year C
Proper 16

Continuous: Jeremiah **1**: 4-10 and Psalm **71**: 1-6 or *Related:* Isaiah **58**: 9b-14 and Psalm **103**: 1-8; Hebrews **12**: 18-29; Luke **13**: 10-17

		AMNS	NEH	HTC	HON	MP	H&P	R&S	BPW	CH3
p1	A safe stronghold/fortress/refuge	114		523		2	661	585	375	406/7
o2	Come, let us to the Lord our God						33	81		69
o1	Come, living God, when least expected							354		
o1	Come, Lord, to our souls come down	348					470	361		
p2	Fill thou/now my/our life	200		541	129	146	792	406	569	457
e	God is a name my soul adores						24	31		
g	Hark the glad sound! The Saviour comes	30	6	193	198	210	82	137	143	160
e	Join all the glorious names			214		392	78	280	557	304
o2	King of glory, King of peace	194	391	603	288	397	499	97	53	364
e	Leader of faithful souls and guide						819			
o1	Master, speak! Thy servant heareth / Your servant's listening					459	535		536	
p2	My soul, repeat his praise							716		
p2	O bless the Lord, my soul, let all			34						
e	O God of our forefathers, hear / With solemn faith		314				554			
p2	Praise to the Lord, the Almighty	207	440	40	427	564	16	74	68	9
p2	Praise, my soul, the King of heaven	192	436	38	422	560	13	104	65	360
e	Rejoice! the Lord is King	139	443	180	432	575	243	657	317	296
p1	Rock of ages	135	445	593	437	582	273	365	545	83
g	She was made in God's image: SS92									
o1	Speak, Lord, in the stillness			253		608			105	
g	The first day of the week	424					576			
g	Thine arm, O Lord, in days of old	285	324		502		397			214
e	Victim divine, thy grace we claim		309				629			

Year A
Proper 17

Continuous: Exodus **3**: 1-15 and Psalm **105**: 1-6, 23-26, 45c or *Related:* Jeremiah **15**: 15-21 and Psalm **26**: 1-8; Romans **12**: 9-21; Matthew **16**: 21-28

		AMNS	NEH	HTC	HON	MP	H&P	R&S	BPW	CH3
o2	A safe stronghold/fortress/refuge	114		523		2	661	585	375	406/7
o1	Be still for the presence / Spirit of the Lord				53	50			5	
g	Beneath the cross of Jesus				59	55	165			684
e	Christ from whom all blessings flow			491			764	561		
o1	Deep in the shadows of the past						447			
g	Father, hear the prayer we offer	113	357	360	120	132	436	495	523	
e	Go forth for God		321							
e	God is love, and where true love is / Here in Christ we gather	465	513				757	473		
e	Gracious Spirit, Holy Ghost / Holy Spirit, gracious Guest	154	367	474	184	198	301	310	288	438
e	Holy Spirit, Truth divine			235			289	301	292	106
e	I was lying in the roadway: SS98									
e	Jesus, Lord, we look to thee	380	481				759	564		
g	Jesus, prince and saviour				274	377				
p2	Lord of the worlds above	165								
o2	Lord, thy word abideth / Lord, your word shall guide us	166	407	251	318	446	476	317	102	130
e	Lord, to you we bring our treasure	495								
p2	Mine hands in innocence, O Lord									564
o1	'Moses, I know you're the man'				338		450	547	489	
g	Never further than thy cross							507		
p2	O praise the Lord, ye servants of the Lord		426							
e	Of all the Spirit's gifts to me	503					320			
o1	Take off your shoes: SS66									
g	Take up thy/your cross	237	76	114	465					430
op1	The God of Abraham praise	331	148	9	478	645	452	121	131	358
g	The head that was once crowned with thorns	141	134	182	480	647	209	257	274	286
p2	We love the place, O God	160	471	558	533	731				15
p1	When Israel was in Egypt's land									
e	Where love and loving-kindness dwell	528								
o2	Your words to me are life and health						482	321		

? 583

Year B
Proper 17

Continuous: Song of Solomon **2**: 8-13 and Psalm **45**: 1-2, 6-9

or *Related:* Deuteronomy **4**: 1-2, 6-9 and Psalm **15**; James 1: 17-27; Mark 7: 1-8, 14-15, 21-23

		AMNS	NEH	HTC	HON	MP	H&P	R&S	BPW	CH3
p2	Almighty Father, who for us thy Son didst give	338					401	621		
o2	Before Jehovah's aweful/awesome throne / Sing to the Lord	197		15			61	119		2
o1	Christian people, raise your song	443					601	435	430	
g	Come, O thou all-victorious Lord / O come, our all-victorious		441				418			
p2	Enthrone thy God within thy heart						692			
e	For the beauty of the earth	104	285	298	137	152	333	41	121	367
g	God who created this Eden of earth	369								
e	Help us, O Lord, to learn	373	370	493			474			
g	In Adam we have all been one	474					420			
o1	Jesus, we thus / Now Jesus we obey	477					614	450	446	
p2	My God, accept my heart this day	279	318	551	341		701			429
p1	My heart is full of Christ, and longs						799			
g	O lift us up, strong Son of God						427	337		
e	Of all the Spirit's gifts to me	503					320			
e	Teach me, my God and King	240	456		466		803	538		692
o2	The Lord is King! lift up thy/your voice	107		183	485	656	58	76	322	36
p2	Within thy tabernacle, Lord									5

Year C
Proper 17

Continuous: Jeremiah **2**: 4-13 and Psalm **81**: 1, 10-16 or *Related:* Ecclesiasticus **10**: 12-18 or Proverbs **25**: 6-7 and Psalm **112**; Hebrews **13**: 1-8, 15-16; Luke **14**: 1, 7-14

		AMNS	NEH	HTC	HON	MP	H&P	R&S	BPW	CH3
g	All praise to thee/Christ, for thou / our Lord and King divine	337	335	204	18		253	750		297
o2	Come down, O Love Divine	156	137	231	90	89	281	294	283	115
o1	Glorious things of thee/you are spoken	172	362	494	158	173	817	560	480	421
p1	God in his love for us lent us this planet						343	85		
g	Jesus, humble was your birth	379						196		
o1	Jesus, lover of my soul	123	383	438	261	372	528	332	345	78
p2	Jesus, my Lord, how rich thy grace / Fountain of good	381					147			459
e	Jesus, these eyes have never seen	245	389					592		674
e	Jesus, thy far-extended fame						148			
e	Leader of faithful souls and guide						819			
p2	Lord Christ, who on thy heart didst bear	388			308		394			
g	Lord God, we see thy power displayed	390								
o2	Lord, that I may learn of thee						737			
e	O Christ the same, through all our story's pages		258	263						
p1	O Father, whose creating hand						349			
o2	O for a heart to praise my God	230	74	483	361	495	536	514	538	85
p1	Praise and thanksgiving, Father, we offer	415					350	48		
g	Tell out, my soul, the greatness of the Lord	422	186	42	467	631	86	740	391	164
p2	We find thee, Lord, in others' need	430								
p1	We plough the fields and scatter	290	262	292	534	732	352	124	135	620

Year A
Proper 18

Continuous: Exodus **12**: 1-14 and Psalm **149** or *Related:* Ezekiel **33**: 7-11 and Psalm **119**: 33-40;
Romans **13**: 8-14; Matthew **18**: 15-20

		AMNS	NEH	HTC	HON	MP	H&P	R&S	BPW	CH3
o1	At the Lamb's high feast we sing	81	104		45					
e	Awake, awake, fling off the night	342			49				404	
p1	Be it my only wisdom here						786			
g	Brother, sister, let me serve you				73			474	473	
p1	Captains of the saintly band / Christian soldiers	299	215							539
o2	Come, let us to the Lord our God						33	81		69
e	Father of all, whose laws have stood		539						335	
g	Forgive our sins as we forgive	362	66	111	141		134	84	83	
o2	Go, tell it on the mountains						.			
o1	If our God had simply saved us: SS35									
o1	Lord, enthroned in heavenly splendour	263	296	416	309	431	616			583
o2	Lord, speak to me, that I may speak			510		444	553	613	611	485
o2	My God, how wonderful thou art / you are	102	410	369	343	468	51	408		356
o1	Now lives the Lamb of God			159					255	
e	O day of God, draw near/nigh In beauty	405						632	635	511
g	O thou not made with hands	174	430				656	617		
e	Soldiers of Christ, arise	219	449	533	449	604	719	370	580	441
p2	Thou art / You are the way	128	464	113	512	695	234	554		121
e	Thy kingdom come! on bended knee	178	500		520					323
p1	Ye/You servants of God, your Master proclaim	149	476	520	565	784	278	293	76	372
e	Ye/You servants of the Lord	150	18	598	566		248			319

Page 142

Year B
Proper 18

		AMNS	NEH	HTC	HON	MP	H&P	R&S	BPW	CH3
g	A stranger once did bless the earth	335						198		
p2	All glory, honour, blessing and power: SS2									
e	Father all-loving, thou rulest in majesty	355ii								
g	Father of mercy, God of consolation		323					645		
p1	Glorious things of thee/you are spoken	172	362	494	158	173	817	560	480	421
p1	God is love: let heaven adore him	365	364		170	187	36	95	374	
o1	Happy are they who walk in God's wise way							669		
o1	Help us to help each other / Jesus, united by thy grace	374		540	208		773	500		
p2	I'll praise my Maker while I've breath			20		320	439	734	127	
e	Jesus, my Lord, how rich thy grace / Fountain of good	381					147			459
o2	Let the desert sing			198						
o2	Lord, we your Church						775			
g	O Christ the healer, we have come						395			
p2	O Christ the Lord, O Christ the King		496				406	630		
o2g	O for a thousand tongues to sing	125	415	219	362	496	744	285	59	371
e	Son of God, eternal Saviour	132	498	102				605	639	454
g	Soundless were the tossing trees: SS93									
e	The Church of Christ in every age						804	636	613	
o2	The day of the Lord shall come							637		
g	The Kingdom of God is justice and joy			333		651	139	200	321	
o2	The voice of God goes out to all the world						140	131		
g	We cannot measure how you heal							653		
e	When Christ was lifted from the earth	525		335				655		
o2	When the King shall come again			200						

Year C
Proper 18

Continuous: Jeremiah **18**: 1-11 and Psalm **139**: 1-6, 13-18 or *Related:* Deuteronomy **30**: 15-20 and Psalm **1**; Philemon 1-21; Luke **14**: 25-33

		AMNS	NEH	HTC	HON	MP	H&P	R&S	BPW	CH3
o1	Before Jehovah's aweful/awesome throne / Sing to the Lord	197		15			61	119		2
o1	Behold the servant of the Lord						788			
e	Brother, sister, let me serve you				73			474	473	
g	God be in my head	236	328	543	166		694	498	592	433
p2	Happy are they who walk in God's wise way							669		
g	I bind unto myself / myself to God today / Christ be with me		159	5	225		695	36		402
o2	I heard the voice of Jesus say	247	376		231	275	136	349		212
p1	In all my vast concerns with thee						72			
g	Let him to whom we now belong						698			
p2	Lord, as I wake I turn to you	485	236	267			634	534		
o2	Lord, I have made thy word my choice	490					475	316		
p1	Lord, you have searched and known my ways						71	70	564	
o2	O happy day that fixed my choice			442	369	499	702	359	539	
g	O Jesus, I have promised	235	420	531	372	501	704	509	352	434
p1	Thou art / You are before me, Lord, thou art behind						543	731		68
e	When Christ was lifted from the earth	525		335				655		

Year A
Proper 19

Continuous: Exodus **14**: 19-31 and Psalm **114** or (Canticle) Exodus **15**: 1b-11, 20-21
or *Related:* Genesis **50**: 15-21 and Psalm **103**: [1-7] 8-13; Romans **14**: 1-12; Matthew **18**: 21-35

		AMNS	NEH	HTC	HON	MP	H&P	R&S	BPW	CH3
g	Amazing grace			28	27	31	215	92	550	
g	And can it be			452/588	30	33	216	366	328	409
e	At the name of Jesus	148	338	172	46	41	74	261	370	300
p1	Be still for the presence / Spirit of the Lord				53	50			5	
o1	Be thou / O Lord, my/our guardian	217	64	374	55					
g	Dear Lord and Father of mankind	115	353	356	106	111	673	492	84	76
g	Father of heaven, whose love profound	97	358	359	124		519			77
g	Forgive our sins as we forgive	362	66	111	141		134	84	83	
p1	Glorious things of thee/you are spoken	172	362	494	158	173	817	560	480	421
g	God is love: let heaven adore him	365	364		170	187	36	95	374	
g	Great is thy/your faithfulness			260	186	200	66	96	553	
op1	Guide me, O thou/my great Redeemer/Jehovah	214	368	528	188	201	437	345	593	89
g	I heard the voice of Jesus say	247	376		231	275	136	349		212
e	Jesus lives! Thy/Your terrors now	82	112	156	272	373	198	239	253	605
g	Jesus, where'er thy people meet / Lord Jesus, when your people	162	390	371	282		549	476		
g	Just as I am, without one plea	246	294	440	287	396	697	364	346	79
o1	Lead us, heavenly Father, lead us	224	393	595	293	400	68	543	597	90
g	Make me a channel of your peace			S19	328	456	776	629	634	
g	O God beyond all praising			36	363					
o1	O God of Bethel / O God of Jacob	216	416	35	364		442	71	599	72
g	O love that will/wilt not let me go			486	384	515	685	511	541	677
o1	O/Our God, our help in ages past	99	417	37	366	498	358	705	389	611
g	Oh, the deep, deep, love of Jesus			465		522				
p2g	Praise, my soul, the King of heaven	192	436	38	422	560	13	104	65	360
g	Rock of ages	135	445	593	437	582	273	365	545	83
o1	The God of Abraham praise	331	148	9	478	645	452	121	131	358
g	The price is paid					663				
o1	Through the night of doubt and sorrow	211	468	466	517		441		546	423
g	Timeless love! we sing the story			47		707	60			
g	When all thy/your mercies	109	472	39	544	751	573	109		150

Year B
Proper 19

Continuous: Proverbs 1: 20-33 and Psalm 19 or (Canticle) Wisdom 7:26 — 8:1
or Related: Isaiah 50: 4-9a and Psalm 116: 1-9; James 3: 1-12; Mark 8: 27-38

		AMNS	NEH	HTC	HON	MP	H&P	R&S	BPW	CH3
g	Be thou / O Lord, my/our guardian	217	64	374	55					
o1	Be thou my vision / Lord be my vision	343	339	545	56	51	378	489	521	87
o1	Can we/man by searching find out God	438					76	80		
p1	Father, Lord of all creation	356			122				620	
p2	God of mercy, God of grace	179	366	293	175			575	48	497
g	God our Father and Creator			562						
o2	He lives in us, the Christ of God			457					554	
g	I danced in the morning	375	375		228			195		
o2	I heard the voice of Jesus say	247	376		231	275	136	349		212
g	I'm not ashamed to own/name my Lord			448	240	323	677	428	343	591
g	It was easy up to Caesarea Philippi: SS27									
g	Jesus our Lord, our King and our God	382								
g	Just as I am, without one plea	246	294	440	287	396	697	364	346	79
g	Light of the minds that know him		400	477				529		
g	Lord Jesus Christ, you have come to us	391	297	417	311	435	617	373	444	
e	Lord, speak to me, that I may speak			510		444	553	613	611	485
g	O Jesus, I have promised	235	420	531	372	501	704	509	352	434
o1	O Lord of every shining constellation	411		314					130	141
o2	O sacred head	68	90	139	389	520	176	220	223	253
p1	O worship the King all glorious above	101	433	24	393	528	28	47	63	35
g	Praise to the Holiest in the height	117	439	140	426	563	231	103	562	238
g	Take my life, and let it be	249		554	464	624	705	371	358	462
g	Take up thy/your cross	237	76	114	465					430
p1	The heavens declare thy/your glory, Lord	168		254			481	320		
p1	The spacious firmament	103	267		493		339			143
g	There is a Redeemer				500	673				
g	Thou art the Christ, O Lord	317	172							
o1	Thou/God whose almighty / Father your mighty word	180	466	506	514	699	29	38	591	494
p2	When all thy/your mercies	109	472	39	544	751	573	109		150
g	Will you come and follow me?				560			558	363	

Year C
Proper 19

Continuous: Jeremiah **4**: 11-12, 22-28 and Psalm **14** or *Related:* Exodus **32**: 7-14 and Psalm **51**: 1-10;
1 Timothy **1**: 12-17; Luke **15**: 1-10

		AMNS	NEH	HTC	HON	MP	H&P	R&S	BPW	CH3
g	All people that on earth do dwell	100	334	14	17	20	1	712	2	1
g	Be thou / O Lord, my/our guardian	217	64	374	55					
g	Before Jehovah's aweful/awesome throne / Sing to the Lord	197		15			61	119		2
g	Christ who knows all his sheep	347						470		672
p1	Come down, O Love Divine	156	137	231	90	89	281	294	283	115
g	Faithful Shepherd, feed me		282	29	117					
g	Father of heaven, whose love profound	97	358	359	124		519			77
p2	Heal me, hands of Jesus			319						
g	I will sing the wondrous story			212	237	315	223		382	381
e	Immortal, invisible, God only wise	199	377	21	242	327	9	67	383	32
g	In heavenly love abiding			458	246	331	678	590	555	681
o2	Jesus calls us: o'er/in the tumult	312	200	104	266	359	141	355		211
e	Jesus, lover of my soul	123	383	438	261	372	528	332	345	78
o2e	King of glory, King of peace	194	391	603	288	397	499	97	53	364
g	Loving Shepherd of thy/your sheep	134		305	325					93
p2	My God, how wonderful thou art / you are	102	410	369	343	468	51	408		356
e	My song is love unknown	63	86	136	346	478	173	207	204	224
e	Name of all majesty			218		481				
p2	O for a heart to praise my God	230	74	483	361	495	536	514	538	85
e	O God of Bethel / O God of Jacob	216	416	35	364		442	71	599	72
g	O thou who at thy eucharist / O Christ at your first eucharist	265	302	420	391		779			492
g	O where, O where's my silver piece: SS97									
g	Oh, the deep, deep, love of Jesus			465		522				
e	Praise, my soul, the King of heaven	192	436	38	422	560	13	104	65	360
o1	Rejoice, O land, in God thy might / your Lord	296	493	331	431					
g	The King of love my shepherd is	126	457	44	484	649	69	552	394	388
o1p	The Lord will come and not be slow	29	15		489		245	128		321
g	Thine/Yours for ever	234	463	556	504					
o2	Through all the changing scenes of life	209	467	46	516	702	73	685	544	
o2g	When all thy/your mercies	109	472	39	544	751	573	109		150

Continuous: Exodus **16**: 2-15 and Psalm **105**: 1-6, 37-45 or *Related:* Jonah **3**:10 — **4**:11 and Psalm **145**: 1-8; Philippians **1**: 21-30; Matthew **20**: 1-16

		AMNS	NEH	HTC	HON	MP	H&P	R&S	BPW	CH3
o1	Bread of heaven, on thee we feed	271	276	398	67			442		
o1	Deck thyself/yourself, my soul, with gladness	257	280	400	108		606	446		567
g	Father, hear the prayer we offer	113	357	360	120	132	436	495	523	
e	Fight the good fight	220	359	526	128	143	710	496	524	442
e	For me to live is Christ							410		
g	Forth in the peace of Christ we go	458	361	542	142			602	607	589
g	From heaven you came (The servant King)				148	162		522	529	
g	God makes his rain to fall: SS96									
g	Great is thy/your faithfulness			260	186	200	66	96	553	
o1	Guide me, O thou/my great Redeemer/Jehovah	214	368	528	188	201	437	345	593	89
e	He/they want/lack not friends	183	371				495	481		
o1	I hunger and I thirst			409			730	449		
e	Jesus lives! Thy/Your terrors now	82	112	156	272	373	198	239	253	605
o1e	Jesus, thou/the joy of loving hearts	255	292	413	265	383	258	389	439	571
e	Jesus, the very thought of thee/you is sweet	120	291,385	478	264	386	265	509	352	377
p2	King of glory, King of peace	194	391	603	288	397	499	97	53	364
g	Lead us, heavenly Father, lead us	224	393	595	293	400	68	543	597	90
o1e	Light of the minds that know him		400	477				529		
o1	Lord, enthroned in heavenly splendour	263	296	416	309	431	616			583
e	Lord, for the years			328	310	428		603	535	
g	Lord/Great God, your love has called us here	489		480			500	339	442	
o1	Lord, speak to me, that I may speak			510		444	553	613	611	485
g	May the mind of Christ my Saviour			550	334	463	739		537	432
e	My gracious Lord, I own thy right						741	535		
p2	O Lord, thou art my God and King							732		346
g	Take my life, and let it be	249		554	464	624	705	371	358	462
g	The Lord is King! lift up thy/your voice	107		183	485	656	58	76	322	36
g	Through all the changing scenes of life	209	467	46	516	702	73	685	544	
g	To him we come			518		709			547	
g	With joy we meditate the grace	530				774	235	206	275	

Year B
Proper 20

Continuous: Proverbs **31**: 10-31 and Psalm **1** or *Related:* Wisdom **1**:16 — **2**:1, 12-22 or Jeremiah **11**: 18-20 and Psalm **54**; James **3**:13 — **4**:3, 7-8a; Mark **9**: 30-37

		AMNS	NEH	HTC	HON	MP	H&P	R&S	BPW	CH3
g	A man there lived in Galilee	334			3					
o2e	All my hope on God is founded	336	333	451	15	16	63	586	327	405
g	And now, O Father, mindful of the love	260	273	392	32		593			580
op2	Behold, the mountain of the Lord						50	130	617	312
g	Christ who welcomed little children							497		
o1	Eternal Father, Lord of life			295						
o1	For the beauty of the earth	104	285	298	137	152	333	41	121	367
g	From heaven you came (The servant King)				148	162		522	529	
e	God of grace and God of glory	367		324	174	192	712	344	572	88
g	Jesus, Friend of little children						146			100
e	Jesus, lover of my soul	123	383	438	261	372	528	332	345	78
o2	Led like a lamb / You're alive, you have risen				294	402		241	254	
p1	Lord, be thy word my rule / Lord, make your word	232		250						
e	Lord, teach us how to pray aright	227	406	367	316		551			
g	Lord/Great God, your love has called us here	489		480			500	339	442	
g	Meekness and majesty				335	465			58	
g	Morning glory, starlit sky	496						99		
g	My song is love unknown	63	86	136	346	478	173	207	204	224
g	O Master, let me walk with thee						802			436
o1	O perfect love	280	320		387	517	370		509	
g	O sing a song of Bethlehem	413						201		220
g	Once, only once, and once for all	261	304		404					
eg	Praise to the Holiest in the height	117	439	140	426	563	231	103	562	238
e	Put thou thy trust / Commit thou all thy griefs	223			429		672	550		669
g	Teach me, my God and King	240	456		466		803	538		692
op2	The Lord will come and not be slow	29	15		489		245	128		321
p1	Thy/Your way, not mine			555	521					
g	We sing the praise of him who died	138	94	146	536	738	182	229	231	258
g	What a friend we have in Jesus			373	541	746	559	413	603	
g	Ye/You servants of the Lord	150	18	598	566		248			319

Year C
Proper 20

Continuous: Jeremiah **8**:18 — **9**:1 and Psalm **79**: 1-9 or *Related:* Amos **8**: 4-7 and Psalm **113**;
1 Timothy **2**: 1-7; Luke **16**: 1-13

		AMNS	NEH	HTC	HON	MP	H&P	R&S	BPW	CH3
o1	Abide with me	13	331	425	6	4	665	336	515	695
g	Be thou my vision / Lord be my vision	343	339	545	56	51	378	489	521	87
p2	Christ is the world's true light	346	494	323	78		456	601	618	505
e	Father, Lord of all creation	356			122				620	
g	Forth in thy/your name, O Lord	239	235	306	143	159	381	521	526	463
p2	From the rising of the sun					163			43	
e	God of gods, we sound his praises			340					46	
p1	Hark, my soul, it is the Lord / Christian, do you hear the Lord	244		472	197	209	521	348		676
e	Jesus, Lord, we look to thee	380	481				759	564		
e	Jesus, where'er thy people meet / Lord Jesus, when your people	162	390	371	282		549	476		
o2	Judge eternal, throned in splendour		490	329	285	395	409	626	627	519
p2	Let all the world in every corner sing	202	394	342	296	404	10	114	54	361
eg	Lord, for the years			328	310	428		603	535	
e	Lord, teach us how to pray aright	227	406	367	316		551			
g	O for a heart to praise my God	230	74	483	361	495	536	514	538	85
g	O Jesus, I have promised	235	420	531	372	501	704	509	352	434
p2	O Lord my God, when I in awesome wonder [How great thou art]				380	506		117	62	
p2	O praise the Lord, ye servants of the Lord		426							
o1	Stay with us, God							338		
g	Take my life, and let it be	249		554	464	624	705	371	358	462
g	Teach me, my God and King	240	456		466		803	538		692
o2	The Kingdom of God is justice and joy		333		651	139	200	321		
g	The Lord is King! I own his power							543		
g	The Lord is King! lift up thy/your voice	107		183	485	656	58	76	322	36
e	Thou art / You are the way	128	464	113	512	695	234	554		121
o2e	Thy/Your kingdom come, O God	177	499	334	519		783	638	644	322
g	To him we come			518		709			547	
g	Who is on the Lord's side?					769	722		615	479

Year A
Proper 21

Continuous: Exodus **17**: 1-7 and Psalm **78**: 1-4, 12-16 or *Related:* Ezekiel **18**: 1-4, 25-32 and Psalm **25**: 1-9; Philippians **2**: 1-13; Matthew **21**: 23-32

		AMNS	NEH	HTC	HON	MP	H&P	R&S	BPW	CH3
e	All hail the power of Jesus' name	140	332	587/203	13	13	252		29	382
e	All praise to thee/Christ, for thou / our Lord and King divine	337	335	204	18		253	750		297
e	And can it be			452/588	30	33	216	366	328	409
eg	At the name of Jesus	148	338	172	46	41	74	261	370	300
e	Before the heaven and earth			612						
g	Christ is the King! O friends rejoice	345	345	492				571	475	474
g	Christ triumphant, ever reigning			173	81	77			306	
g	Crown him with many crowns	147	352	174	103	109	255	262	37	298
e	Empty he came			127						
e	From heaven you came (The servant King)				148	162		522	529	
op1	Guide me, O thou/my great Redeemer	214	368	528	188	201	437	345	593	89
g	Hark the glad sound! The Saviour comes	30	6	193	198	210	82	137	143	160
e	Help us to help each other / Jesus, united by thy grace	374		540	208		773	500		
p2	Lead us, heavenly Father, lead us	224	393	595	293	400	68	543	597	90
g	Lo, from the desert homes	316								
g	Lo, in the wilderness a voice	384	170							
e	May the mind of Christ my Saviour			550	334	463	739		537	432
e	Meekness and majesty				335	465			58	
o2	O for a heart to praise my God	230	74	483	361	495	536	514	538	85
g	O Jesus, I have promised	235	420	531	372	501	704	509	352	434
e	O Lord my God, when I in awesome wonder [How great thou art]				380	506		117	62	
e	O loving Lord, you are / who art for ever seeking						798		354	
g	On Jordan's bank the Baptist's cry	27	12	601	401	538	84	134	147	208
p2	Praise the Lord! ye heaven(s), adore him	195	437	583	425		15	116	67	37
g	Rejoice! the Lord is King	139	443	180	432	575	243	657	317	296
op1	Rock of ages	135	445	593	437	582	273	365	545	83
g	Sing we the praises of the great forerunner / On this high feast day	315	168							
p2	Tell out, my soul, the greatness of the Lord	422	186	42	467	631	86	740	391	164
e	There's no greater name than Jesus			S27		684			396	
e	Thou who wast rich / Lord, you were rich			63		700				

Continuous: Esther **7**: 1-6, 9-10, **9**: 20-22 and Psalm **124**

or *Related:* Numbers **11**: 4-6, 10-16, 24-29 and Psalm **19**: 7-14; James **5**: 13-20; Mark **9**: 38-50

		AMNS	NEH	HTC	HON	MP	H&P	R&S	BPW	CH3
e	'Lift up your hearts!' We lift them	241	398	366	304		405			440
o2p1	A safe stronghold/fortress/refuge	114		523		2	661	585	375	406/7
e	Be thou / O Lord, my/our guardian	217	64	374	55					
g	Be thou my vision / Lord be my vision	343	339	545	56	51	378	489	521	87
g	Dear Lord and Father of mankind	115	353	356	106	111	673	492	84	76
eg	Father of heaven, whose love profound	97	358	359	124		519			77
e	Father, hear the prayer we offer	113	357	360	120	132	436	495	523	
g	For the beauty of the earth	104	285	298	137	152	333	41	121	367
g	Great is thy/your faithfulness			260	186	200	66	96	553	
op2	Guide me, O thou/my great Redeemer/Jehovah	214	368	528	188	201	437	345	593	89
g	How sweet the name of Jesus sounds	122	374	211	220	251	257	277	339	376
g	I heard the voice of Jesus say	247	376		231	275	136	349		212
e	I lift my eyes to the quiet hills					281		64	595	
g	Jesus, where'er thy people meet / Lord Jesus, when your people	162	390	371	282		549	476		
g	Lord of all hopefulness	394	239	101	313		552	531	517	92
g	Lord, I was blind			437		433	423	358	558	
e	Lord, teach us how to pray aright	227	406	367	316		551			
p2	Lord, thy word abideth / Lord, your word shall guide us	166	407	251	318	446	476	317	102	130
e	New every morning is the love	2	238	270	349	480	636	536		47
e	O God of Bethel / O God of Jacob	216	416	35	364		442	71	599	72
p	O worship the King all glorious above	101	433	24	393	528	28	47	63	35
op1	O/Our God, our help in ages past	99	417	37	366	498	358	705	389	611
g	Praise, my soul, the King of heaven	192	436	38	422	560	13	104	65	360
e	Prayer is the soul's sincere/supreme desire		442	372		567	557			
g	Son of God, eternal Saviour	132	498	102				605	639	454
g	Strengthen for service, Lord, the hands	421	306	423	460		626	461	453	588
o1	Tell out, my soul, the greatness of the Lord	422	186	42	467	631	86	740	391	164
g	The price is paid					663				
op1	Through all the changing scenes of life	209	467	46	516	702	73	685	544	
g	When all thy/your mercies	109	472	39	544	751	573	109		150

Continuous: Jeremiah **32**: 1-3a, 6-15 and Psalm **91**: 1-6, 14-16 or *Related:* Amos **6**: 1a, 4-7 and Psalm **146**;
1 Timothy **6**: 6-19; Luke **16**: 19-31

		AMNS	NEH	HTC	HON	MP	H&P	R&S	BPW	CH3
p1e	All my hope on God is founded	336	333	451	15	16	63	586	327	405
g	Amazing grace			28	27	31	215	92	550	
g	Blest are the pure in heart	238	341	110	63		724		588	113
g	Brother, sister, let me serve you				73			474	473	
g	Christ is the world's light	440		321			455	600	34	
g	Father of mercies, in thy/your word	167	247						99	
g	Father, Lord of all creation	356			122				620	
e	Fight the good fight	220	359	526	128	143	710	496	524	442
g	For the healing of the nations	361			139		402	620	621	
g	God has spoken — by his prophets			248			64		100	
g	God is love: let heaven adore him	365	364		170	187	36	95	374	
p1	God is our strength and refuge			527		188			308	
p2	I'll praise my Maker while I've breath			20		320	439	734	127	
g	Immortal Love, for ever full	133	378	105	243	328	392	267	198	306
e	Immortal, invisible, God only wise	199	377	21	242	327	9	67	383	32
g	Jesus, Lord, we look to thee	380	481				759	564		
p2	Jesus, the name high over all			213		385	264			
g	Lord, speak to me, that I may speak			510		444	553	613	611	485
e	Rejoice! the Lord is King	139	443	180	432	575	243	657	317	296
e	Rise up, O men of God	418								
p1	Safe in the shadow of the Lord			445		583				
g	Tell out, my soul, the greatness of the Lord	422	186	42	467	631	86	740	391	164
e	The head that was once crowned with thorns	141	134	182	480	647	209	257	274	286
g	'The Kingdom is upon you!'	512								
g	The Kingdom of God is justice and joy		333			651	139	200	321	
e	The Lord is King! lift up thy/your voice	107		183	485	656	58	76	322	36
g	We find thee, Lord, in others' need	430								
g	What does the Lord require	432					414			
g	When I needed a neighbour	433			548					
g	Ye that know the Lord is gracious	175	477							

Year A
Proper 22

Continuous: Exodus **20**: 1-4, 7-9, 12-20 and Psalm **19** or *Related:* Isaiah **5**: 1-7 and Psalm **80**: 7-15; Philippians **3**: 4b-14; Matthew **21**: 33-46

		AMNS	NEH	HTC	HON	MP	H&P	R&S	BPW	CH3
g	A man there lived in Galilee	334			3					
g	Ah, holy Jesus, how hast thou offended		62	123	8		164	215	215	251
g	At the name of Jesus	148	338	172	46	41	74	261	370	300
g	Christ is made the sure foundation / Blessed city, heavenly Salem	283/332	204/205	559	76		485	559	474	10
g	Christ is our corner-stone	161	206	564	77					
p1	Christ, whose glory fills the skies	4	234	266	82	79	457	380		114
e	Come, let us with our Lord arise	449	254	375			575	383		
p2	Creator of the earth and skies	351		320			419	82		
o1	Father of all, whose laws have stood			539					335	
e	Fight the good fight	220	359	526	128	143	710	496	524	442
p2	God of mercy, God of grace	179	366	293	175			575	48	497
e	Here, O my Lord, I see thee/you	274		406		230	608		436	573
g	How firm a foundation			430	216	243		589	380	
g	I danced in the morning	375	375		228			195		
g	It is a thing most wonderful	70	84	131	255	346	224	503	219	385
e	Jesus, the name high over all			213		385	264			
e	Jesus, the very thought of thee/you is sweet	120	291,385	478	264	386	265	509	352	377
e	Jesus, thou/the joy of loving hearts	255	292	413	265	383	258	389	439	571
g	My Lord, what love is this				345	476				
g	My song is love unknown	63	86	136	346	478	173	207	204	224
g	Nature with open volume stands	497	87				174	219		
g	O sacred head	68	90	139	389	520	176	220	223	253
g	Praise to the Holiest in the height	117	439	140	426	563	231	103	562	238
g	The head that was once crowned with thorns	141	134	182	480	647	209	257	274	286
p1	The heavens declare thy/your glory, Lord	168		254			481	320		
g	The price is paid					663				
p1	The spacious firmament	103	267		493		339			143
eg	To him we come			518		709			547	
g	We have a gospel to proclaim	431	486	519	532	728	465		585	
e	We sing the praise of him who died	138	94	146	536	738	182	229	231	258
eg	When I survey the wondrous cross	67	95	147	549	755	180	217	233	254

Year B
Proper 22

Continuous: Job 1: 1, **2**: 1-10 and Psalm **26** or *Related:* Genesis **2**: 18-24 and Psalm **8**;
Hebrews 1: 1-4, **2**: 5-12; Mark 10: 2-16

		AMNS	NEH	HTC	HON	MP	H&P	R&S	BPW	CH3
g	Blest are the pure in heart	238	341	110	63		724		588	113
e	Christ is the world's light	440		321			455	600	34	
e	Christ triumphant, ever reigning			173	81	77			306	
g	Christ who welcomed little children								497	
g	Father on high, to whom we pray			296					499	
g	Father, Lord of all creation	356			122				620	
e	God has spoken — by his prophets			248			64		100	
g	Happy are they, they that/who love God	176	369	473	195		711			408
g	Happy the home that welcomes you			300			366			
g	He/they want/lack not friends	183	371				495	481		
p2	How excellent in all the earth									138
g	It fell upon a summer day				254					213
g	Jesus, good above all other	378	387	96	269		732	528		111
g	Lead us, heavenly Father, lead us	224	393	595	293	400	68	543	597	90
g	Lord Jesus Christ, you have come to us	391	297	417	311	435	617	373	444	
o2g	Lord of all hopefulness	394	239	101	313		552	531	517	92
g	Lord of the home, your only Son	494					367		500	
o2g	Love divine, all loves excelling	131	408	217	321	449	267	663	559	437
g	Loving Shepherd of thy/your sheep	134		305	325					93
g	May the grace of Christ our Saviour	181		370	333		762		110	634
g	Now thank we all our God	205	413	33	354	486	566	72	128	368
o1	O for a heart to praise my God	230	74	483	361	495	536	514	538	85
p2	O Lord of every shining constellation	411		314					130	141
g	Seek ye first the Kingdom of God				442	590	138	512	357	
e	The brightness of God's glory			221						
e	The Lord is King! lift up thy/your voice	107		183	485	656	58	76	322	36
g	The Lord's my shepherd, I'll not want	426	459	591/45	490	660	70	679	395	387
g	Thine/Yours for ever	234	463	556	504					
p1	We love the place, O God	160	471	558	533	731				15
g	Will you come and follow me?				560			558	363	

Year C
Proper 22

Continuous: Lamentations 1: 1-6; (Canticle) Lamentations 3: 19-26 or Psalm 137
or Related: Habakkuk 1: 1-4, 2: 1-4 and Psalm 37: 1-9; 2 Timothy 1: 1-14; Luke 17: 5-10

		AMNS	NEH	HTC	HON	MP	H&P	R&S	BPW	CH3
g	Almighty Father, who for us thy Son didst give	338					401	621		
p2	Be thou my vision / Lord be my vision	343	339	545	56	51	378	489	521	87
g	Come, praise the name of Jesus			538					331	
g	Dear Lord and Father of mankind	115	353	356	106	111	673	492	84	76
g	Father, hear the prayer we offer	113	357	360	120	132	436	495	523	
g	Fight the good fight	220	359	526	128	143	710	496	524	442
o2g	Fill thou/now my/our life	200		541	129	146	792	406	569	457
g	Firmly I believe and truly	118	360	429	133					400
g	Give me/us the wings of faith	324	225		156		815	664		
o2	God is working his purpose out		495	191	172	189	769	573		303
g	Have faith in God, my heart	372		431	201		675	499	336	
g	Help us to help each other / Jesus, united by thy grace	374		540	208		773	500		
o2	I cannot tell why/how he whom angels worship			194	226	266	238	265	381	
e	I know not why God's wondrous grace					279			532	
e	I'm not ashamed to own/name my Lord			448	240	323	677	428	343	591
op1	Lead, kindly light	215	392		292	399	67	544		682
op1	Maker of Earth, to thee alone		71							
l	New every morning is the love	2	238	270	349	480	636	536		47
o1	O come, O come, Emmanuel	26	11	66	358	493	85	126	144	165
eg	O thou/Lord who came[st]	233	431	552/596	392	525	745	433	355	110
o1g	Put thou thy trust / Commit thou all thy griefs	223			429		672	550		669
g	Safe in the shadow of the Lord			445		583				
g	Strengthen for service, Lord, the hands	421	306	423	460		626	461	453	588
g	Teach me, my God and King	240	456		466		803	538		692
o1g	Through all the changing scenes of life	209	467	46	516	702	73	685	544	
o2	Thy/Your kingdom come, O God	177	499	334	519		783	638	644	322
e	To God be the glory			584	522	708	463	289	566	374
e	We have a gospel to proclaim	431	486	519	532	728	465		585	

Year A
Proper 23

Continuous: Exodus **32**: 1-14 and Psalm **106**: 1-6, 19-23 or *Related:* Isaiah **25**: 1-9 and Psalm **23**; Philippians **4**: 1-9; Matthew **22**: 1-14

		AMNS	NEH	HTC	HON	MP	H&P	R&S	BPW	CH3
g	Bread of heaven, on thee we feed	271	276	398	67			442		
g	Christians, lift your hearts and voices	447							431	
g	Come, risen Lord, and deign to be our guest	349	279		96		605	445		572
g	Faithful Shepherd, feed me		282	29	117					
g	From glory to glory advancing	276	286		147			462		325
g	Here, O my Lord, I see thee/you	274		406		230	608		436	573
o2	How bright these glorious spirits shine	306	227	572						533
g	I come with joy to meet my Lord	473		408	227		610	447	437	
p2	I know that my Redeemer lives, what joy			169	232	278	196	278	251	
g	Jerusalem the golden	184	381	573	259			662	312	537
o2	Jesus, lover of my soul	123	383	438	261	372	528	332	345	78
g	Light's abode, celestial Salem	185	401		305					
e	Like a mighty river flowing			32		419			632	
g	Lord/Great God, your love has called us here	489		480			500	339	442	
e	May the mind of Christ my Saviour			550	334	463	739		537	432
g	My God, and/now is thy table spread	259		418	342					
o1	O for a closer walk with God	231	414	368	360	494		551		663
g	O what their joy / What of those sabbaths	186	432					659		535
e	Rejoice, rejoice, Christ is in you					572				
e	Rejoice! the Lord is King	139	443	180	432	575	243	657	317	296
g	Spread the table of the Lord						625		450	
p1	The King of love my shepherd is	126	457	44	484	649	69	552	394	388
g	The Kingdom of God is justice and joy			333		651	139	200	321	
p2	The Lord's my shepherd, I'll not want	426	459	591/45	490	660	70	679	395	387
g	To him we come			518		709			547	
g	We come as guests invited			602		723				
o2	We trust in you, our shield and our defender			446						
g	Ye watchers and ye holy ones	532	478		567					

Year B
Proper 23

Continuous: Job **23**: 1-9, 16-17 and Psalm **22**: 1-15 or *Related:* Amos **5**: 6-7, 10-15 and Psalm **90**: 12-17; Hebrews **4**: 12-16; Mark **10**: 17-31

723

		AMNS	NEH	HTC	HON	MP	H&P	R&S	BPW	CH3
e	Amazing grace			28	27	31	215	92	550	
g	Be thou my vision / Lord be my vision	343	339	545	56	51	378	489	521	87
o1g	Can we/man by searching find out God	438					76	80		
g	Come Holy Spirit, heavenly dove							299		
g	Come, praise the name of Jesus			538					331	
o2	Eternal Ruler of the ceaseless round	353	355		115			623	477	514
g	Glorious things of thee/you are spoken	172	362	494	158	173	817	560	480	421
p2eg	God of mercy, God of grace	179	366	293	175			575	48	497
e	How sure the Scriptures are		249							
g	Jesus calls us: o'er/in the tumult	312	200	104	266	359	141	355		211
g	Jesus, lover of my soul	123	383	438	261	372	528	332	345	78
p2	Judge eternal, throned in splendour		490	329	285	395	409	626	627	519
g	Just as I am, without one plea	246	294	440	287	396	697	364	346	79
g	Lord, be thy word my rule / Lord, make your word	232		250						
e	Lord, enthroned in heavenly splendour	263	296	416	309	431	616			583
g	My God, accept my heart this day	279	318	551	341		701			429
e	O God of Bethel / O God of Jacob	216	416	35	364		442	71	599	72
g	O Jesus, I have promised	235	420	531	372	501	704	509	352	434
g	O thou/Lord who came[st]	233	431	552/596	392	525	745	433	355	110
g	Rejoice, rejoice, Christ is in you					572				
g	Safe in the shadow of the Lord			445		583				
g	Take my life, and let it be	249		554	464	624	705	371	358	462
o2	The day of the Lord shall come							637		
g	Thine/Yours for ever	234	463	556	504					
o2	Thy/Your kingdom come, O God	177	499	334	519		783	638	644	322
e	Where high the heavenly temple stands	130		184				259		295
g	Will you come and follow me?				560			558	363	
e	With joy we meditate the grace	530				774	235	206	275	
g	Ye/You servants of God, your Master proclaim	149	476	520	565	784	278	293	76	372

Year C
Proper 23

Continuous: Jeremiah **29**: 1, 4-7 and Psalm **66**: 1-12 or *Related:* 2 Kings **5**: 1-3, 7-15c and Psalm **111**; 2 Timothy **2**: 8-15; Luke **17**: 11-19

		AMNS	NEH	HTC	HON	MP	H&P	R&S	BPW	CH3
g	A man there lived in Galilee	334			3					
p1	All people that on earth do dwell	100	334	14	17	20	1	712	2	1
g	As pants the hart	226	337		38		416	689		
e	Be thou / O Lord, my/our guardian	217	64	374	55					
p1	Before Jehovah's aweful/awesome throne / Sing to the Lord	197		15			61	119		2
e	Christ's Church shall glory in his power			522						
g	How sweet the name of Jesus sounds	122	374	211	220	251	257	277	339	376
g	I'll praise my Maker while I've breath			20		320	439	734	127	
e	I'm not ashamed to own/name my Lord			448	240	323	677	428	343	591
g	Immortal Love, for ever full	133	378	105	243	328	392	267	198	306
o2	Just as I am, without one plea	246	294	440	287	396	697	364	346	79
e	Lead, kindly light	215	392		292	399	67	544		682
g	Lord Christ, who on thy heart didst bear	388			308		394			
e	Lord of our life, and God of our salvation		404	529	315	441				491
g	Now thank we all our God	205	413	33	354	486	566	72	128	368
g	O for a thousand tongues to sing	125	415	219	362	496	744	285	59	371
p2	O praise the Lord, ye servants of the Lord		426							
e	Oft in danger, oft in woe / Christian soldiers, onward go	210	434	524	396	533	715			
p2g	Praise to the Lord, the Almighty	207	440	40	427	564	16	74	68	9
g	Praise, my soul, the King of heaven	192	436	38	422	560	13	104	65	360
o2	Rock of ages	135	445	593	437	582	273	365	545	83
e	Stand up, stand up for Jesus	221	453	535	457	617	721			481
e	Take up thy/your cross	237	76	114	465					430
g	The crippled hands reached out: SS95									
e	The head that was once crowned with thorns	141	134	182	480	647	209	257	274	286
g	Thine arm, O Lord, in days of old	285	324		502		397			214
e	Through the night of doubt and sorrow	211	468	466	517		441		546	423
g	To God be the glory			584	522	708	463	289	566	374
g	When all thy/your mercies	109	472	39	544	751	573	109		150

Year A
Proper 24

Continuous: Exodus 33: 12-23 and Psalm 99 or Related: Isaiah 45: 1-7 and Psalm 96: 1-9 [10-13]; 1 Thessalonians 1: 1-10; Matthew 22: 15-22

		AMNS	NEH	HTC	HON	MP	H&P	R&S	BPW	CH3
g	All my hope on God is founded	336	333	451	15	16	63	586	327	405
g	At the name of Jesus	148	338	172	46	41	74	261	370	300
e	Christ is the King! O friends rejoice	345	345	492				571	475	474
g	Christ triumphant, ever reigning			173	81	77			306	
g	City of God, how broad and far	173	346		85		809			422
g	Crown him with many crowns	147	352	174	103	109	255	262	37	298
e	Firmly I believe and truly	118	360	429	133					400
g	Give to our God immortal praise	460		31	155	171	22	94	47	
g	Glorious things of thee/you are spoken	172	362	494	158	173	817	560	480	421
e	God of gods, we sound his praises			340					46	
o1	Great is thy/your faithfulness			260	186	200	66	96	553	
o2	Immortal, invisible, God only wise	199	377	21	242	327	9	67	383	32
p2	In beauty of his holiness									311
o2g	Jesus shall reign where'er the sun	143	388	516	277	379	239	269	313	413
p2	Join all the glorious names			214		392	78	280	557	304
g	Judge eternal, throned in splendour		490	329	285	395	409	626	627	519
o2	Lift up your heads, ye gates of brass						227			471
g	Name of all majesty			218		481				
p2	O sing a new song to the Lord									22
e	O thou/Lord who came[st]	233	431	552/596	392	525	745	433	355	110
p2	O worship / Worship the Lord in the beauty of holiness	49	52	344	394	529	505	187	22	40
p1g	Rejoice! the Lord is King	139	443	180	432	575	243	657	317	296
o1	Rock of ages	135	445	593	437	582	273	365	545	83
g	The Kingdom of God is justice and joy			333		651	139	200	321	
p1g	The Lord is King! lift up thy/your voice	107		183	485	656	58	76	322	36
o2	Thou/God whose almighty / Father your mighty word	180	466	506	514	699	29	38	591	494
e	Through all the changing scenes of life	209	467	46	516	702	73	685	544	
g	Thy/Your kingdom come, O God	177	499	334	519		783	638	644	322
e	We have a gospel to proclaim	431	486	519	532	728	465		585	
g	Ye that know the Lord is gracious	175	477							
g	Ye/You servants of the Lord	150	18	598	566		248			319

Year B
Proper 24

Continuous: Job **38**: 1-7 [34-41] and Psalm **104**: 1-9, 24, 35c or *Related:* Isaiah **53**: 4-12 and Psalm **91**: 9-16; Hebrews **5**: 1-10; Mark **10**: 35-45

		AMNS	NEH	HTC	HON	MP	H&P	R&S	BPW	CH3
g	All praise to thee/Christ, for thou / our Lord and King divine	337	335	204	18		253	750		297
g	Almighty Father, who for us thy Son didst give	338					401	621		
o2e	Christ triumphant, ever reigning			173	81	77			306	
g	Come down, O Love Divine	156	137	231	90	89	281	294	283	115
g	Father of heaven, whose love profound	97	358	359	124		519			77
g	From heaven you came (The servant King)				148	162		522	529	
g	God of gods, we sound his praises			340					46	
o2e	Hail thou/our once-despisèd/rejected Jesus			175	192	203	222		273	
g	Help us to help each other / Jesus, united by thy grace	374		540	208		773	500		
o2	I will sing the wondrous story			212	237	315	223		382	381
e	It is a thing most wonderful	70	84	131	255	346	224	503	219	385
g	Jesus is Lord! creation's voice proclaims it			S17	270	367	260	268	384	
o2	Led like a lamb / You're alive, you have risen				294	402		241	254	
o1	Lord of beauty, thine the splendour	106	265		314					120
g	Lord, speak to me, that I may speak			510		444	553	613	611	485
g	Lord/Great God, your love has called us here	489		480			500	339	442	
o2	My song is love unknown	63	86	136	346	478	173	207	204	224
o2	O sacred head	68	90	139	389	520	176	220	223	253
op1	O worship the King all glorious above	101	433	24	393	528	28	47	63	35
g	Praise, my soul, the King of heaven	192	436	38	422	560	13	104	65	360
p2	Safe in the shadow of the Lord			445		583				
o2	See, Christ was wounded for our sake			137					229	
o2	The price is paid					663				
op1	The spacious firmament	103	267		493		339			143
g	There is a green hill far away	137	92	148	499	674	178	223	230	241
o2e	We sing the praise of him who died	138	94	146	536	738	182	229	231	258
e	Where high the heavenly temple stands	130		184				259		295

Year C
Proper 24

Continuous: Jeremiah **31**: 27-34 and Psalm **119**: 97-104 or *Related:* Genesis **32**: 22-31 and Psalm **121**; 2 Timothy **3**:14 — **4**:5; Luke **18**: 1-8

		AMNS	NEH	HTC	HON	MP	H&P	R&S	BPW	CH3
o1	A debtor to mercy alone			449						
g	Be thou / O Lord, my/our guardian	217	64	374	55					
g	Behold, the mountain of the Lord						50	130	617	312
g	Father all-loving, thou rulest in majesty	355ii								
g	Father, hear the prayer we offer	113	357	360	120	132	436	495	523	
g	Father of heaven, whose love profound	97	358	359	124		519			77
p1e	Father of mercies, in thy/your word	167		247					99	
g	Give to our God immortal praise	460		31	155	171	22	94	47	
g	Great Shepherd of thy/your people, hear	164		363			490	387		
o1	Hail to the Lord's anointed	142	55	190	193	204	125	127	142	317
o2	Here, O my Lord, I see thee/you	274		406		230	608		436	573
o1g	Immortal, invisible, God only wise	199	377	21	242	327	9	67	383	32
g	'Lift up your hearts!' We lift them	241	398	366	304		405			440
e	Lord, be thy word my rule / Lord, make your word	232		250						
g	Lord, for the years			328	310	428		603	535	
g	Lord, teach us how to pray aright	227	406	367	316		551			
e	Lord, thy word abideth / Lord, your word shall guide us	166	407	251	318	446	476	317	102	130
e	Lord, you sometimes speak in wonders								101	
po1	My hope is built on nothing less			462		473				411
g	O God beyond all praising			36	363					
o2	O love that will/wilt not let me go			486	384	515	685	511	541	677
e	Powerful in making us wise to salvation			252			479			
g	Prayer is the soul's sincere/supreme desire		442	372		567	557			
o1	Restore, O Lord, the honour of your name				434	579			324	
e	Thou/God whose almighty / Father your mighty word	180	466	506	514	699	29	38	591	494
o1	We are called to be God's people								583	
g	Ye that know the Lord is gracious	175	477							

Year A
Proper 25

Continuous: Deuteronomy **34**: 1-12 and Psalm **90**: 1-6, 13-17 or *Related:* Leviticus **19**: 1-2, 15-18 and Psalm **1**; 1 Thessalonians **2**: 1-8; Matthew **22**: 34-46

		AMNS	NEH	HTC	HON	MP	H&P	R&S	BPW	CH3
e	A safe stronghold/fortress/refuge	114		523		2	661	585	375	406/7
g	Come down, O Love Divine	156	137	231	90	89	281	294	283	115
g	Father of all, whose laws have stood			539					335	
e	Father, hear the prayer we offer	113	357	360	120	132	436	495	523	
p2	Father of mercies, in thy/your word	167		247					99	
g	Firmly I believe and truly	118	360	429	133					400
o1e	Forth in thy/your name, O Lord	239	235	306	143	159	381	521	526	463
g	Hail to the Lord's anointed	142	55	190	193	204	125	127	142	317
o1	If our God had simply saved us: SS35									
o1e	Lead, kindly light	215	392		292	399	67	544		682
p2	Lord, be thy word my rule / Lord, make your word	232		250						
g	Lord of all power, I give you my will / Lord of creation, to you be all praise	395		547		440	699	532		428
p1	Lord, thou hast been our dwelling-place									102
o1	O God of Bethel / O God of Jacob	216	416	35	364		442	71	599	72
e	O Jesus, I have promised	235	420	531	372	501	704	509	352	434
e	O thou/Lord who came[st]	233	431	552/596	392	525	745	433	355	110
p1	O/Our God, our help in ages past	99	417	37	366	498	358	705	389	611
o1	Put thou thy trust / Commit thou all thy griefs	223			429		672	550		669
g	Rejoice! the Lord is King	139	443	180	432	575	243	657	317	296
g	Take my life, and let it be	249		554	464	624	705	371	358	462
p1	The Church's one foundation	170	484	501	473	640	515	566	393	420
o1	The God of Abraham praise	331	148	9	478	645	452	121	131	358
o1	There is a land of pure delight	190	460	575			822	668	323	536
o1	There was a man who had a dream: SS63									
e	Through all the changing scenes of life	209	467	46	516	702	73	685	544	
e	Through the night of doubt and sorrow	211	468	466	517		441		546	423
e	Thy/Your hand, O God, has guided	171	485	536	518	705	784	567	398	424
p2	Thy/Your way, not mine			555	521					
e	Who would true valour / He who would valiant / Who honours courage	212	372	537/590	205	224	688	557	362	443

Year B
Proper 25

Continuous: Job **42**: 1-6, 10-17 and Psalm **34**: 1-8, 19-22 or *Related:* Jeremiah **31**: 7-9 and Psalm **126**; Hebrews **7**: 23-28; Mark **10**: 46-52

		AMNS	NEH	HTC	HON	MP	H&P	R&S	BPW	CH3
e	All for Jesus!		272	469	10		251		332	
e	Alleluia! sing to Jesus	262	271	170	26	207	592		270	
g	Amazing grace			28	27	31	215	92	550	
g	Come, Lord, to our souls come down	348					470	361		
o1	Dear Lord and Father of mankind	115	353	356	106	111	673	492	84	76
g	Firmly I believe and truly	118	360	429	133					400
e	Forth in the peace of Christ we go	458	361	542	142			602	607	589
o1	God moves in a mysterious way	112	365		173	193	65	59	122	147
g	Have faith in God, my heart	372		431	201		675	499	336	
o2	Hills of the north, rejoice	470	7		209		237		311	
p1	Holy, holy, holy, Lord God almighty	95	146	7/594	212	237	7	34	51	352
g	I heard the voice of Jesus say	247	376		231	275	136	349		212
g	I know that my Redeemer lives, and ever prays						731			
g	Immortal Love, for ever full	133	378	105	243	328	392	267	198	306
g	Jesus, lover of my soul	123	383	438	261	372	528	332	345	78
e	Lord, enthroned in heavenly splendour	263	296	416	309	431	616			583
g	My Lord, I did not choose you			107						
g	O for a thousand tongues to sing	125	415	219	362	496	744	285	59	371
g	O God, by whose almighty plan	406					396	651		
g	O Master, let me walk with thee						802			436
e	Once, only once, and once for all	261	304		404					
o2	Praise, my soul, the King of heaven	192	436	38	422	560	13	104	65	360
g	Put thou thy trust / Commit thou all thy griefs	223			429		672	550		669
e	The Lord ascendeth up on high		135				210			287
g	Thine arm, O Lord, in days of old	285	324		502		397			214
p1	Through all the changing scenes of life	209	467	46	516	702	73	685	544	
p2	To God be the glory			584	522	708	463	289	566	374
e	We hail thy presence glorious	266	310		531					
g	When all thy/your mercies	109	472	39	544	751	573	109		150
g	Ye/You servants of God, your Master proclaim	149	476	520	565	784	278	293	76	372

Year C
Proper 25

Continuous: Joel **2**: 23-32 and Psalm **65** or *Related:* Ecclesiasticus **35**: 12-17 or Jeremiah **14**: 7-10, 19-22 and Psalm **84**: 1-7; 2 Timothy **4**: 6-8, 16-18; Luke **18**: 9-14

		AMNS	NEH	HTC	HON	MP	H&P	R&S	BPW	CH3
e	A safe stronghold/fortress/refuge	114		523		2	661	585	375	406/7
p2	A sovereign protector I have							54	325	651
g	All praise to thee/Christ, for thou / our Lord and King divine	337	335	204	18		253	750		297
g	Amazing grace			28	27	31	215	92	550	
eg	And can it be			452/588	30	33	216	366	328	409
o1	Breathe on me, Breath of God	157	342	226	69	67	280	295	282	103
e	Christ the Lord is risen today / Love's redeeming work is done / All creation	83	113	150	324	76	193	232	246	275
g	Come down, O Love Divine	156	137	231	90	89	281	294	283	115
o2g	Father of heaven, whose love profound	97	358	359	124		519			77
e	Fight the good fight	220	359	526	128	143	710	496	524	442
e	For all the saints	305	197	567	134	148	814	658	478	534
01	God as Fire, send your Spirit: SS52									
e	Guide me, O thou/my great Redeemer	214	368	528	188	201	437	345	593	89
p2	Here, O my Lord, I see thee/you	274		406		230	608		436	573
p2	How lovely is thy dwelling place — tabernacles							703		4
o1	I will pour out my Spirit						292			
g	I will sing the wondrous story			212	237	315	223		382	381
g	Jesus, lover of my soul	123	383	438	261	372	528	332	345	78
g	Just as I am, without one plea	246	294	440	287	396	697	364	346	79
g	King of glory, King of peace	194	391	603	288	397	499	97	53	364
o2g	'Lift up your hearts!' We lift them	241	398	366	304		405			440
g	Name of all majesty			218		481				
o1	O Breath of life, come sweeping / O Breath of love, come breathe			237	356	488	777	302	293	339
o2	O for a closer walk with God	231	414	368	360	494		551		663
g	Praise, my soul, the King of heaven	192	436	38	422	560	13	104	65	360
p1	Praise waits for thee in Zion, Lord									28
g	Tell out, my soul, the greatness of the Lord	422	186	42	467	631	86	740	391	164
g	To the Name of our / that brings salvation	121	470	222	523		80	291		373
e	Who would true valour / He who would valiant / Who honours courage	212	372	537/590	205	224	688	557	362	443
eg	Ye that know the Lord is gracious	175	477							

Year A
Bible Sunday

Nehemiah **8**: 1-4a [5-6] 8-12; Psalm **119**: 9-16; Colossians **3**: 12-17; Matthew **24**: 30-35

		AMNS	NEH	HTC	HON	MP	H&P	R&S	BPW	CH3
e	All for Jesus!		272	469	10		251		332	
e	Angel-voices ever singing	163	336	307	33	34	484	405	1	455
g	Christ is the King! O friends rejoice	345	345	492				571	475	474
e	Come down, O Love Divine	156	137	231	90	89	281	294	283	115
s	Come, Holy Ghost, our hearts inspire (Wesley)	448	348		91		469	312	97	122
s	Father of mercies, in thy/your word	167		247					99	
e	Forgive our sins as we forgive	362	66	111	141		134	84	83	
o	God has spoken — by his prophets			248			64		100	
s	God who hast caused to be written						472			
s	How lovely on the mountains are the feet of him				219	249			310	
g	How sure the Scriptures are			249						
e	How sweet the name of Jesus sounds	122	374	211	220	251	257	277	339	376
g	I cannot tell why/how he whom angels worship			194	226	266	238	265	381	
e	Let all the world in every corner sing	202	394	342	296	404	10	114	54	361
g	Lo, he / Jesus comes with clouds descending	28	9	196	307	424	241	656	314	314
o	Lord, be thy word my rule / Lord, make your word	232		250						
o	Lord, I have made thy word my choice	490					475	316		
pg	Lord, thy word abideth / Lord, your word shall guide us	166	407	251	318	446	476	317	102	130
s	Lord, you sometimes speak in wonders								101	
e	May the mind of Christ my Saviour			550	334	463	739		537	432
s	Powerful in making us wise to salvation			252			479			
g	Rejoice! the Lord is King	139	443	180	432	575	243	657	317	296
g	Songs of praise the angels sang	196	451	350			512	667		38
s	Speak, Lord, in the stillness			253		608			105	
s	Thanks/Praise to God whose word was spoken (5 verse version)	423	438					319		
s	The heavens declare thy/your glory, Lord	168		254			481	320		
s	The prophets spoke in days of old	513								
s	Thou/God whose almighty / Father your mighty word	180	466	506	514	699	29	38	591	494

Year B
Bible Sunday

Isaiah **55**: 1-11; Psalm **19**: 7-14; 2 Timothy 3:14 — 4:5; John 5: 36b-47

		AMNS	NEH	HTC	HON	MP	H&P	R&S	BPW	CH3
o	At even[ing], ere/when the sun was/had set	9	243	315	43	43	142	644	616	52
g	Break thou/now the bread of life					64	467	314	98	
s	Come, Holy Ghost, our hearts inspire (Wesley)	448	348		91		469	312	97	122
p	Creator of the earth and skies	351		320			419	82		
s	Father of mercies, in thy/your word	167		247					99	
p	God be in my head	236	328	543	166		694	498	592	433
s	God has spoken — by his prophets			248			64		100	
s	God who hast caused to be written						472			
s	How lovely on the mountains are the feet of him				219	249			310	
g	How sure the Scriptures are			249						
g	Immortal, invisible, God only wise	199	377	21	242	327	9	67	383	32
s	Lord, be thy word my rule / Lord, make your word	232		250						
e	Lord, for the years			328	310	428		603	535	
s	Lord, I have made thy word my choice	490					475	316		
oeg	Lord, thy word abideth / Lord, your word shall guide us	166	407	251	318	446	476	317	102	130
s	Lord, you sometimes speak in wonders								101	
e	Powerful in making us wise to salvation			252			479			
s	Speak, Lord, in the stillness			253		608			105	
s	Thanks/Praise to God whose word was spoken (5 verse version)	423	438					319		
s	The heavens declare thy/your glory, Lord	168		254			481	320		
s	The prophets spoke in days of old	513								
s	Thou/God whose almighty / Father your mighty word	180	466	506	514	699	29	38	591	494

Year C
Bible Sunday

Isaiah **45**: 22-25; Psalm **119**: 129-136; Romans **15**: 1-6; Luke **4**: 16-24

		AMNS	NEH	HTC	HON	MP	H&P	R&S	BPW	CH3
o	At the name of Jesus	148	338	172	46	41	74	261	370	300
g	Christ is the world's true light	346	494	323	78		456	601	618	505
g	Christ on whom the Spirit rested			228						
s	Come, Holy Ghost, our hearts inspire (Wesley)	448	348		91		469	312	97	122
o	Come, let us to the Lord our God						33	81		69
g	Come, thou/O long-expected Jesus	31	3	52	98	102	81	138	139	320
s	Father of mercies, in thy/your word	167		247					99	
s	God has spoken — by his prophets			248			64		100	
s	God's Spirit is deep in my heart				180		315	576	574	
g	Hail to the Lord's anointed	142	55	190	193	204	125	127	142	317
g	Hark the glad sound! The Saviour comes	30	6	193	198	210	82	137	143	160
e	Help us, O Lord, to learn	373	370	493			474			
g	I cannot tell why/how he whom angels worship			194	226	266	238	265	381	
p	Lord, thy word abideth / Lord, your word shall guide us	166	407	251	318	446	476	317	102	130
g	O changeless Christ, for ever new			108					206	
g	O for a thousand tongues to sing	125	415	219	362	496	744	285	59	371
g	Son of God, eternal Saviour	132	498	102				605	639	454
s	Thanks/Praise to God whose word was spoken (5 verse version)	423	438					319		
p	The heavens declare thy/your glory, Lord	168		254			481	320		
g	'The Kingdom is upon you!'	512								
g	The Kingdom of God is justice and joy			333		651	139	200	321	
o	The prophets spoke in days of old	513								
g	The voice of God goes out to all the world						140	131		
s	The world is full of stories: SS1									
g	There is a Redeemer				500	673				
s	Thou/God whose almighty / Father your mighty word	180	466	506	514	699	29	38	591	494
g	When Jesus walked upon this earth			317						

Year A
Dedication Festival

1 Kings **8**: 22-30 or Revelation **21**: 9-14; Psalm **122**; Hebrews **12**: 18-24; Matthew **21**: 12-16

		AMNS	NEH	HTC	HON	MP	H&P	R&S	BPW	CH3
o	Angel-voices ever singing	163	336	307	33	34	484	405	1	455
s	Be thou my vision / Lord be my vision	343	339	545	56	51	378	489	521	87
p	Before Jehovah's aweful/awesome throne / Sing to the Lord	197		15			61	119		2
g	Bright the vision that delighted / Round the Lord	96	343	578	70		445	665	71	353
s	Christ is made the sure foundation / Blessed city, heavenly Salem	283/332	204/205	559	76		485	559	474	10
s	Christ is our corner-stone	161	206	564	77					
er	Glorious things of thee/you are spoken	172	362	494	158	173	817	560	480	421
s	God is here! As we his people	464		560			653			
g	God our Father and Creator			562						
o	Great Shepherd of thy/your people, hear	164		363			490	387		
s	Here within this house of prayer			563						
o	Holy, holy, holy, Lord God almighty	95	146	7/594	212	237	7	34	51	352
p	How pleased and blest was I						497	563	10	
g	Immortal Love, for ever full	133	378	105	243	328	392	267	198	306
pr	Jerusalem the golden	184	381	573	259			662	312	537
r	Jerusalem, my happy home / thou city blest	187	225	569	258					
g	Jesus shall reign where'er the sun	143	388	516	277	379	239	269	313	413
g	My song is love unknown	63	86	136	346	478	173	207	204	224
s	Now thank we all our God	205	413	33	354	486	566	72	128	368
s	O praise the Lord, ye servants of the Lord		426							
s	Only-begotten, Word of God eternal		210							
s	The Church of God a kingdom is	169	483		472					
s	The Church's one foundation	170	484	501	473	640	515	566	393	420
g	Thine arm, O Lord, in days of old	285	324		502		397			214
o	This is the day the Lord hath/has made	22	257	379			577	376		
s	Thy/Your hand, O God, has guided	171	485	536	518	705	784	567	398	424
s	We have a gospel to proclaim	431	486	519	532	728	465		585	
og	We love the place, O God	160	471	558	533	731				15
s	Who are we who stand and sing	529								
s	Ye that know the Lord is gracious	175	477							

Year B
Dedication Festival

Genesis **28**: 11-18 or Revelation **21**: 9-14; Psalm **122**; 1 Peter **2**: 1-10; John **10**: 22-29

		AMNS	NEH	HTC	HON	MP	H&P	R&S	BPW	CH3
o	As Jacob with travel was weary one day	435			36		444			
s	Be thou my vision / Lord be my vision	343	339	545	56	51	378	489	521	87
p	Before Jehovah's aweful/awesome throne / Sing to the Lord	197		15			61	119		2
e	Christ is made the sure foundation / Blessed city, heavenly Salem	283/332	204/205	559	76		485	559	474	10
e	Christ is our corner-stone	161	206	564	77					
e	Church of God, elect and glorious			504					406	
s	Father, Lord of all creation	356			122				620	
r	For all the saints	305	197	567	134	148	814	658	478	534
e	Forth in the peace of Christ we go	458	361	542	142			602	607	589
r	Glorious things of thee/you are spoken	172	362	494	158	173	817	560	480	421
s	God is here! As we his people	464		560			653			
e	Hail to the Lord's anointed	142	55	190	193	204	125	127	142	317
s	Here within this house of prayer			563						
e	How firm a foundation			430	216	243		589	380	
pr	Jerusalem the golden	184	381	573	259			662	312	537
g	Loving Shepherd of thy/your sheep	134		305	325					93
s	Now thank we all our God	205	413	33	354	486	566	72	128	368
o	O God of Bethel / O God of Jacob	216	416	35	364		442	71	599	72
o	O happy band of pilgrims	208	418	530	368					
s	O praise the Lord, ye servants of the Lord		426							
p	I joyed when to the house of God / Pray that Jerusalem		441				510	727		489
o	Prayer to a heart of lowly love								601	
s	The Church of God a kingdom is	169	483		472					
s	The Church's one foundation	170	484	501	473	640	515	566	393	420
e	Through all the changing scenes of life	209	467	46	516	702	73	685	544	
s	Thy/Your hand, O God, has guided	171	485	536	518	705	784	567	398	424
e	To him we come			518		709			547	
r	Wake, O wake / Sleepers, wake	32	16	199	529		249	132		315
s	We have a gospel to proclaim	431	486	519	532	728	465		585	
s	Who are we who stand and sing	529								
s	Ye that know the Lord is gracious	175	477							

Year C
Dedication Festival

1 Chronicles **29**: 6-19; Psalm **122**; Ephesians **2**: 19-22; John **2**: 13-22

		AMNS	NEH	HTC	HON	MP	H&P	R&S	BPW	CH3
p	All people that on earth do dwell	100	334	14	17	20	1	712	2	1
s	Be thou my vision / Lord be my vision	343	339	545	56	51	378	489	521	87
e	Christ is made the sure foundation / Blessed city, heavenly Salem	283/332	204/205	559	76		485	559	474	10
e	Christ is our corner-stone	161	206	564	77					
e	Christ is the world's light	440		321			455	600	34	
e	City of God, how broad and far	173	346		85		809			422
s	Father, Lord of all creation	356			122				620	
s	Forth in thy/your name, O Lord	239	235	306	143	159	381	521	526	463
s	Glorious things of thee/you are spoken	172	362	494	158	173	817	560	480	421
s	God is here! As we his people	464		560			653			
s	Here within this house of prayer			563						
o	Holy, holy, holy, Lord God almighty	95	146	7/594	212	237	7	34	51	352
p	How pleased and blest was I						497	563	10	
g	I danced in the morning	375	375		228			195		
o	Immortal, invisible, God only wise	199	377	21	242	327	9	67	383	32
p	Jerusalem the golden	184	381	573	259			662	312	537
g	Lead us, heavenly Father, lead us	224	393	595	293	400	68	543	597	90
e	Light's abode, celestial Salem	185	401		305					
s	O praise the Lord, ye servants of the Lord		426							
s	Only-begotten, Word of God eternal		210							
p	I joyed when to the house of God / Pray that Jerusalem		441				510	727		489
s	The Church of God a kingdom is	169	483		472					
s	The Church's one foundation	170	484	501	473	640	515	566	393	420
o	This is the day the Lord hath/has made	22	257	379			577	376		
s	Thy/Your hand, O God, has guided	171	485	536	518	705	784	567	398	424
s	Thy kingdom come! on bended knee	178	500		520					323
s	We have a gospel to proclaim	431	486	519	532	728	465		585	
g	We love the place, O God	160	471	558	533	731				15
s	Who are we who stand and sing	529								
e	Ye that know the Lord is gracious	175	477							

Years A, B, C

All Saints' Day (Seasonal material)

		AMNS	NEH	HTC	HON	MP	H&P	R&S	BPW	CH3
s	Behold what witnesses unseen									531
s	Blest be the everlasting God						669	588		530
s	By every nation, race and tongue			579						
s	For all the saints	305	197	567	134	148	814	658	478	534
s	For all thy saints, O Lord	308	224							
s	For those we love within the veil									538
s	Give me/us the wings of faith	324	225		156		815	664		
s	Glory to thee, O God, for all thy saints	363			163					
s	Hark how the adoring hosts									532
s	Hark! the sound of holy voices	304	226		200					
s	Here from all nations, all tongues, and all peoples			571					309	
s	How bright these glorious spirits shine	306	227	572						533
s	Joy and triumph everlasting		229							
s	Let saints on earth / Come let us join our friends above	182	396	574	297	409	812	472		543
s	Lo, round the throne a glorious band	303								
s	Lord God, we give you thanks for all your saints	488								
s	O heavenly Jerusalem	322								
s	O what their joy / What of those sabbaths	186	432					659		535
s	Rejoice in God's saints	508								
s	Sing alleluia forth in duteous praise / ye saints on high	188	446							542
s	Sing we the song of those who stand						821	666		
s	Soldiers, who are Christ's below	302	450		450					
s	Ten thousand times ten thousand	189		576						
s	There is a land of pure delight	190	460	575			822	668	323	536
s	We praise, we worship thee/you, O God						443	755	490	
s	Who are these, like stars appearing	323	231		555					
s	Ye watchers and ye holy ones	532	478		567					

Year A
All Saints' Day (Lectionary material)

Revelation **7**: 9-17; Psalm **34**: 1-10; 1 John **3**: 1-3; Matthew **5**: 1-12

		AMNS	NEH	HTC	HON	MP	H&P	R&S	BPW	CH3
e	Behold the amazing gift of love						666	587		396
g	Blest are the pure in heart	238	341	110	63		724		588	113
o	Father, if justly still we claim						299			
p	God will I bless at all times									391
o	Help us, O Lord, to learn	373	370	493			474			
g	How blest the poor who love the Lord							197		
gl	Lord, once you spoke upon the plain									
g	Seek ye first the Kingdom of God			442	590	138	512	357		
g	Show me thy ways, O Lord									74
p	Tell his praise in song and story			41					563	
p	Through all the changing scenes of life	209	467	46	516	702	73	685	544	

Year B
All Saints' Day (Lectionary material)

Wisdom **3**: 1-9 or Isaiah **25**: 6-9; Psalm **24**: 1-6; Revelation **21**: 1-6a; John **11**: 32-44

		AMNS	NEH	HTC	HON	MP	H&P	R&S	BPW	CH3
e	Christ is made the sure foundation / Blessed city, heavenly Salem	283/332	204/205	559	76		485	559	474	10
e	City of God, Jerusalem			187						
e	Father of everlasting grace						300			
e	Jerusalem, my happy home / thou city blest	187	225	569	258					
e	Jerusalem on high			565						
e	Jerusalem the golden	184	381	573	259			662	312	537
e	O holy City, seen of/by John	409						628		509
e	Songs of praise the angels sang	196	451	350			512	667		38
p	The earth belongs unto the Lord									566

Year C
All Saints' Day (Lectionary material)

Daniel 7: 1-3, 15-18; Psalm 149; Ephesians 1: 11-23; Luke 6: 20-31

		AMNS	NEH	HTC	HON	MP	H&P	R&S	BPW	CH3
p	All praise to our redeeming Lord					19	753		401	
e	And he shall reign: LPB 237									
e	At the name of Jesus	148	338	172	46	41	74	261	370	300
p	Bring to the Lord a glad new song			336					30	
e	Christ from whom all blessings flow			491			764	561		
e	Come, Holy Ghost, our souls inspire	93	138	589	92	90	283	751		342
e	Come, thou/most Holy Spirit, come / Come, thou Holy Paraclete	92	139	227	97		284	297		105
e	Head of the Church, our risen Lord						547	562		
o	Immortal, invisible, God only wise	199	377	21	242	327	9	67	383	32
el	Jesus invites his saints						612	434	438	
e	O King enthroned on high	158	421		373		311	296		
o	O worship the King all glorious above	101	433	24	393	528	28	47	63	35
e	Our blest/great Redeemer	151		241	410	548	312	330		336
p	Rejoice! the Lord is King	139	443	180	432	575	243	657	317	296
e	Ride on Jesus, all-victorious						272			
e	See where our great High Priest						622			
e	Spirit of wisdom, turn our eyes						385			
o	The head that was once crowned with thorns	141	134	182	480	647	209	257	274	286

Year A
CLC: The Fourth Sunday before Advent
RCL: Proper 26

Micah 3: 5-12; Psalm 43; 1 Thessalonians 2: 9-13; Matthew 24: 1-14

		AMNS	NEH	HTC	HON	MP	H&P	R&S	BPW	CH3
g	All my hope on God is founded	336	333	451	15	16	63	586	327	405
el	Author of life divine	258	274	395	48		596	440		587
e	Brother, sister, let me serve you				73			474	473	
e	Christ from whom all blessings flow			491			764	561		
g	Christ is coming! Let creation									313
e	God is love, and where true love is / Here in Christ we gather	465	513				757	473		
g	Hark what a sound, and too divine for hearing						236	660		
e	Head of the Church, our risen Lord						547	562		
e	Jesus, Lord, we look to thee	380	481				759	564		
g	Jesus, priceless treasure			461	262		259			
e	Jesus, where'er thy people meet / Lord Jesus, when your people	162	390	371	282		549	476		
o	Judge eternal, throned in splendour		490	329	285	395	409	626	627	519
g	Lo, he / Jesus comes with clouds descending	28	9	196	307	424	241	656	314	314
o	Lord of all hopefulness	394	239	101	313		552	531	517	92
e	Love divine, all loves excelling	131	408	217	321	449	267	663	559	437
e	My God, how wonderful thou art / you are	102	410	369	343	468	51	408		356
e	My spirit longs for thee	57	299					333		
o	Now that the daylight fills the sky		151							45
o	O Christ the Lord, O Christ the King		496				406	630		
p	O send thy/your light forth						537	690	18	7
o	O Spirit of the living God			513			322	577	579	496
e	The Church's one foundation	170	484	501	473	640	515	566	393	420
g	The day of the Lord shall come							637		
g	The king shall come when morning dawns								320	
o	The Kingdom of God is justice and joy			333		651	139	200	321	
o	The voice of God goes out to all the world						140	131		
o	Thy/Your kingdom come, O God	177	499	334	519		783	638	644	322
e	We are your people	519						483		
e	Ye/You servants of God, your Master proclaim	149	476	520	565	784	278	293	76	372

Year B
CLC: The Fourth Sunday before Advent
RCL: Proper 26

Deuteronomy 6: 1-9; Psalm 119: 1-8; Hebrews 9: 11-14; Mark 12: 28-34

		AMNS	NEH	HTC	HON	MP	H&P	R&S	BPW	CH3
e	All praise to thee/Christ, for thou / our Lord and King divine	337	335	204	18		253	750		297
g	Can we/man by searching find out God	438					76	80		
g	Come, let us to the Lord our God						33	81		69
e	Come, my soul, thy suit prepare						546			
e	Come, thou everlasting Spirit						298	315		
e	Eternal Light! Eternal Light!			454			458	83	85	357
o	Father of all, whose laws have stood		539						335	
g	Fill thou/now my/our life	200		541	129	146	792	406	569	457
e	Glory be to Jesus	66	83	126	159					
o	God has spoken — by his prophets			248			64		100	
s	Join all the glorious names			214		392	78	280	557	304
s	Now that the daylight fills the sky		151							45
o	O Lord my / Thee will I love, my strength, my tower			485						678
e	Souls of men / Restless souls / There's a wideness	251	461	443	501	607,683	230	353	573	218
o	Spirit of God, descend upon my heart						313	305		108
o	The prophets spoke in days of old	513								
o	Thee will I love, my God and King						40			403
e	Victim divine, thy grace we claim		309				629			
e	What offering shall we give			439						
e	With joy we meditate the grace	530				774	235	206	275	

Year C
CLC: The Fourth Sunday before Advent
RCL: Proper 26

Isaiah 1: 10-18; Psalm 32: 1-7; 2 Thessalonians 1: 1-12; Luke 19: 1-10

		AMNS	NEH	HTC	HON	MP	H&P	R&S	BPW	CH3
g	All ye who seek a comfort / for sure relief	64	63		22					
gl	Deck thyself/yourself, my soul, with gladness	257	280	400	108		606	446		567
g	God makes his rain to fall: SS96									
g	He gave his life in selfless love			405		214		435		
e	Head of thy Church triumphant						818			
gl	I come with joy to meet my Lord	473		408	227		610	447	437	
g	I heard the voice of Jesus say	247	376		231	275	136	349		212
o	I'll praise my Maker while I've breath			20		320	439	734	127	
g	Jesus who walked beside the lake: SS81									
g	Jesus, whose all-redeeming love	383								215
g	Just as I am, without one plea	246	294	440	287	396	697	364	346	79
gl	Let all mortal flesh keep silence	256	295	61	295		266	454	441	577
g	Little Zacchaeus: SS64									
e	Lo, he / Jesus comes with clouds descending	28	9	196	307	424	241	656	314	314
e	Lord, save thy world; in bitter need	397					425			
g	My Lord, you wore no royal crown			118						
o	O day of God, draw near/nigh In beauty	405						632	635	511
g	O for a closer walk with God	231	414	368	360	494		551		663
e	O thou/Lord who came[st]	233	431	552/596	392	525	745	433	355	110
g	This is the day the Lord hath/has made	22	257	379			577	376		
g	When Christ was lifted from the earth	525		335				655		

Remembrance: also National, Peace, Justice; seasonal

		AMNS	NEH	HTC	HON	MP	H&P	R&S	BPW	CH3
s	Almighty Father, who for us thy Son didst give	338					401	621		
s	Beneath the shade of our vine and fig tree							622		
s	Christ is the world's light	440		321			455	600	34	
s	Christ is the world's true light	346	494	323	78		456	601	618	505
s	Creator of the earth and skies	351		320			419	82		
s	Eternal Ruler of the ceaseless round	353	355		115			623	477	514
s	Father eternal, Ruler of creation							624		507
s	For the healing of the nations	361			139		402	620	621	
s	God of freedom, God of justice							625	623	
s	God of grace and God of glory	367		324	174	192	712	344	572	88
s	God of love and truth and beauty	368					403			
s	God save and bless our nation			325						
s	Grant us your peace: SS14									
s	'I have a dream,' a man once said							625		
s	It is God who holds the nations						404			
s	Judge eternal, throned in splendour		490	329	285	395	409	626	627	519
s	Lead me from death to life							627	628	
s	Let there be peace on earth								629	
s	Lord of lords and King eternal	396								
s	Lord, save thy world; in bitter need	397					425			
s	Lord, while for all mankind we pray		491							518
s	Make me a channel of your peace			S19	328	456	776	629	634	
s	O Christ the Lord, O Christ the King		496				406	630		
s	O day of God, draw near/nigh In beauty	405						632	635	511
s	O holy City, seen of/by John	409						628		509
s	O let us spread the pollen of peace							633		
s	O Lord our God, arise		497					631		495
p	O/Our God, our help in ages past	99	417	37	366	498	358	705	389	611
s	Pray for the Church, afflicted and oppressed						556	634		
s	Son of God, eternal Saviour	132	498	102				605	639	454
s	The Church of Christ in every age						804	636	613	
s	The Kingdom of God is justice and joy			333		651	139	200	321	
s	The Saviour's precious blood						410			
s	This we can do for justice and for peace							639		
s	Thy love, O God, has all mankind created						411			503
s	Thy/Your kingdom come, O God	177	499	334	519		783	638	644	322
s	We pray for peace						413	641		
s	We turn to you, O God of every nation	522					412	654	641	
s	We utter our cry: that peace may prevail							642		
s	What does the Lord require	432					414			

Year A
CLC: The Third Sunday before Advent
RCL: Proper 27

Wisdom **6**: 12-16 and (Canticle) Wisdom **6**: 17-20 or Amos **5**: 18-24 and Psalm **70**;
1 Thessalonians **4**: 13-18 and Matthew **25**: 1-13

		AMNS	NEH	HTC	HON	MP	H&P	R&S	BPW	CH3
o1	Be thou my vision / Lord be my vision	343	339	545	56	51	378	489	521	87
o2	Command thy blessing from above						488	385		117
o2	Great Shepherd of thy/your people, hear	164		363			490	387		
o1	Happy the man that finds the grace						674			
g	Here, O my Lord, I see thee/you	274		406		230	608		436	573
e	Leader of faithful souls and guide						819			
e	Let saints on earth / Come let us join our friends above	182	396	574	297	409	812	472		543
e	Lord, it belongs not to my care	242	402				679	545		679
e	Love divine, all loves excelling	131	408	217	321	449	267	663	559	437
o2	O Christ the Lord, O Christ the King		496				406	630		
o2	O day of God, draw near/nigh In beauty	405						632	635	511
o2	O Lord our God, arise		497					631		495
o2	O worship / Worship the Lord in the beauty of holiness	49	52	344	394	529	505	187	22	40
e	Rejoice! the Lord is King	139	443	180	432	575	243	657	317	296
e	Shepherd divine, our wants relieve	228					558			
g	The day of the Lord shall come							637		
e	The Lord will come and not be slow	29	15		489		245	128		321
o1	Thou hidden love of God, whose height						544			96
e	Thou Judge of quick and dead						247			
g	Wake, O wake / Sleepers, wake	32	16	199	529		249	132		315
e	Ye faithful souls who Jesus know						751			
g	Ye/You servants of the Lord	150	18	598	566		248			319
o1	Your words to me are life and health						482	321		

For seasonal hymns see Remembrance, page 178

Year B

CLC: The Third Sunday before Advent
RCL: Proper 27

Jonah **3**: 1-5, 10; Psalm **62**: 5-12; Hebrews **9**: 24-28; Mark **1**: 14-20

		AMNS	NEH	HTC	HON	MP	H&P	R&S	BPW	CH3
e	Alas! and did my Saviour bleed			124						
g	And can it be			452/588	30	33	216	366	328	409
el	And now, O Father, mindful of the love	260	273	392	32		593			580
l	Christ, whose glory fills the skies	4	234	266	82	79	457	380		114
o	Come, let us to the Lord our God						33	81		69
g	Come, living God, when least expected							354		
o	Forgive our sins as we forgive	362	66	111	141		134	84	83	
g	From heaven you came (The servant King)				148	162		522	529	
o	God, who stretched the spangled heavens							86		
g	Here comes Jesus: SS79									
g	I want to walk with Jesus Christ			S16		302		367		
g	James and Andrew, Peter and John				257					
g	Jesus who walked beside the lake: SS81									
el	Lord, enthroned in heavenly splendour	263	296	416	309	431	616			583
g	O happy day that fixed my choice			442	369	499	702	359	539	
g	O Jesus, I have promised	235	420	531	372	501	704	509	352	434
g	O thou/Lord who came[st]	233	431	552/596	392	525	745	433	355	110
el	Once, only once, and once for all	261	304		404					
p	Only on God do thou, my soul									25
p	Put thou thy trust / Commit thou all thy griefs	223			429		672	550		669
e	See, Christ was wounded for our sake			137					229	
g	Take my life, and let it be	249		554	464	624	705	371	358	462
o	The love of God comes close							107		
l	Thy/Your hand, O God, has guided	171	485	536	518	705	784	567	398	424
g	We are your people	519						483		
e	We sing the praise of him who died	138	94	146	536	738	182	229	231	258
o	When all thy/your mercies	109	472	39	544	751	573	109		150
g	When the Son of Mary: SS80 HSN82									
g	Will you come and follow me?				560			558	363	

For seasonal hymns see Remembrance, page 178

Year C
CLC: The Third Sunday before Advent
RCL: Proper 27

Job **19**: 23-27a; Psalm **17**: 1-9; 2 Thessalonians **2**: 1-5, 13-17; Luke **20**: 27-38

		AMNS	NEH	HTC	HON	MP	H&P	R&S	BPW	CH3
p	Be thou / O Lord, my/our guardian	217	64	374	55					
g	Christ the Lord is risen today / Love's redeeming work is done / All creation	83	113	150	324	76	193	232	246	275
g	Christian people, raise your song	443					601	435	430	
gl	Come, let us with our Lord arise	449	254	375			575	383		
g	Come on and celebrate				95	99				
e	Father almighty / Wherefore O Father, we thy/your humble servants	275	313	402						
gl	Forth in the peace of Christ we go	458	361	542	142			602	607	589
o	He's alive									
o	I know that my Redeemer lives, and ever prays						731			
o	I know that my Redeemer lives, what joy			169	232	278	196	278	251	
o	Jesus Christ, our great Redeemer					356				
o	Led like a lamb / You're alive, you have risen				294	402		241	254	
o	My God, how wonderful thou art / you are	102	410	369	343	468	51	408		356
g	My Lord, I did not choose you			107						
g	Now is eternal life	402	114		351		203	432		
o	Walking in a garden	518	123					334		
e	With glorious clouds encompassed round						184			
g	You, living Christ, our eyes behold	533	487							

For seasonal hymns see Remembrance, page 178

Year A
CLC: The Second Sunday before Advent
RCL: Proper 28

Zephaniah 1: 7, 12-18; Psalm 90: 1-8 [9-11] 12; 1 Thessalonians 5: 1-11; Matthew 25: 14-30

		AMNS	NEH	HTC	HON	MP	H&P	R&S	BPW	CH3
e	Almighty Lord, the holy one			273						
e	As sons of the day and daughters of light			490						'
o	Be thou / O Lord, my/our guardian	217	64	374	55					
e	Be thou my vision / Lord be my vision	343	339	545	56	51	378	489	521	87
e	Captains of the saintly band / Christian soldiers	299	215							539
e	From heaven you came (The servant King)				148	162		522	529	
g	God makes his rain to fall: SS96									
e	Help us to help each other / Jesus, united by thy grace	374		540	208		773	500		
e	Jesus lives! Thy/Your terrors now	82	112	156	272	373	198	239	253	605
e	Let us talents and tongues employ	481		414	301			453		
p	Lord, thou hast been our dwelling-place									102
e	No weight of gold or silver			138						
e	O Holy Ghost, thy people bless / O Holy Spirit, come to bless	155		238	370					
p	O/Our God, our help in ages past	99	417	37	366	498	358	705	389	611
e	Soldiers of Christ, arise	219	449	533	449	604	719	370	580	441
e	Soldiers of the cross, arise			534						478
o	The day of the Lord shall come							637		

Year B
CLC: The Second Sunday before Advent
RCL: Proper 28

Daniel 12: 1-3; Psalm 16; Hebrews 10: 11-14 [15-18] 19-25; Mark 13: 1-8

		AMNS	NEH	HTC	HON	MP	H&P	R&S	BPW	CH3
g	All my hope on God is founded	336	333	451	15	16	63	586	327	405
3	And can it be			452/588	30	33	216	366	328	409
g	Christ is our corner-stone	161	206	564	77					
o	Christ, the fair glory	321	190		79					
p	Christ, whose glory fills the skies	4	234	266	82	79	457	380		114
e	Come, ye faithful / Alleluia, raise the anthem	145	351	205	99	103	813		269	
e	Crown him with many crowns	147	352	174	103	109	255	262	37	298
el	Father almighty / Wherefore O Father, we thy/your humble servants	275	313	402						
g	Fight the good fight	220	359	526	128	143	710	496	524	442
o	For all the saints	305	197	567	134	148	814	658	478	534
p	Forth in thy/your name, O Lord	239	235	306	143	159	381	521	526	463
l	From glory to glory advancing	276	286		147			462		325
g	Glorious things of thee/you are spoken	172	362	494	158	173	817	560	480	421
e	Happy the souls to Jesus joined						816			
g	Head of thy Church triumphant						818			
p	Holy Spirit, Truth divine			235			289	301	292	106
e	Jesus, our hope, our hearts' desire			178						302
g	Oft in danger, oft in woe / Christian soldiers, onward go	210	434	524	396	533	715			
e	Praise, my soul, the King of heaven	192	436	38	422	560	13	104	65	360
g	Souls of men / Restless souls / There's a wideness	251	461	443	501	607,683	230	353	573	218
l	The first day of the week	424					576			
e	The head that was once crowned with thorns	141	134	182	480	647	209	257	274	286
e	The Lord ascendeth up on high		135				210			287
g	Through all the changing scenes of life	209	467	46	516	702	73	685	544	
g	Through the night of doubt and sorrow	211	468	466	517		441		546	423
e	Where high the heavenly temple stands	130		184				259		295
o	Who are these, like stars appearing	323	231		555					
el	O God of our forefathers, hear / With solemn faith		314				554			

Year C
CLC: The Second Sunday before Advent
RCL: Proper 28

Malachi 4: 1-2a; Psalm 98; 2 Thessalonians 3: 6-13; Luke 21: 5-19

		AMNS	NEH	HTC	HON	MP	H&P	R&S	BPW	CH3
e	Christ from whom all blessings flow			491			764	561		
g	Christ is our corner-stone	161	206	564	77					
gl	Christ, whose glory fills the skies	4	234	266	82	79	457	380		114
g	For the healing of the nations	361			139		402	620	621	
e	God of love and truth and beauty	368					403			
e	Help us to help each other / Jesus, united by thy grace	374		540	208		773	500		
o	Hills of the north, rejoice	470	7		209		237		311	
p	Joy to the world, the Lord is come			197	283	393	77	135	315	
o	Judge eternal, throned in splendour		490	329	285	395	409	626	627	519
el	Lord, as we rise to leave the shell of worship	385							608	
e	My gracious Lord, I own thy right						741	535		
p	New songs of celebration render	498		343	350		491	709		
el	Now let us from this table rise	403		419	352		619	463	451	
g	O Christ the Lord, O Christ the King		496				406	630		
p	Sing a new song to Jehovah									348
o	Sometimes a light surprises	108					571	595		
el	Strengthen for service, Lord, the hands	421	306	423	460		626	461	453	588
o	The race that long / The people that in darkness	52	57	71	491		89	129		168
g	The Saviour's precious blood						410			
o	Thou/God whose almighty / Father your mighty word	180	466	506	514	699	29	38	591	494
g	We turn to you, O God of every nation	522					412	654	641	
e	What does the Lord require	432					414			

Year A
CLC: Christ the King
RCL: Proper 29

Ezekiel **34**: 11-16, 20-24; Psalm **95**: 1-7a; Ephesians **1**: 15-23; Matthew **25**: 31-46

		AMNS	NEH	HTC	HON	MP	H&P	R&S	BPW	CH3
e	At the name of Jesus	148	338	172	46	41	74	261	370	300
s	Christ is the King! O friends rejoice	345	345	492				571	475	474
e	Crown him with many crowns	147	352	174	103	109	255	262	37	298
gl	Deck thyself/yourself, my soul, with gladness	257	280	400	108		606	446		567
g	Glorious the day when Christ was born							263		
g	God is love: his the care			311	169		220	274	45	416
e	God of love and truth and beauty	368					403			
g	He is Lord, he is Lord			S7	204	220	256	264	378	
g	Help us to help each other / Jesus, united by thy grace	374		540	208		773	500		
g	I cannot tell why/how he whom angels worship			194	226	266	238	265	381	
g	Jesus, my Lord, how rich thy grace / Fountain of good	381					147			459
gl	Let all mortal flesh keep silence	256	295	61	295		266	454	441	577
g	Lord Christ, who on thy heart didst bear	388			308		394			
gl	Lord, as we rise to leave the shell of worship	385							608	
g	Lord, to you we bring our treasure	495								
p	O come, and let us to the Lord						567	707		19
g	O King enthroned on high	158	421		373		311	296		
o	Praise the Lord! rise up	416			424					
el	Rejoice! the Lord is King	139	443	180	432	575	243	657	317	296
g	Ride on Jesus, all-victorious						272			
g	Son of God, eternal Saviour	132	498	102				605	639	454
g	The day of the Lord shall come									
o	The King of love my shepherd is	126	457	44	484	649	69	552	394	388
s	'The Kingdom is upon you!'	512								
s	The Kingdom of God is justice and joy			333		651	139	200	321	
o	Thou Shepherd of Israel and mine						750			
s	Thy/Your kingdom come, O God	177	499	334	519		783	638	644	322
g	We find thee, Lord, in others' need	430								
g	When I needed a neighbour	433			548					
g	Where love and loving-kindness dwell	528								

Year B
CLC: Christ the King
RCL: Proper 29

Daniel 7: 9-10, 13-14; Psalm 93; Revelation 1: 4b-8; John 18: 33-37

		AMNS	NEH	HTC	HON	MP	H&P	R&S	BPW	CH3
g	Ah, holy Jesus, how hast thou offended		62	123	8		164	215	215	251
g	Alleluia, Jesus is Lord				23					
e	At the name of Jesus	148	338	172	46	41	74	261	370	300
s	Christ is the King! O friends rejoice	345	345	492				571	475	474
o	Great God, what do I see and hear			189						
g	Hark what a sound, and too divine for hearing						236	660		
g	He stood before the court			129						
o	Immortal, invisible, God only wise	199	377	21	242	327	9	67	383	32
o	Jesus came — the heavens adoring			195						
g	Jesus in the olive grove						169			
e	Let all mortal flesh keep silence	256	295	61	295		266	454	441	577
o	Let all the world in every corner sing	202	394	342	296	404	10	114	54	361
e	Lo, he / Jesus comes with clouds descending	28	9	196	307	424	241	656	314	314
g	Lord of the boundless curves of space	493	405				335	44		
g	Lord, enthroned in heavenly splendour	263	296	416	309	431	616			583
g	Man of sorrows			130	330	458	228		350	380
g	Mine eyes have seen the glory				336		242			318
g	My song is love unknown	63	86	136	346	478	173	207	204	224
g	Nature with open volume stands	497	87				174	219		
o	O worship / Worship the Lord in the beauty of holiness	49	52	344	394	529	505	187	22	40
o	O worship the King all glorious above	101	433	24	393	528	28	47	63	35
g	Praise to the living God						56	118		
g	Rejoice! the Lord is King	139	443	180	432	575	243	657	317	296
o	The God of Abraham praise	331	148	9	478	645	452	121	131	358
g	The head that was once crowned with thorns	141	134	182	480	647	209	257	274	286
s	'The Kingdom is upon you!'	512								
s	The Kingdom of God is justice and joy			333		651	139	200	321	
p	The Lord doth reign and clothed is he									140
p	The Lord Jehovah reigns						59			
s	Thy/Your kingdom come, O God	177	499	334	519		783	638	644	322
e	To God be the glory			584	522	708	463	289	566	374
g	Unto us a Child / boy/ Jesus Christ the Lord is born		39	83	526	714	127	169	181	187
g	Ye/You choirs of new Jerusalem	73	124	168	563		823			

Year C
CLC: Christ the King
RCL: Proper 29

Jeremiah **23**: 1-6; Psalm **46**; Colossians **1**: 11-20; Luke **23**: 33-43

		AMNS	NEH	HTC	HON	MP	H&P	R&S	BPW	CH3
p	A safe stronghold/fortress/refuge	114		523		2	661	585	375	406/7
o	All hail the power of Jesus' name	140	332	587/203	13	13	252		29	382
p	Be still and know that I am God				52	48			280	
s	Christ is the King! O friends rejoice	345	345	492				571	475	474
e	From glory to glory advancing	276	286		147			462		325
p	God is our refuge and our strength							691		24
g	He gave his life in selfless love			405		214			435	
e	How shall I sing that majesty	472	373				8	661		
g	It was on a Friday morning: SS43									
e	Lord, enthroned in heavenly splendour	263	296	416	309	431	616			583
e	Lord, teach us how to pray aright	227	406	367	316		551			
g	Meekness and majesty				335	465			58	
e	O Christ the same, through all our story's pages		258	263						
o	O come, O come, Emmanuel	26	11	66	358	493	85	126	144	165
g	O sacred head	68	90	139	389	520	176	220	223	253
eg	So dies this man, this carpenter: SS41									
e	Soldiers of Christ, arise	219	449	533	449	604	719	370	580	441
s	'The Kingdom is upon you!'	512								
s	The Kingdom of God is justice and joy			333		651	139	200	321	
g	There is a green hill far away	137	92	148	499	674	178	223	230	241
s	Thy/Your kingdom come, O God	177	499	334	519		783	638	644	322
g	Were you there	523	93		540	745	181	227	232	

The Naming and Circumcision of Jesus

Numbers **6**: 22-27; Psalm **8**; Galatians **4**: 4-7; Luke **2**: 15-21

		AMNS	NEH	HTC	HON	MP	H&P	R&S	BPW	CH3
e	All hail the power of Jesus' name	140	332	587/203	13	13	252		29	382
e	At the name of Jesus	148	338	172	46	41	74	261	370	300
o	God of mercy, God of grace	179	366	293	175			575	48	497
e	How sweet the name of Jesus sounds	122	374	211	220	251	257	277	339	376
s	I'm not ashamed to own/name my Lord			448	240	323	677	428	343	591
e	Jesus! the name high over all			213		385	264			
e	Name of all majesty			218		481				
e	O for a thousand tongues to sing	125	415	219	362	496	744	285	59	371
p	O Lord my God, when I in awesome wonder [How great thou art]				380	506		117	62	
p	O Lord of every shining constellation	411		314					130	141
sp	Tell out, my soul, the greatness of the Lord	422	186	42	467	631	86	740	391	164
e	To the Name of our / that brings salvation	121	470	222	523		80	291		373
e	To us a child of royal birth	45		64						
g	Unto us a Child / boy/ Jesus Christ the Lord is born		39	83	526	714	127	169	181	187

See also New Year, page 18

The Conversion of St Paul

Jeremiah 1: 4-10, Psalm 67 and Acts 9: 1-22

or Acts 9: 1-22, Psalm 67 and Galatians 1: 11-16a; Matthew 19: 27-30

		AMNS	NEH	HTC	HON	MP	H&P	R&S	BPW	CH3
o	All my hope on God is founded	336	333	451	15	16	63	586	327	405
e	Amazing grace			28	27	31	215	92	550	
e	And can it be			452/588	30	33	216	366	328	409
ae	At the name of Jesus	148	338	172	46	41	74	261	370	300
I	Captains of the saintly band / Christian soldiers	299	215							539
s	Children of the heavenly King	213	344	566	63					
s	Christ is made the sure foundation / Blessed city, heavenly Salem	283/332	204/205	559	76		485	559	474	10
ae	Christ is the world's light	440		321			455	600	34	
s	Disposer supreme and judge of the earth	298	216		110					
s	Eternal Spirit of the living Christ							300		
a	Fight the good fight	220	359	526	128	143	710	496	524	442
s	Give praise for famous men			568						
p	God of mercy, God of grace	179	366	293	175			575	48	497
s	It is a thing most wonderful	70	84	131	255	346	224	503	219	385
a	Just as I am, without one plea	246	294	440	287	396	697	364	346	79
e	Light of the minds that know him		400	477				529		
e	Lord of all power, I give you my will / Lord of creation, to you be all praise	395		547		440	699	532		428
e	Lord, speak to me, that I may speak			510		444	553	613	611	485
o	My Lord, I did not choose you			107						
e	Stand up, stand up for Jesus	221	453	535	457	617	721			481
g	Take my life, and let it be	249		554	464	624	705	371	358	462
s	The eternal gifts of Christ the King	297	213		476					540
s	Thy/Your hand, O God, has guided	171	485	536	518	705	784	567	398	424
s	To God be the glory			584	522	708	463	289	566	374
I	We sing the glorious conquest	313	155							
s	Who would true valour / He who would valiant / Who honours courage	212	372	537/590	205	224	688	557	362	443
e	Will you come and follow me?				560			558	363	
s	Ye/You servants of God, your Master proclaim	149	476	520	565	784	278	293	76	372

The Blessed Virgin Mary

Isaiah **61**: 10, 11 or Revelation **11**:19 — **12**:6, **12**:10; Psalm **45**: 10-17; Galatians **4**: 4-7; Luke **1**: 46-55

		AMNS	NEH	HTC	HON	MP	H&P	R&S	BPW	CH3
s	Blest are the pure in heart	238	341	110	63		724		588	113
g	For Mary, Mother of our/the Lord	360	161		136					
s	Hail, O star that pointest		180		190					
s	Her Virgin eyes	310	182							
s	Alleluia, alleluia, give thanks to the risen Lord			S3	24	30	250	234	31	
s	Mary, blessed grieving mother				331					
s	Mary, blessed teenage mother				332					
p	My heart is full of Christ, and longs						799			
o	O Christ the Lord, O Christ the King		496				406	630		
s	O glorious Maid, exalted far		183							
e	Of the Father's love/heart begotten / God of God	33	33	56	395		79	181	145	198
g	Sing we a song of high revolt	419							638	
s	Sing we of the blessed Mother		185		448					
g	Tell out, my soul, the greatness of the Lord	422	186	42	467	631	86	740	391	164
g	The angel Gabriel from heaven came				471		87	139	177	
p	The Church's one foundation	170	484	501	473	640	515	566	393	420
s	The Lord/God whom earth and sea and sky	309	181							
e	To the Name of our / that brings salvation	121	470	222	523		80	291		373
s	Virgin-born, we bow before thee	311	187		527					
g	When our God came to earth				552					
s	Who better than Mary: SS73									
s	Ye who own the faith of Jesus		188		568					

Rogationtide Years A, B, C

Deuteronomy **8**: 1-10; 1 Kings **8**: 35-40; Job **28**: 1-11; Philippians **4**: 4-7; 2 Thessalonians **3**: 6-13;
1 John **5**: 12-15; Psalms **104**: 21-30, **107**: 1-9 or **121**; Matthew **6**: 1-15; Mark **11**: 22-24; Luke **11**: 5-13

		AMNS	NEH	HTC	HON	MP	H&P	R&S	BPW	CH3
p	All creatures of our God and King	105	263	13	9	7	329	39	28	30
p	All people that on earth do dwell	100	334	14	17	20	1	712	2	1
p	All things bright and beautiful	116	264	283	21	23	330		116	154
p	Before Jehovah's aweful/awesome throne / Sing to the Lord	197		15			61	119		2
s	By the rutted roads we follow									619
s	For the beauty of the earth	104	285	298	137	152	333	41	121	367
g	For the fruits of his/all creation	457		286	138	153	342	42	123	
p	Forth in thy/your name, O Lord	239	235	306	143	159	381	521	526	463
s	God of light and life's creation			561						
s	God of mercy, God of grace	179	366	293	175			575	48	497
s	God, whose farm is all creation	370		282	179		344	612	124	
s	God, you have / who hast given us power	469					345			452
s	Great God, we sing that mighty / your guiding hand						356	63	552	613
s	Great is thy/your faithfulness			260	186	200	66	96	553	
p	Immortal, invisible, God only wise	199	377	21	242	327	9	67	383	32
p	Judge eternal, throned in splendour		490	329	285	395	409	626	627	519
s	Lord, in thy name thy servants plead		126							
s	Lord of the changing year			261						
g	Lord, teach us how to pray aright	227	406	367	316		551			
s	Morning has broken		237	265	337	467	635	45	132	
g	O God of Bethel / O God of Jacob	216	416	35	364		442	71	599	72
s	O Lord of every shining constellation	411		314					130	141
s	O Lord of heaven and earth and sea	287	422	287			337		387	145
p	O worship the King all glorious above	101	433	24	393	528	28	47	63	35
s	Praise to the Lord, the Almighty	207	440	40	427	564	16	74	68	9
g	Rejoice, O land, in God thy might / your Lord	296	493	331	431					
s	The earth is yours, O God			290						
s	To thee, our God, we fly	330	127							
p	Unto the hills around			48						
g	We plough the fields and scatter	290	262	292	534	732	352	124	135	620

See also Sixth Sunday of Easter

Harvest Years A, B, C

Year A: Deuteronomy **8**: 7-18 or **28**: 1-14; Psalm **65**; 2 Corinthians **9**: 6-15; Luke **12**: 16-30 or **17**: 11-19

Year B: Joel **2**: 21-27; Psalm **126**; 1 Timothy **2**: 1-7 or **6**: 6-10; Matthew **6**: 25-33

Year C: Deuteronomy **26**: 1-11; Psalm **100**; Philippians **4**: 4-9 or Revelation **14**: 14-18; John **6**: 25-35

		AMNS	NEH	HTC	HON	MP	H&P	R&S	BPW	CH3
s	All people that on earth do dwell	100	334	14	17	20	1	712	2	1
s	All things bright and beautiful	116	264	283	21	23	330		116	154
s	All things praise thee, Lord most high					24	331			
s	Come, ye/you thankful people, come	289	259	284	101	106	355	40	120	627
s	Fair waved the golden corn		260		116					629
s	For the beauty of the earth	104	285	298	137	152	333	41	121	367
s	For the fruits of his/all creation	457		286	138	153	342	42	123	
s	Fountain of mercy, God of love									628
s	Glory, love, and praise, and honour	461	287		160		35			
s	God in his love for us lent us this planet						343	85		
s	God of all ages					190				
s	God of mercy, God of grace	179	366	293	175			575	48	497
s	God, whose farm is all creation	370		282	179		344	612	124	
s	Great is thy/your faithfulness			260	186	200	66	96	553	
s	In humble gratitude, O God	377								
s	Let us, with a gladsome mind / Let us gladly with one mind	204	397	23	302	415	27		56	33
s	Lord, by whose breath all souls and seeds	486								
s	My father was a wandering Aramean: SS54									
s	Now thank we all our God	205	413	33	354	486	566	72	128	368
s	O Father, whose creating hand						349			
s	O Lord of heaven and earth and sea	287	422	287			337		387	145
s	O worship the King all glorious above	101	433	24	393	528	28	47	63	35
s	Praise and thanksgiving, Father, we offer	415					350	48		
s	Praise God for the harvest of farm and of field			288			351			
s	Praise God from whom all blessings flow	1	232	586	417	557	632	21	113	658
s	Praise, O praise our God and King	288			423		359			
s	See the farmer sow the seed									621
s	The earth is yours, O God			290						
s	To thee/you, O Lord, our hearts we raise	291	261	291	524		362	53		
s	We plough the fields and scatter	290	262	292	534	732	352	124	135	620

Christian Initiation

Infant Baptism

		AMNS	NEH	HTC	HON	MP	H&P	R&S	BPW	CH3
I	Eternal God, we consecrate	452								
I	Glory and praise to God who loves						581	464		
I	God the Father, name we treasure	466		385						
I	In the name of God the Father NSC3									
I	Lord Jesus, as you came NSC5									
I	Lord Jesus, once a child						585	417		
I	Now in the name of him who sent						590	425		
I	Sing to the Lord glad hymns of praise		316							
I	This child from God above						589			
I	We praise you, Lord, for Jesus Christ	521						418		
I	Word of the Father, the life of creation							419		

Adult or Family Baptism

		AMNS	NEH	HTC	HON	MP	H&P	R&S	BPW	CH3
I	Awake, awake, fling off the night	342			49				404	
I	Christ, when for us you were baptized	442					129		405	
I	Come, Father, Son and Holy Ghost						580			
I	Lord, here is one to be baptized						584			
I	Praise and thanksgiving be to our creator	506								
I	Praise to God, almighty Maker						582	430	414	
I	Stand, soldier of the cross						591			
I	We bring our children, Lord, today NSC10									

Re-affirmation of Baptismal Faith
(see also Confirmation)

		AMNS	NEH	HTC	HON	MP	H&P	R&S	BPW	CH3
I	A mighty mystery we set forth						579		403	
I	All who believe and are baptized							421	402	
I	Jesus, we follow thee						583			
I	Light of the minds that know him		400	477				529		
I	This is the truth which we proclaim			388						
I	We know that Christ is raised and dies no more			389				426		

Confirmation

		AMNS	NEH	HTC	HON	MP	H&P	R&S	BPW	CH3
I	Forth in thy/your name, O Lord	239	235	306	143	159	381	521	526	463
I	God be in my head	236	328	543	166		694	498	592	433
I	I bind unto myself / myself to God today / Christ be with me		159	5	225		695	36		402
I	I'm not ashamed to own/name my Lord			448	240	323	677	428	343	591
I	Jesus, our Lord and King							429		
I	Lift high the cross	72		508	303	417	170	422	575	550
I	Lord, for the years			328	310	428		603	535	
I	Lord, let your grace descend on those						587		412	
I	Lord of all power, I give you my will / Lord of creation, to you be all praise	395		547		440	699	532		428
I	Lord of the love that in Christ							431		
I	My God, accept my heart this day	279	318	551	341		701			429
I	Now is eternal life	402	114		351		203	432		
I	O happy day that fixed my choice			442	369	499	702	359	539	
I	O Jesus, I have promised	235	420	531	372	501	704	509	352	434
I	O thou/Lord who came[st]	233	431	552/596	392	525	745	433	355	110
I	Take my life, and let it be	249		554	464	624	705	371	358	462
I	Thine/Yours for ever	234	463	556	504					
I	Will you come and follow me?				560			558	363	